THE UNITED NATIONS UNIVERSITY/T

STUDIES IN AFRICAN POLITIC

African Agriculture

THE UNITED NATIONS UNIVERSITY/THIRD WORLD FORUM

STUDIES IN AFRICAN POLITICAL ECONOMY
General Editor: Samir Amin

The United Nations University's Project on Transnationalization or Nation-Building in Africa (1982–1986) was undertaken by a network of African scholars under the co-ordination of Samir Amin. The purpose of the Project was to study the possibilities of and constraints on national autocentric development of African countries in the context of the world-system into which they have been integrated. Since the 1970s the world-system has been in a crisis of a severity and complexity unprecedented since the end of the Second World War; the Project examines the impact of this contemporary crisis on the political, economic and cultural situation of Africa today. Focusing on the complex relationship between transnationalization (namely, the dynamics of the world-system) and nation-building, which is seen as a precondition for national development, the Project explores a wide range of problems besetting Africa today and outlines possible alternatives to the prevailing development models which have proved to be inadequate.

TITLES IN THIS SERIES

Other titles in preparation.

THE UNITED NATIONS UNIVERSITY/THIRD WORLD FORUM

STUDIES IN AFRICAN POLITICAL ECONOMY

African Agriculture:

The Critical Choices

Edited by
Hamid Aït Amara
and
Bernard Founou-Tchuigoua

With a Preface by
Samir Amin

United Nations University Press
Tokyo

Zed Books Ltd.
London and New Jersey

African Agriculture: The Critical Choices was first published
in 1990 by:
Zed Books Ltd., 57 Caledonian Road, London N1 9BU, UK, and
171 First Avenue, Atlantic Highlands, New Jersey 07716, USA
and:
United Nations University Press, Toho Seimei Building,
15-1 Shibuya 2-chome, Shibuya-ku, Tokyo 150, Japan
in co-operation with
The Third World Forum, B.P. 3501, Dakar, Senegal.

Copyright © The United Nations University, 1990.

Translation by A. M. Berrett.
Cover designed by Andrew Corbett.
Typeset by EMS Photosetters, Rochford, Essex.
Printed and bound in the United Kingdom
at Bookcraft (Bath) Ltd, Midsomer Norton.

British Library Cataloguing in Publication Data

African agriculture : the critical choices.
(The United Nations university studies in African economy)
1. Africa. Agricultural industries. Social aspects.
I. Amara, Hamid Aït. II. Founou-Tchuigoua, Bernard. III. Series.
305.9'631'096

ISBN 0-86232-798-9
ISBN 0-86232 799-7 pbk

Library of Congress Cataloging-in-Publication Data

African agriculture, the critical choices/edited by Hamid Aït Amara and
Bernard Founou-Tchuigoua with a preface by Samir Amin.
p.   cm. – (Studies in African political economy)
ISBN 0-86232-798-9   ISBN 0-86232-799-7 (pbk.)
1. Agriculture and state – Africa – Case studies. 2. Food supply –
Government policy – Africa – Case studies. 3. Produce trade –
Government policy – Africa – Case studies.
I. Amara, Hamid Aït. II. Founou-Tchuigoua, Bernard. III. Series.
HD2118.A33   1989.   89-35869
338.1'86–dc20   CIP

Contents

Tables

Acknowledgements

This book was produced in the framework of the United Nations University 'African Regional Perspectives' programme under the auspices of the Third World Forum. We wish to thank the UNU, the Italian Cooperation Agency and the Swedish Agency SAREC whose financial support made this work possible. Nevertheless, in accordance with the usual formula, the opinions expressed here are those of the authors alone and not of those institutions.

1. The Agricultural Revolution and Industrialization

Samir Amin

This chapter starts with the recognition that globally, the development strategies implemented in Africa since independence have neither aimed at achieving the priority task of an agricultural revolution, nor really aimed at any significant industrialization, but basically extended the colonial pattern of integration in the world capitalist system. The catastrophic results are now obvious; moreover the Western inspired policies of so-called 'readjustment' to the new conditions created by the global crisis (through the IMF and World Bank recipes) would only worsen the case. Hence another development, fundamentally based on a popular alliance, is the only acceptable alternative. The priority target of achieving the agricultural revolution clearly calls for industrialization, but a pattern of industrialization quite different from the conventional one. This chapter attempts to show the ways in which this pattern presupposes some form of 'delinking' from the system governing the economic global expansion of capitalism. This national and popular content of development, in its turn, is virtually inconceivable without significant change toward democratization of the society, allowing for an autonomous expression of the various social forces and creating the basis for a real civil society. Simultaneously, the weakness of African states, referred to here, calls for co-operation and unity without which any national and popular attempt would remain extremely limited and vulnerable.

The failure of the modernization strategies

Twenty years ago when most African countries were acceding to independence, the view prevailing at that time, even among Africans, attributed under-development on the continent to an historical backwardness which was to be overcome simply by redoubling efforts aimed at progress in a previously defined and known direction. The national liberation movement, such as it was, blamed the colonizers precisely for the fact that they were not up to the task.

African 'left' and 'right' were hence convinced that independence was a sure guarantee of, and a sufficient precondition for, the acceleration of modernization rates. The liberal thesis considered that the means to accelerate growth was to maintain a large opening to foreign capital. The government's role was to create more favourable conditions likely to generate new opportunities for capital investments by accelerating education and training, so feared by the colonizers, as well as modernizing both infrastructure and administration. The socialist thesis of the time, suspicious of foreign capital, argued that the government was itself to compensate for the lack of capital, specifically with a view to effectively speeding up the modernization process. In other words, the socialist thesis was not rejecting either the 'modernization' perspective or that of integration into the international division of labour.

Both theses shared the same basic views concerning the neutrality of technology: both were arguing that the direction of modernization could be and was known. A mere glance at both Western and Eastern advanced societies would convince of the similarity of a number of objectives in terms of consumption, organization of production, administration, and education. The 'socialists' were probably more sensitive to such issues as national independence, which is why they were on their guard against the recourse to foreign capital. They were also probably more sensitive to issues related to income distribution and the priority of collective services. But the 'liberals' retorted that capitalism would also solve these problems and moreover, would gradually lead to a democratization of social and political life. Both theses were finally based on the same West-centred and technico-economistic view, the common denominator of a popular version of Marxism and the best of bourgeois social science.

Only 15 years ago protests were still rare and unwelcome, considered as peasant utopias and culturalist nationalisms. It is true that, because of a lack of sufficient support, the protestors were often guilty of such weaknesses. The outcome of the real history of the last two decades has been such that the two theses are systematically called into question today. It is this twofold historical 'frustration' that gives the thesis of unequal development the strength it is gaining.

The thesis of unequal development began by the affirmation that underdevelopment, far from being 'backwardness', was the result of integration into the world capitalist system as an exploited and dominated periphery, fulfilling specific functions in the process of accumulation at the centre of the system. This integration, contrary to superficial points of view, did not date from the colonial scramble of Africa at the end of the 19th century, but from the very beginning of mercantilism in the 18th century, a period when Africa was 'specialized', through the slave trade, in the supply of labour power which, exploited in America, was to speed up the process of capital accumulation in Atlantic Europe. This 'specialization' – apart from its horrors – was not only leading to a regression of local production systems as well as state organizations, and marking the ideology of the societies involved in this shameful trade with features that will remain for a long time, but was also impoverishing Africa.

The thesis of unequal development continued its analysis by trying to understand the mechanisms by which capital, dominant on the world scale, was subordinating pre-capitalist modes of production while distorting them. Whereas the ethnological mainstream was carrying on its research on the singularities of African societies, trying to isolate them conceptually, the thesis of unequal development was laying stress on the integration of apparently 'traditional' rural societies in the process of capital accumulation. This is how, in the first half of the 1960s, the essential characteristics of the modes of formal domination of capital over the African rural world were defined. It was shown how in the 'trade economy', the technical and commercial systems of control were depriving peasant producers of their control over the means of production they still formally owned, in order to extract a surplus of labour, transformed through commodity trade into profit for the capital of the dominating monopolies. It was shown how driving back the peasants into intentionally small reserves in South Africa and Zimbabwe was intended to supply cheap labour power to industries, mines and plantations. These analyses lead to a consideration of the fundamentally different alternative of a development, based on popular alliance between workers and peasants.

The way was thus opened for a positive rethinking of all the issues of development: orientations of industrialization, the question of state and nation, and so on. Within this perspective industry is meant to support the technical and social revolution in the rural area. This inversion of priorities also, by force of circumstances, involved fundamental revisions at the level of reflection on consumption models, the articulation of big and small industries, modern techniques and artisanal and traditional techniques, and so on. A positive content could be given to a strategy of delinking, that is, to refuse the imperatives of the international division of labour, heretofore considered as inevitable necessities.

The seed was sown. But it could not germinate unless it had fallen on fertile soil. Ideas become realities only if they are supported by effective social forces; the ground is, however, becoming increasingly solid. The old movement of national liberation, whose objective was political independence, has exhausted its potentials. The 50-state Africa to whose creation it contributed finds itself in a dilemma: of economic development whose contrasted effects are ever more explosive: urbanization and mass unemployment, agricultural stagnation, soil deterioration, famines and massive imports of food products, growing external dependency. A dilemma of national construction; a political dilemma: imitative democracies give way to tyrannies, single parties of national construction give place to military and bureaucratic cliques. An ideological dilemma: capitalist liberalism and bureaucratic socialism do not answer any needs of the popular masses; a cultural dilemma: imitative education shows all its dysfunctionality, the imposition of the foreign languages of colonization is a vehicle of alienation as ineffective as it is unsupportable.

The reason is that the old movement of national liberation was, in fact, a bourgeois movement even though it was able to mobilize peasant masses and its *petit bourgeois* component had given the illusion of a possible socialist prospect. The newly emerging movement will, necessarily, be one of peasants and workers; and probably, inevitably assume populist forms in a first stage before the seed sown has germinated.

The present crisis of the imperialist system obviously enhances all these contradictions. The solutions offered by the system imposing its 'adjustment' policies do not answer the real questions. There is no alternative to a strategy of national and popular reconstruction, self-centred and delinked from the world capitalist system.

The agricultural revolution, but how?

The failure of 'development' has been more dramatic for Africa as a whole than for any other region. Africa has not yet started its agricultural revolution without which no further stage of development can be considered. The production and productivity per rural family have been almost stagnant for long and might have even begun to decline in many places. Out-village migration is not the result of a relatively surplus population created by some agricultural progress, even if socially unequal, but is a desperate attempt by the whole population to escape from famine. This type of migration generates a monstrous type of urbanization with no hope of industrial employment, since it provides no means of financing new activities. Simultaneously, African countries, with very few exceptions, have not begun to enter the industrial age from any viewpoint. There is neither a minimal network of inter-related industries, nor a minimal financial and technological capacity to pursue any consistent industrial policy. Elsewhere, in many areas of Latin America and South, South-East and East Asia, such minimal tasks have already been accomplished, even if in a chaotic, regionally and socially unequal way, hence inadequate from a national and popular viewpoint.

Of course, this failure has deep roots, both pre-colonial and colonial, but in no way can it be considered that the post-colonial decades have begun reversing the negative processes.

Achieving the agricultural revolution is, therefore, the priority target for the decades to come. This is a very complex, multi-dimensional undertaking. It has technological dimensions: what type of equipment and other inputs (for example, control of water, use of chemicals) may bring, simultaneously, significant increases in production per capita and per acre. These technological choices imply the production per capita and per acre. These technological choices imply the design of adequate supportive economic policies: of price and income systems ensuring the rationality of the choices they induce; of the supportive industrialization priorities, the pattern of financing among others. These policies in their turn bear complex social and political consequences: how the various types of social control in rural areas (land property and use, rent and wage system, co-operatives of producers of a variety of types, from lower to higher forms, and so on) command the direction of change (or make it impossible); how the types of social control in place are the historical result of social power balances and imbalances (particularly the result of the relation of the State to the rural communities and their components). And, through which political moves they could be changed, how the various types of social control on trade systems and industry (state, basic collectivities, private national capital, transnationals) combine with the need for agricultural changes.

On none of these aspects, and on how they interrelate, are the lessons from the historical experiences – either of the developed West, the East or of Latin American and Asian regions – transferable to Africa today. There are many reasons for this: differences in the availability of disposable land, differences in pre-modern patterns of social organization and levels of productivities, differences in available industrial technologies, are some. Similarly, the lessons from other experiences of industrialization, whether conceived in the perspective of the world division of labour or 'delinked' from it, based on private capital initiative or state intervention, are of a limited significance for Africa.

Yet perhaps because the task is totally new and the challenges too complex, recipes are suggested hurriedly by agencies (notably from the UN family, World Bank and major bilateral agencies) few of which pass the test of experience. Hence the flow of short-lived 'fashions'. In the name of 'immediate efficiency', those who do not recognize our deep ignorance of what can be done, easily substitute for deeper studies their 'theological' beliefs, whether in market efficiency (as if some minor changes in prices would create *ipso facto* adequate incentives), or in the state efficiency (without questioning enough the historical, political, cultural dimensions of the state).

Considered from the global perspective of today's world system, the failure of African development bears further dramatic consequences. The continent's weakness both at economic and financial levels and, perhaps consequently, at political and military levels, encourages cynical attitudes, allowing the powers to give priority to their geo-strategic views without being compelled to consider local forces and interests. This weakness, combined with the global strategies of the powers, thus creates an additional set of conditions unfavourable for internal changes.

A glaring example of how 'theology' is substituted for scientific analysis of the roots of Africa's failure to achieve its agricultural revolution is provided by the famous World Bank Report on 'Accelerated Development in Sub-Saharan Africa'.

It was to be expected that the World Bank would produce a critique of local social and economic systems and the world system of the division of labour, responsible for this failure. Or even that the Bank would make some sort of self-criticism, since for the past 20 years it has supported most of the basic principles underlying the development system now being called into question. But instead, the Bank attributes the failure entirely to the African governments, accusing them of having held agriculture in contempt and given far too much priority to industry!

The Bank's proposed strategy can be accurately summed up as follows:

The internal structural problems and external constraints impeding African economic growth have been exacerbated by domestic policy inadequacies

... trade and exchange-rate policies [which] have overprotected industry, held back agriculture ... the public sector has become over-extended.

Upon which, the Bank goes on to suggest a strategy of adjustment to the demands of the world system, based on exports (agricultural and mining commodities), supported mainly by devaluation measures and resort to a larger measure of liberalism, these to be accompanied by offering greater scope to private initiative. A carrot, that of doubling external aid in real terms during the 1980s, is dangled to encourage countries to accept these principles of 'healthy' management.

Low agricultural productivity in Africa is a platitude. What the World Bank report does not say is that this low productivity, which goes hand in hand with the land-extensive type of agriculture, was – and still is – economic from the point of view of the world system of the division of labour. It allowed the West to acquire raw materials without having to invest in its colonies. It has been clearly shown that this mechanism is responsible for the impoverishment of the land that has resulted in poorer yields. The transition to intensive agriculture, a necessity today, implies an increase in the world prices of raw materials, if they are to be exported: land, like oil or water, is no longer an 'unlimited' resource. Yet the Bank has managed to discover only three ills from which Africa suffers: overvalued exchange rates; too high a level of taxation of farmers; and excessive growth in administrative expenditure.

Obviously, if prices in foreign currencies are maintained, devaluation would allow the exporter to obtain more in the local currency. But it cannot be assumed either that devaluation would bring about equilibrium in the balance of payments without control or that prices in foreign currencies would remain stable if the African countries devalued their own currency. Experience has repeatedly shown that in many Third World countries the whole range of local prices tends to adjust to the import prices and that, therefore, the effect of devaluation both on comparative price structures and on the balance of payments is cancelled out. The absence of a self-reliant and autonomous economic structure explains this generalized contagion, which reflects how local price systems are dependent on the world price system.

It is true that peasants in Africa are subjected to a considerable degree of 'hidden taxation' – the difference between the export price, the real cost of internal marketing deducted, and the price paid to the producer. But where else would the state raise these resources if this margin were abolished and if the country were to give priority in its development to the production of such export commodities as suggested by the Bank? Why not reduce consumer taxes (for example, on coffee) in the developed countries for the benefit of the African peasant? Clearly, such hidden taxation reflects the local states' 'anti-peasant' bias, but this bias is a consequence of the nature of the states' relations with the world system. The anti-peasant feature is not that of the local state alone, but that of the global system of exploitation within which it functions.

By failing to extend the analysis of the system further, the World Bank condemns itself, on the subject of public expenditure as on others, to distribute advice that is hardly efficient and to suggest ways and means of tinkering with the economy in order to reduce this expenditure (by very little). Such savings are invariably made at the expense of the poor, in contradiction to the fine speeches about 'basic needs'. Moreover, does not the IMF, a close partner of the World Bank, always impose devaluation, austerity and a reduction in the standard of living of the poorest sections of the population? 'Real prices' (world prices being the supreme reference) and the abolition of subsidies for the most basic consumer goods always operate against the interest of peoples.

Conversely, is industry in Africa really over-protected? Will not reducing such 'over-protectionism' of an industry which is still the most fragile in the world reduce even further its already negligible rate of growth?

Wages in Africa are said to be too high and those of Bangladesh are held up as a model. Does the World Bank see the future in terms of the Bangladeshization of the Third World? How does one reconcile this statement with that on satisfying 'basic needs'? In addition, there is no discussion on industrialization strategies, and import substitution is considered as by far the superior option (no attention is paid to the fact that this strategy reproduces and reinforces inequalities in income distribution) although it is said to have been 'badly applied' in Africa because it too often required state intervention (without which, despite the Bank's pious hopes concerning 'entrepreneurs', the rate of industrialization would have been even lower). The Bank also recommends processing mineral resources for export, although it is a known fact that such processing swallows up considerable capital without leading to interaction between the exploitation of the resources and national development. It also recommends light export industries. Have the disasters of the textile industries in Morocco and Tunisia been forgotton which, after having followed such 'recommendations', saw the doors of Western market firmly closed to their products? As for the industrialization required to ensure agricultural development, this is one aspect of which the Bank is, apparently, quite unaware.

The alternative strategy

Instead of the false, and metaphysical, opposition between agriculture and industry, consideration should be given to how they are interlinked in 'modernization' theory and practices and how they should be linked in an alternative national and popular strategy. For the agricultural revolution needs industry to make it possible, but not the type of industries so far developed (poorly) in Africa.

To try to schematize the opposing autocentred model/extraverted model, a four sector analysis had been proposed: 1) production of the means of production; 2) production of goods for mass consumption; 3) luxury production/consumption; 4) exports. The autocentred model is defined as one mainly governed by the interlinkage of sectors 1) and 2), and the extraverted model as one mainly determined by the interlinkage of sectors 3) and 4). This analysis leads to a major conclusion: in the autocentred model labour remuneration (wages and peasants' incomes) must necessarily increase according to the pace of the progress of productivity; in the extraverted model the labour remuneration can be delinked from the productivity growth.

Therefore:

(i) the development of a contemporary Third World country cannot be achieved through the adjustment of its economy to the requirements of the international division of labour, but through delinking this economy from the international division of labour;

(ii) this delinking is a necessary (but not sufficient) condition for an autocentred development which remains impossible if it is not intended for the people (that is, if the benefits of the productivity rise do not go straight to the greater majority);

(iii) conversely, a growth, mainly of benefit to a minority, is possible on the basis of an extraverted development (not always and everywhere possible), but such development is more effective for this objective than is an autocentred model.

In the contemporary Third World, autocentred development is synonymous with a national and popular content. It is now possible to see that the policies implemented in Africa during the 1960s and 1970s have been mainly 'extraverted'. In Africa, bearing in mind the contrasts and differences, and different political regimes and numerous changes, there have been four sets of experience:

a) 'Stagnation', associated with a lack of natural resources and/or a stagnant world demand for these resources.
b) 'Stagnation', despite the existence of such resources either potential (but well-known), or even exploited (and at times on a large scale).
c) 'Relatively marked growth', at times even high, associated with the exploitation of these resources, either by the multinationals or by the national state.

d) 'Marked growth', despite the fact that the exploited resources (often agricultural rather than mining) are moderate, due in general to an extensive opening to the exterior; this marked growth being associated with an uneven distribution of its benefits.

Within that framework of conventional economic analysis some motors of effective growth (when it has existed) may be identified: (1) oil and mines; (2) export agriculture (relatively rich: coffee, cocoa; or poor: groundnut); (3) light consumption industries managed in an acceptable way, established by multinationals or the state, modern in techniques, responding to the internal market (import substitution); (4) a lively building sector (linked to the accelerated urbanization and 'prosperity'); (5) administrative expenditures conceived in very classical terms, miming the West in its form and, to some degree, so-called social (education first), growing at a sustained pace; (6)

tertiary activities (trade, finance) almost always stronger in growth than the other sectors.

When the global growth has been slight (or zero, or negative) it seems attributed to an insufficient dynamism of (1) and (2) and/or to a doubtful character of (3). If, in addition, (5) and (6) have been pushed, then the linked double crisis of public finances and balance of payments ineluctably worsens the situation. The lack of dynamism of (1), (2) and (3) is attributed either to the evident shortcomings of the country or to its lofty nationalism that refuses foreign capital, a rare factor. It is, or can be, aggravated by the unconcern of the elite, its corruption, and so on.

A steadily backward agriculture almost always stagnant (except in export products) is incapable of releasing a marketed food surplus up to the standard of the effective urban demand. In the most extreme cases, it becomes increasingly difficult for the rural world to feed itself. These disasters or shortages are easily attributed to the climate (drought) or to the careless administrative bureaucracy of the rural world. The policies draining the rural world, which these conventional global strategies of growth necessarily imply, are rarely analysed.

In these experiences, industry has rarely been the driving force of the growth, but the product of a response adjusting to growth, whose chain effects are limited: (i) upstream, through the shortage of basic industries and the weak inter-industrial integration; (ii) downstream, through the uneven character of the incomes it distributes. If the industry restricts itself to a definite number of production units in a position of quasi-monopoly on a small market, and these units provide consumption goods for middle classes, then, even if efficiently managed (that is, without need of subsidies and with prices competitive with those of imports), this industry is derived, and not a driving force.

The alternative option of a national and popular autocentred strategy rests first on the principle of an equitable distribution of income, especially between rural and urban sectors, between the modern sectors with higher productivity and the backward ones. The surplus of the production over the remuneration of labour thus equalized constitutes an excess which, if it is national and retained for accumulation, guarantees a marked growth and a parallel and even progression of popular consumption. Constituted in this way, the structure of demand would show priority in basic needs and orient the productive system towards their satisfaction.

Without entering into an illusory description of concrete details of the measures necessary to implement a development pattern of this type, it can be assumed that:

a) It not only implies a declaration of an agricultural priority, but also its effective implementation. This priority requires that other activities with higher productivity should not provide an opportunity for the distribution of incomes in excess of those distributed in agriculture. The reason for this is that to structure demand in such a way would satisfy the needs expressed by the privileged at the expense of agriculture.

b) It implies that industrialization be first conceived to maintain the progress of productivity in agriculture: production of adequate inputs; infrastructural works; preserving and processing the produce, and so on. It then ensures that industry satisfies the non-food consumption needs of the rural and urban population, on as egalitarian a basis as possible. This national industry cannot be abandoned by substitution through imports, because imports must be paid for through exports, and the comparative advantages are those resulting from the price and income system of the world order, in conflict with the political coherence outlined above. Therefore, imports must be reduced to a strict minimum.

c) It thus implies national and popular forms of social organization of the production: peasants' control over agricultural projects; real co-operatives (which should not be a way of draining the rural areas, depriving the peasants of their hold on production); institutions for collective bargaining of agricultural prices; national control of industries; a national wage policy; redistribution of the financing means on a country scale, and so on. It is difficult to imagine how, for instance, multinationals would find a place in this organizational pattern, except, in time and under the strict national control, to provide some limited production or organizational models.

d) It implies that technology is not reduced to its transfer. It is in fact a matter of creating an inventive capacity, not for reasons of cultural nationalism, but because available techniques, especially the more advanced ones, are specific with regard to the range of products, the structure of demand to be satisfied (Western patterns), the price and income structures which control the profitability of these techniques.

e) It implies limited external relations radically different from those derived from the various industrialization strategies, import substitution, or export industrialization. Import substitution is based on an already actual demand in a structure of income distribution characterized by inequality, and on this basis respects the principles of the profitability (with at most some arguments of 'moderate protection of infant industries' during a brief transition). It can, therefore, only displace imports towards the intermediate goods (the industrial apparatus remaining non-integrated) and sophisticated capital goods (as the demand to be satisfied, in competition with the imports reproduces the Western capital's exacting consumption model): it thus remains extraverted. National and popular autocentred industry, however, is not built in response to a pre-existing demand, but is created on the basis of the satisfaction of peoples' needs (incomes policy) and intermediate and derived capital needs. Imports aim at filling the gaps in the range of these derived needs, but progressively reducing their relative importance (but not necessarily their absolute bulk). External relations are therefore bound to the logic of internal accumulation. The export industry, by its very definition, is extraverted, especially as, forced to compete with advanced countries' industry in their own homeland, advanced technology must be extensively imported. This explains why the newly industrializing countries (NICs), which are the most advanced in that direction, are also the most indebted: the export industry does not alleviate the balance of foreign trade (contrary to the argument put forward to that effect, by the World Bank in particular), it aggravates it.

f) It implies building up a national structure of interdependence price/financing means which is in conflict with the principles of the criterion of micro-economic profitability. In fact, the autocentred industry, to comply with the peoples' needs, must accept the juxtaposition of diverse productive units – modern industries, semi-mechanized manufactures, handicrafts manufactures. The unit of labour remuneration and that of prices thereby entail unequal surplus, which must be redistributed in order to avoid the polarization of progress in the modern units; and to finance progressive modernization of the backward sectors with the modern sectors' surplus. This is hardly possible on a large scale without big public property: the private national enterprise and, *a fortiori*, the multinational sub-company cannot at this level accept loss of profitability. In fact, such enterprises act in a directly opposite sense: by destroying the non-competitive cottage industry, they have contributed to increasing unemployment and simultaneously depriving the population of useful products.

2.   The Role of the Export Sector

Hamid Aït Amara

Today, all African countries are facing the limitations of a development strategy based on expanding the export sector. The 1970s were marked by an almost universal slowing down of growth in GNP and economic expansion came to a halt, or became negative in many countries. This happened in Chad and Uganda whose problems are well known; but it has also affected mineral-rich countries such as Zaire, Liberia and Zambia and even the Ivory Coast which, in the 1960s and the first half of the 1970s, had registered high growth rates.

In these countries, GNP has regressed in absolute terms as a result of a decline in both agricultural and industrial production. On average, per capita income in sub-Saharan Africa fell by 0.4% per annum during the 1970s, and the end or slowing down of economic growth has led to growing unemployment, increased pressure on land, and unproductive tertiary sectors.

The 'modern' economic system's capacity to absorb a labour force that is growing rapidly as a result of population growth and urbanization is reaching breaking point. This trend is appearing at a very low level of industrialization, such that the proportion of the economically active population employed in industry is still very low, compared to what can be observed in other Third World regions.

The decline in agricultural production

Paradoxically, the fact that most of the labour force is in agriculture has not prevented the decline in food production and the growth of imports. The food production index fell from 100 to 91 during the 1970s (World Bank, 1981).

Africa south of the Sahara – although the Arab countries of Africa should also be included – is thus the only region in the world where per capita food production has fallen over the last two decades. Furthermore, the rate of cover of Africa's (including North Africa and Egypt) external agricultural trade (export receipts as a percentage of expenditure on imports) is declining rapidly, falling from an index of 216 in 1970–71 to 134.2 in 1976–77 and 68.8 in 1983–84; and for sub-Saharan African countries alone, 138.2, 223.6 and 128.5 over the same periods.

This downward trend in the food balance reflects the situation of the vast majority of countries, including those such as the Ivory Coast or Kenya, which recorded a smaller fall in their agricultural surplus.[1] In the Ivory Coast, rice imports rose from 149,000 metric tons in 1973 to 382,500 metric tons in 1982, and wheat imports from 139,000 metric tons in 1973 to 200,000 metric tons in 1983.

Globally, the period 1975–85 saw a large increase in food imports, cereal imports rose from six to 21 million metric tons.[2] This development was due mainly to rapid urban growth which reached an average rate of 6 or 7% per annum; but in a growing number of countries, such imports have also become necessary to cover the needs of the rural areas.[3] This new situation arises from the increasing integration of agricultural production into both the local and the external market and increased monetization of the rural economy.

Faced with the aggravation of the food crisis, most countries have, on the recommendations of the IMF, implemented policies aimed at extending private exploitation and control of agricultural resources, and further promoting the role of the market in both the production and distribution of agricultural inputs and commodities. Additionally, in many countries the state has disbanded public agencies that had previously performed major economic functions in the organization of production and exchange.

Official aid and the grant of new loans are being made subject to measures designed to promote the further liberalization of African economies. Thus the EC intervenes directly in the formulation of agricultural and food policies in countries to which it gives aid.[4] Raising producer prices, input subsidies, and reorganizing the collection of local products are designed to create conditions favourable to a growth of production for the market.

These policies have been in effect for a few years, but it appears that the situation has not greatly changed. The fall in the standard of living of urban workers consequent upon increased prices of foodstuffs has had no counterpart in a measurable improvement in peasant incomes. While the relative prices of food crops and export crops have, in a number of countries, shifted in favour of food crops, they have been insufficient to slow down the growth of wheat, rice and maize imports. Food production rose by only 1.5% per annum during the 1970s, whereas population was rising by 2.7%.

With the rise of agricultural food prices and the deepening of the urban food supply crisis, trends have emerged towards the control of land and the principal means of production and exchange by small groups of capitalist farmers, traders or entrepreneurs. This development is marked in countries where the food deficits are large, where the rise in prices has been highest (Nigeria, Kenya, Egypt, Algeria) and where the reduction in the availability of foreign exchange for external procurement has given more scope for local production for the market.

In countries where the 'green revolution' has occurred, government measures, especially in the area of price rises, mainly benefit the big farmers. Experience, particularly Africa's, shows that transfers of the social product in favour of agriculture through a pricing policy, operate, in practice, to the benefit of a particular category of farmers and that the mass of small or landless peasants who must substitute insufficient production with foodstuffs bought on the market are penalized by higher agricultural prices just as much as urban workers.

The increase in the role of the market and reference to prices have generally led to African agriculture becoming more closely integrated into the international division of labour and their dependence.

Reducing the areas in which the state intervened heavily, notably in the trade in cereal products,[5] has not led to an improvement in the conditions of supply to the cities, or the collection and stocking of products. Overall, after the implementation of a series of measures, the situation of agriculture has not improved. This is the message of the report drawn up by the *Comité permanent Inter-Etats de la lutte contre la sécheresse au Sahel*[6] meeting in 1986 in Cape Verde; it also observed that in regions where a co-ordinated and systematic effort had been made to promote food production, the situation had barely improved. The Sahel's dependence had even deepened, and production everywhere was growing more slowly than population. Finally, the Comité stressed 'that the efforts made at the technical level of the production of inputs, production infrastructures, and intensification . . . have not borne the fruits expected of them'.

The difficulties in promoting agricultural production by sectoral measures alone show quite clearly that the problem of agricultural failure must be looked at in a more global context, that of the choice of development. As Samir Amin notes, *famine and rural poverty are the product of the relations of the subsistence sector with other sectors and with the international economy.*

The fact is that, beyond the sectoral crisis of agriculture, what needs to be examined is the validity of accumulation strategies based on expanding the export sector (whether agricultural, mining or energy exports) and the effects of a process of accumulation and the development dynamic.

Failure of the export model

The case study by Aly Traoré, on the Ivory Coast, represents the typical example of the agricultural export model implemented by most African countries at varying economic levels, depending on the potential of agricultural natural resources. Today it is quite clear that after a high growth rate during the 1970s and relatively high industrial growth, the Ivorian economy since 1978 has entered a period of unbroken recession; GDP growth after 1980 and 1985 became negative. There was a fall in external receipts, and a deficit in the current balance of payments with a debt service ratio that rose from 24% in 1980 to almost 39% in 1985, leading the Ivory Coast to turn to the IMF. In March 1981, a first stabilization plan was put into effect, and this was soon followed by a second programme in 1984.[7]

Theoretically, as Traoré points out, expansion of the export sector is supposed to fulfill a double function: to provide a financial base for the construction of an import-substitution industry: and to lead an increase in production by the food sub-sector so as to increase the supply of foodstuffs to meet urban demand.

Generally, in the long term, the growth of peasant incomes formed the basis for an enlargement of the domestic market for the products of a gradual industrialization. The analyses presented by Traoré and Kosura bring out the factors that slow down and distort the growth of the Ivorian and Kenyan economies and which, in varying degrees, mark all African economies of this type.

Western countries have a monopoly of the demand for coffee and cocoa, and their industrial processing and marketing leaves only a small proportion of the surplus realized to the Ivory Coast and Kenya. Traoré observes a falling trend of export receipts, which is as much the direct consequence of the decline of world market prices for the Ivory Coast as it is of an unequal distribution of the added value as a result of the unfavourable movement of the terms of trade.

The world market's limited absorptive capacity and the sharp competition between Third World countries for the export of tropical products mean that supplies are increasing much more rapidly than demand, leading to falling prices. In the last ten years, with a diminution of global receipts of the order of 20%, prices have fallen rapidly. The deterioration in trade terms now affects all export products. Thus, compared to the prices of wheat and rice, increasing quantities of which have to be purchased, the terms of trade have deteriorated for tea, groundnuts, rubber, pepper, sugar, among others (since 1984), cotton and oilseeds.[8]

Wide variations in prices on world markets have constituted another source of fragility for African economies that have specialized in an agriculture sector to take account of comparative advantage. Most export crops which, in the 19th-century framework of colonial policy had a comparative advantage, are today suffering the backlash of import-restricting policies practised by the developed capitalist countries, and the development of import-substituting crops. This is the case, for example, with the advance of sweeteners at the expense of sugar. In 1974–76 world consumption of high fructose maize syrup was equivalent to 700,000 metric tons of raw sugar, in 1979–81 to three million metric tons, in 1982 to over four million metric tons, and in 1985 to 5.5 million metric tons.[9]

Transnational companies have also embarked on the use of biological engineering to create substitutes for coffee and cocoa, the two principal agricultural products exported by Third World countries. Finally, a reorientation of the trade of the former colonial powers in the framework of Atlantic integration, has replaced the earlier colonial integration. Africa's share in France's external trade, for example, continues to fall, 13.3% in 1981 as against 17.6% in 1970 and 30% in 1960.[10] The shift in France's agricultural trade policy has taken place in favour of its partners in the EC and the USA.

A varying proportion of external receipts has been reinvested in the expansion of the export sector. This has happened in the Ivory Coast which, given the large amount of land available and favourable climatic conditions, has encouraged the extension and diversification of crops and preliminary industrial processing activities in order to maximize its foreign exchange receipts. In order to accelerate the growth rate of exports it had to resort to massive external financing and accept a high level of indebtedness. Thus the Ivory Coast appears among the most indebted countries in Africa. In 1984, the debt-service ratio amounted to approximately 39%. This development reflects the situation of all African countries that have chosen to promote the extraversion of their economy through recourse to external capital.

During the 1970s, with the rise in international liquidity, the banks had no difficulty in financing exports from industrialized to Third World countries. In many cases they even pushed some countries further into debt than was necessary. Thus the Ivory Coast had no difficulty in raising large loans to carry out a programme to produce 550,000 metric tons of sugar, 450,000 of which would be for export despite the collapse in the world market price of sugar. In 1984, at the request of the IMF and the World Bank, two sugar complexes were closed.[11]

Sub-Saharan Africa's global debt of between US\$ 100 and 200 million represents a per capita burden similar to that of Latin America; and if the level of poverty is taken into account, it represents an even greater burden. Total external public debt represents a proportion of GNP that varies from 20% for Ethiopia and Zimbabwe to 146% for Mauritania, most countries falling between 30 and 80% of GNP. The yield on capital borrowed and invested in agro-export projects, notably the high foreign exchange costs for exploitation, considerably reduces the available net resources produced by the export activities that are the source of the mechanisms transferring value to the developed capitalist countries. One of the most obvious consequences of the export-led development model is the high level of the external debt which is directly proportional to the economy's degree of openness.

A more or less important function of the surplus derived from exports is to finance the establishment of industries. Industrialization strategies are based on the growth of industries to add value to export products and on import-substitution industries. The food, beverages and textile sectors, plus perhaps units manufacturing various consumer items, provide most of the value of industrial production. The mining sector (bauxite, copper, phosphates, and so on) remains in the hands of the big foreign companies.

Generally speaking, industry has been conceived of as a mere supplement to the traditional import–export economy.[12] Given that domestic markets are small and people's purchasing power is low, particularly in the rural areas, the limits to substitution were soon reached. In Hirschman's words, 'industry ran out of steam before having achieved very much'. The export resources devoted to investment have been insufficient to finance the backward linkage towards the production of intermediate and capital goods that are the basis of a diversified process of industrialization. The Ivory Coast has had to abandon its projects to develop iron ore and paper industries.

In Senegal, the government doubled the price of fertilizers, leading to a massive fall in consumption. Fertilizer production in the Ivory Coast fell from

100,000 metric tons in 1981 to 50,000 metric tons in 1984, and cement production from 1,156,000 metric tons in 1980 to 500,000 metric tons in 1981. Peasant incomes are everywhere insufficient to fuel a demand for capital and manufactured goods that could constitute a significant domestic outlet for existing industries, and even less constitute a potential basis for industrialization.

Clearly, the expansion of the export sectors had no linkage effect on the rest of the economy and particularly no knock-on effect on *food* production. The concept of consumption linkage which, according to Hirschman,[13] applies to 'the surplus of food production that arises from the increase in exports', is more relevant to the economies in the centre than to the local economy, where the increase in revenues from exports simply means an increase in imports of foodstuffs. Local agriculture, particularly food agriculture, as illustrated by the case of Nigeria, and to a lesser degree, that of the Ivory Coast, derives no advantage from a widening of domestic demand. The paradox could even be argued that it is where export revenues are reduced that local food production is encouraged. The under-utilized agricultural potential is then more efficiently mobilized through transfers of part of the factors of production from the export to the foodstuff sector.

The question of the repercussions of a policy of promoting exports over food production is a very vexed one. The World Bank (1981), argues that export crops represent the channel through which features of modernization can be introduced into food crop activities. Cash crops make possible the purchase of implements, fertilizers and pest-control agents which can be used to improve labour productivity and the yield per hectare of food crops.

Numerous studies have, however, demonstrated the absence of any knock-on effect of cash crops on food crops. More recent observations (Rwanda 1985) even report a deterioration in the daily calorie intake, almost 20% in peasant smallholder families that grow food crops, as compared to those which devote themselves exclusively to food production. The stagnation, or even regression, of food crops is more the consequence of the dualism of the structures of production brought about by the system of export crops.[14]

The expansion of the agro-export sector was in fact accompanied by a distinct shift in agricultural structures in favour of large mechanized holdings. The orientation of production towards world markets, writes A. Basler, 'may lead to changes in the structure of farmholdings in favour of "plantation"-type holdings exclusively oriented towards export crops and the retreat of family holdings growing both food and cash crops'.

In many countries a growth in the number of large holdings in commercial production and exports can be observed, while small-scale subsistence agriculture encounters increasing difficulties in reproducing itself. In Malawi, the government pursues a systematic policy in favour of large farms comprising between 100 and 9,000 hectares[15] while smallholdings average 1.5 hectares.

Adding value to the main agricultural export products continues overwhelmingly to be done abroad, as Traoré shows for the Ivory Coast. Those that are processed on the spot, coconuts, oil palm, pineapples, all second rank products, are processed by foreign technology and capital. There has been no great development of the agricultural foodstuffs industry for the processing of products intended for the local market – millet, cassava and maize semolina and flour – despite a few attempts to do so in Nigeria, Sudan, Senegal and the Ivory Coast.

Although having the necessary resources (iron ore, petroleum, gas, phosphate, for example) African countries have not equipped themselves with industries producing capital goods for agriculture. With a few rare exceptions (1   Algeria, Zimbabwe) local production takes the form of assembly activities and processing chemical products (Kenya, the Ivory Coast) more than processing local raw materials or semi-finished products by a true backward-linking industrial sector.

Most of the equipment intended for agriculture is acquired from abroad. A UNIDO report estimates that between now and the year 2000, of 10 agricultural implements, Africans will have to import more than eight. This indicates that the fall in export receipts has had a negative impact on supplies to the agricultural sector. Fertilizer consumption, already very low, fell even further, contrary to what can be observed in other Third World countries where fertilizer consumption rose from 17 kg (1976) to 32 kg (1982) per hectare.

The use of fertilizers, a major factor in the increase in yields, is thus 8.8 kg in Africa, according to the FAO, less than 3 kg in half the countries of the continent, as against 33 kg for the Third World as a whole and 110 kg in developed countries.

In Kenya, the largest farms, those over 20 hectares in area, number 3,700 and cover 2.7 million hectares, while 1.7 million smallholdings have to share 3.5 million hectares; or an average of two per holding. In Zimbabwe, large-scale agriculture, modern profitable commercial agriculture, is in the hands of some 3,500 European farmers (1977) employing 350,000 workers.

In most African countries, the share of large farms in overall marketed production increased considerably during the 1970s. Large farms accounted for over 70% of the increase in agricultural export volumes in Malawi, while the disparities in relative incomes between large farms and smallholders has continued to grow (Malawi, Kenya, Sudan, the Ivory Coast, amongst others). The corollary of such a trend is not only the economic weakening of small, increasingly marginalized farms, but the accentuation of the process of differentiation within the peasantry and increasing control by a small number of owners of the land and other means of production. It also implies, as in Kenya, the growing proletarianization of agricultural labourers as part and parcel of the development of a capitalist agriculture and movement towards the individualization of property rights. In many countries, stress is placed on consolidating a kulak-based agriculture, better equipped to increase production for the market, although peasant agriculture remains the essential productive base.[16]

The example of Cuba, however, shows that there is no contradiction between export production and food production. Cuba has maintained its sugar exports, and even sought to increase them (1970) by achieving a high growth rate. For the period 1981–83, despite the collapse in sugar prices, it managed to secure an increase in per capita production of 5.9%, whereas over the same period the other Latin American countries recorded a fall of 10% in their GNP (CEPAL). With much less land than the Ivory Coast, and more limited external financing, Cuba has pursued its development, improving the food, health and education levels of the population, achieving full employment of the labour force through diversifying agricultural production and developing its industry.[17]

Alternative strategies: Algeria and Ethiopia

The extraverted pattern of accumulation has finally led to blocking the development dynamic and an irreducible dualism of economic and social structures. Promotion of the export sector has produced 'structural effects', a trend to social and economic polarization that marginalizes the vast majority of the rural population.

The alternative experiences, illustrated by the Algerian and Ethiopian cases, have concentrated on building up relations between agriculture and industry and meeting rural demand for producer and consumer goods. Modernizing agriculture and improving rural labour's productivity are thus placed at the very centre of the development problematic.

In Algeria, the stress on industrialization, in a first phase, aimed 1) to set up industries capable 'of bringing technological progress to the heart of the most backward sector, agriculture';[18] and, 2) by diversifying economic activities, to create sufficient jobs eventually to absorb the surplus of rural labour, without which rapid growth of agricultural productivity is impeded.

The relationship between agriculture and industry has thus been accorded special attention and priority has been given to investment designed to provide agriculture with the means to modernize its techniques of production. The development of iron and steel and petro-chemical industries, which form the backbone of the industrialization process, served as the focus for the construction of engineering, electrical and chemical sectors designed to meet agriculture's demand for producer goods: agricultural implements, machinery, fertilizers, irrigation equipment and so on. After a decade and a half, large quantities of various capital goods have been delivered to agriculture, notably in the area of mechanization.

But relations between agriculture and industry could intensify only in so far as conditions of productivity in the employment of capital and labour existed, enabling agriculture to develop and finance purchases from industry and raise the purchasing power of rural households. The question of the evolution of agricultural productivity thus becomes of fundamental importance.

In Algeria, where the land is relatively overpopulated, improving labour productivity necessarily involves an increase in physical production per unit of surface area. Raising peasant incomes is then possible only if agricultural productivity is rising faster than agricultural employment. For it is possible to increase production per hectare without altering labour productivity if agriculture has proportionally to absorb as many new workers as it creates extra goods.

In China, for example, labour productivity calculated in man-days appears to have declined considerably between 1950 and 1975, most of the increase in incomes having been provided by an increase in the number of days worked per worker in agriculture; from 175 days in the late 1950s to 275 days per worker per annum in 1975.[19]

The movement of employment is thus a strategic variable, determining the productivity gains of labour in agriculture and final demand by sector. Agriculture will perform its role in the development process all the better when other sectors, and principally industry, are in a position to reduce population pressure on the land.

The numerous criticisms of the Algerian strategy 'based on priority for industry and the abandonment of agriculture', criticisms generally directed at countries which attempt to escape from the import-substitution industrialization model, thus fundamentally misunderstand the basic facts about its development model. Algeria has based its industrialization on an internal dynamic that makes growth of the local market a condition of the development process, and agriculture's demand, both for producer and industrially produced consumer goods, is an essential dimension of that process.

Contrary to what has often been written, the autocentred strategy is a true 'rehabilitation of agriculture and the rural areas' that starts from the need for purchasing power in the rural areas in order to extend the local market and pursue development.[20] It is also necessary to emphasize that Algeria is half-way along in its industrialization process. The phase of capital goods industries 'whose size testifies to the capacity for self-transformation of the economic system'[21] has not yet reached a significant level. The 1980–84 and 1985–89 plans proposed to continue the establishment of capital goods industries and thus reduce dependence on imports necessary for the functioning of the production apparatus. Capital and intermediate goods still represent almost 50% of total imports. It thus appears that the inter-sectoral and intra-sectoral integration project has not been pushed far enough to give the economy a (relative) autonomy in its accumulation project.

The more or less rapid and sizeable transfer of the surplus rural labour force to non-agricultural activities can help or hinder the growth of productivity, and thus determine the intensity of relations between agriculture and industry. In other words, the development problematic consisted in seeking the conditions of a continuous improvement of rural labour productivity, given the specific constraints of the economy.

Naturally, given Algeria's demographic situation, an absolute reduction of the rural population in order to accelerate the process of labour productivity growth, such as happened in Europe from the late 19th century, was ruled out. In the most favourable circumstances, agriculture will have to absorb a proportion of the annual growth of the labour force for an indeterminate period.

This explains the strategic role of industrialization and the growth of non-agricultural employment, in realizing a growth rate of productivity per worker in agriculture that would make it possible both to fuel agriculture's demand for industrial goods and to improve the producers' standard of living.

Globally, the analysis suggested by Aït Amara shows that the industry-led development dynamic has had positive effects on the growth of the agricultural sector, notably in employment and incomes. Throughout the 1970s and the first half of the 1980s, job creation was sufficiently sustained to absorb the whole of the additional demand for jobs both in the towns and in the countryside, thus making it possible to stabilize the numbers of those working in agriculture at the 1960s level, at the same time as extending mechanization. The industrialization process also made it possible to widen the domestic outlets for agriculture and to increase agricultural incomes as a result of rising demand and prices. In addition, it contributed to keeping the majority of the small peasantry, living on holdings that were too small, in the rural areas by providing them with extra jobs and incomes without which they could not have remained in the countryside.

Analysis of the Algerian case, however, shows that in countries with strong population pressure on the land, if industrialization is a necessary prior condition, then an increase in yields is essential; by itself, industrialization is not sufficient to sustain a lasting process of agricultural growth.[22] Progress cannot be limited to the material factors of production, it also concerns the biological aspects that influence the evolution of yields and the capacity of peasants to master new production techniques. This interdependence, or interaction, of different links in 'the chain of agricultural progress' explains the very slow diffusion of technological change in agriculture, and the importance of structural policies that attempt to accelerate its spread. Structural reforms are thus a fundamental aspect of the problematic of the modernization of agriculture, 'in so far as concerns both the ownership of land and the performance of labour itself'.[23]

In Algeria, the process of structural reform was deliberately limited, and in addition interrupted, in the 1980s. In 1982, the government dissolved the agrarian reform sector established in the 1970s, and terminated aid provided to the subsistence sector through service co-operatives. The collective sector that had emerged from the nationalization of settler lands in 1963 was once again reorganized, stressing intervention by the state in the functioning and management of the 'socialist agricultural estates'. The policy of gradually reducing the agrarian dualism inherited from the colonial period, initiated by the 1971 agrarian reform through a gradual reorganization of labour and ownership, has been abandoned in favour of a path for developing agriculture that seeks to rely on individual exploitation of the land and a greater role given to the market.

The result is a limited employment of agricultural resources, despite a very high rate of food dependency and the maintenance of distortions in the productive structure compared to the demand for food, notably in order to contain the rise in farm prices within limits that do not excessively compromise the global economic balances. This evolution of agrarian relations further accentuates the importance of the oil rent in the development process and neglects the mobilization of a domestic surplus generated by a broad development of productive forces in agriculture. It also testifies to the class limits that may impede the full realization of an autocentred development model. Ethiopia appears not to have set such limits, but bases the accumulation dynamic on the effects of a radical reform of agrarian structures.

Ethiopia completely reversed its approach to development after the advent of people's power. The agro-export model of import-substitution industrialization pursued until 1974 was abandoned and replaced by a strategy of mobilizing the principally agricultural domestic surplus. This surplus, writes M. Douri, can result only from increasing the yields and labour productivity of the whole peasant sector. This explains the vital importance of the agrarian reform in Ethiopia in opening up access to all of technological progress. The abolition of the feudal tenure system simultaneously transformed both the ownership regime and the social relations of production. It created a new mode of organization and production that literally liberated the rural productive forces and cast aside the obstacles to intensifying labour and improving productivity. This movement rests on peasant associations, which are responsible for allocating land and promoting service co-operatives.

Since 1976, the peasant associations have been developing forms of co-operation between their members and embarking on a process of rural industrialization built around peasant needs. Service co-operatives constitute an increasing source of employment and accumulation that benefits the development of the rural economy. The key question, writes M. Douri, is how to meet the new peasant demand consequent upon the agrarian reform and the changes in the distribution of the country's wealth. Thus, the agrarian reform has been accompanied by a process of industrialization more closely subordinated to meet the needs of agriculture whose social, structural and technical transformation it sustains.

The Ethiopian experience testifies to the key role of structural reforms, in the broad sense, in the dynamic of relations between agriculture and industry and brings out the importance of the knock-on effects peasant demand and new modes of organizing labour and agricultural production can have on the development process. Which types of social relations should be chosen in order to accelerate the development of agriculture thus reappears as an essential question in the problematic of the modernization of agriculture.

Social relations and agricultural development

In this context, Africa finds itself showered with advice from all quarters to apply the social forms of agricultural production that have historically accompanied the development of capitalism. It is alleged that these forms would make possible the provision of a basic calorie intake for all cheaply, an unprecedented increase in the volume of output and the mobilization of an agricultural surplus for industrial investment. They thus offer the example of a successful integration of agriculture into overall development. One is led to believe, writes C. Servolin, 'that this model of agricultural policy is the only one that has succeeded throughout past and present history, the only one whose adoption can be recommended to developing countries'.[24]

But, apart from the fact these forms imposed themselves only after agrarian structures had been evolving for two centuries – the first agricultural revolution dates from the 18th century, the second and more decisive one from the 1950s – the conditions that favoured their realization quite clearly do not exist in Africa. In Western Europe the process of restructuring the rural areas around the farms best suited by their economic scale and their size went on for over a century, a process favouring a concentration of production in the hands of a certain type of 'achieving' farmer capable of developing production for the market. The others, the majority of small peasants, gradually had to stop working their best situated farms.[25]

For reasons as much economic (protection of local agriculture) as political (as a counterweight to the growing working class), the disintegration of the peasantry was curbed in many countries, except for Britain where the process of expelling the majority of the peasantry was carried out with all its well known brutality. By the 19th century, the rural population already accounted for scarcely one-third of the total labour force. Generally speaking, only after the Second World War, in the early 1950s, did agricultural policies begin to favour a stepping-up of the movement to modernize agriculture.

Industry was by then in a position to provide massive quantities of all the mechanical, chemical and biochemical means necessary for a rapid growth of agricultural productivity. As M. Mazoyer stresses, modern industry, which provides the mechanical, chemical, energy and civil engineering means, plays a considerable role in the establishment of new agricultural systems; 'moreover, the elimination of the peasant economy is carried out in conditions that are consistent with industrial development which avoids brutal ruptures and generalized crises'. There is consistency in two senses, since the rate at which agricultural producers are removed continues to be related to the creation of jobs outside agriculture and, conversely, the transformation of equipment makes it possible to increase the efficiency of agricultural labour.

The relative fall in the price of agricultural foodstuffs consequent upon the rapid improvement in labour productivity thus makes it possible to limit the proportion of household expenditure on food in favour of expenditure on manufactured goods. This model of 'agricultural modernization' benefited from specific conditions that Third World countries cannot reproduce today. The movement of the rural population into non-agricultural activities rested on sustained industrial expansion.

In addition, from the second half of the 19th century to the end of the Second World War, 40 million Europeans moved, for example, to America, Australia, New Zealand.[26] In 40 years (1860–1900) there were 14 million new arrivals in the United States, of whom Europeans were the vast majority: 86.5% of immigrants in 1860; 58.1% in 1880; 73.4% in 1890; 86.2% in 1900.[27]

This meant that in most West European countries, from the second half of the 19th century, the agricultural population fell in absolute numbers making it possible to increase the size of farms and improve farm area per worker. Finally, the European population growth rate was in no way comparable to that of African countries. Population growth did not exceed 1.5% to 2% throughout the 19th century, as against 3 to 3.4% in Africa and even 4% in Kenya, and, in contrast to a downward trend in the birth rate in China, Brazil or Indonesia, which can be observed today, Africa's still shows no sign of peaking.

In spite of the very high urban expansion of recent years, the agricultural population has continued to rise, leading to a marked deterioration in the available land/population ratio in those countries without further large areas of land to bring into cultivation.

The FAO's report on the potential of land in Africa reveals very high agricultural densities in a number of countries (350 per km^2 of agricultural land in Rwanda, for example) which will have to cope with a serious land shortage. Even the best endowed countries (the Ivory Coast, Sudan, Nigeria) are seeing their cultivable land diminish rapidly following the mechanization of farming or the adoption of new forms of cultivation,[28] as well as ecological changes due to massive deforestation. Over the last two decades the Ivory Coast has cut down over 7,000,000 hectares of forest, and soil deterioration is leading many people to extend their crops to ecologically fragile regions and to shorten or eliminate fallow periods, thus further contributing to rapid deterioration of the soil. According to the UN world desertification map, 43% of the land in Africa that is not already desert is threatened with becoming so.[29]

As the Economic Commission for Africa stresses, probably in future, in a majority of African countries, the rural population will be faced with an almost disastrous shortage of cultivable land, and whole families will have to subsist on scarcely one hectare.[30] The question of how to modernize agriculture must fundamentally be posed in relation to the crucial problem of employment and the need to find a permanent solution to it.

It is a fact that the type of industrialization introduced in most African countries has only rarely absorbed a significant fraction of the available labour force. It is equally likely that the pursuit of current development policies will not lead to more non-agricultural employment on such a scale as to slow down the growth of the economically active agricultural population. Agriculture thus finds itself in a situation of retaining all or part of the additional numbers of workers entering the labour market each year. African economies must both create more jobs in agriculture and increase net output per worker.

In that situation, the issue is not, as in the capitalist pattern of agriculture, one of seeking to expand production through the gradual removal of the economically active agricultural population, but, on the contrary, of expanding employment and stepping up exploitation of all agricultural natural resources.

What social forms of organizing production are best suited to a rational and intensive use of space and labour? This question is vital in dry farming countries where the scale of the tasks of soil conservation and improvement requires strict social discipline at all levels of agricultural activity. What is needed is a process of 'ecological reconstruction'. Experience shows that peasants individually cannot undertake such tasks nor integrate the conditions of long-term reproduction into their everyday activities. The individual smallholding system can, in Erik Eckholm's words, lead only to a 'suicidal use of the land', with the peasants seeking to ward off declining soil fertility and the consequences of erosion with even wider destruction of the natural environment. What is required, therefore, is a large-scale reorganization of agricultural work through co-operation between producers in order to avoid the negative phenomena of land concentration and soil destruction. In countries with a relative scarcity of cultivable land such an evolution would soon lead to a blocking of the productive forces by the minority that held a monopoly over landownership.

Unfortunately, the notion of co-operation has been largely discredited in Africa by the way states have used it. Co-operatives have usually served as a means of authoritarian organization of the peasantry and have sometimes (as in Senegal, Mali, Tanzania) been envisaged as a reformist alternative to socialism. But past errors must not be allowed completely to condemn co-operative living as a democratic framework in which peasant producers can organize and express themselves. The development of co-operation remains, however, closely subordinated to the capacity of political forces to embark on a real process of social transformation, in particular to revamp rural social structures and institute a new distribution of power. Failing such a programme, the evolution of agriculture, under the effect of the laws of the market and monetization of the rural economy, will lead to the impoverishment of the majority of the peasantry excluded from access to the means of agricultural modernization.

The policies introduced to stem the agricultural crisis already give a glimpse of the development of a dualistic dynamic of agrarian structures. The raising of agricultural prices and the concessions granted to promote production have the effect of strengthening the groups that already have the most resources and the largest amount of land and which can take on wage labour: in other words they promote big farmers working for the market and capable of more efficient production. They also favour the penetration of speculative urban capital attracted by the inducements and prospects of quick, high profits. There are numerous reports pointing in this direction.

Many surveys show that projects initiated by governments have rather benefited a minority in which the urban elites, businessmen, bureaucrats or retired soldiers were the majority.[31] At the same time, in some countries, aid to small-scale subsistence agriculture, which is finding it increasingly hard to sustain itself, has been abolished. The new agricultural strategies rest rather on the groups with the capacity to increase commercial production and improve the supply of food to the towns.

It is today clear, after over two decades of experience, that export-led growth, whether the exports be of agricultural or mineral products, has not led to the construction of an autonomous basis of accumulation that would make the pursuit of development possible. Most African countries are unable to maintain employment at its previous levels and it even seems that a process of de-industrialization and economic decline is underway. There can be no solution to the external development crisis because no external development dynamic has been created. The most pronounced trend consists in yielding to the pressures of the world market and seeking greater integration into the capitalist economy in order to safeguard the interests of dominant groups. In order to compensate for the fall in external receipts, African countries are seeking to increase their exports, usually by restricting the consumption of the mass of the population rather than by embarking on mobilizing resources and labour to the benefit of the local market.

The example of Cuba's development shows that the essential problem lies in social control of the surplus realized from exports. Being open to external markets remains indispensable if speeding up the modernization and development of the productive forces through imports of equipment and technology is desired. But in African countries, the economic surplus derived from exports contributes mostly to increasing and diversifying the consumption of the ruling classes through the importation and local assembly of new products. Openness to the outside world makes it easy to fill the gaps in local production and leads to neglect of the development of activities that are yet essential for the establishment of economic equilibria.

The mobilization of external resources for development implies, however, a consistent accumulation strategy that necessarily involves a complete overhaul of the price system. Delinking, as Samir Amin points out, does not mean autarky, but the construction of a price system on the basis of the law of national value.[32] Clearly the inherited price system was organized to assist accumulation in the home countries in order to ensure the functioning of the colonial system. After the restructuring of the world economy and the direct integration of the colonial countries into the general movement of capital, the domestic price system conformed even more closely to the development needs of the productive forces of the dominant countries.

For this reason, in the long run, the prices that have relatively fallen least are those of agricultural machinery, wheat prices falling faster than those of equipment. This price ratio is, of course, central to the process of the concentration of production, land and capital in the industrialized countries of the North. Transferred to the countries of the Third World, through import prices, agricultural equipment prices are rising much faster than those of locally produced cereals and thus tend to hinder the diffusion of technological progress in agriculture (animal-drawn farming for example).

Finally, emerging from the crisis will inevitably involve gaining control of the local market and *articulating industrial and agricultural development*. Gaining control requires removal of the bottlenecks that hamper the processing of such local products as millet, sorghum, yams and so on (processing them into flour) which would make possible and facilitate the storage, processing, distribution and consumption of local products. Experiments in this area have been made in, for example, Senegal, Nigeria,

Sudan, the Ivory Coast, aimed at using blended flours incorporating local cereals for making bread, modernizing the process of preparing cassava (in the Congo) for making cassava bread and cassava couscous. Industry should thus ensure the promotion of technological methods to process local products, notably maize, which has a very large production potential in Africa (maize chips). Numerous industrial processes can thus develop downstream from production for the treatment of by-products (oil-mills, cotton, coffee) and meat.

Notes

1. A. Basler, 'L'agriculture d'éxportation en Afrique et les répercussions pour la production vivrière: un essai d'évolution', *Economie rurale*, No 173, May–June 1986.

2. J. Alibert, 'Problèmes socio-économiques de l'autosuffisance et de l'alimentation des villes en Afrique Noire', *Afrique contemporaine*, No 140, 1986.

3. Yabice Kinimo, 'Autosuffisance alimentaire en Côte d'Ivoire: paradoxe ou réalisme socio-économique', *Economie rurale*, No 175, September–October 1986. See also M. A. Savané and P. Cappagne, 'Quel avenir pour les nouvelles stratégies alimentaires des paysanneries du Sahel', *Economie et société* Cahier de l'ISMEA, July 1975.

4. 'It is conditional aid, rather than contractual aid, which must commit the receiving country to respect the targets and the discipline that they have set in formulating food strategies.'

5. 'In most countries trade liberalization enhances the role of private traders in the exchange of food products. Nevertheless, this shift involves risks that some well placed groups will organize so as to exercise a monopoly over the cereal market', *Mise en oeuvre des stratégies alimentaires et perspectives d'avenir*, EEC. Rome, Brussels, April 1986.

6. See 'La lettre de Sologral', No 14, January–February 1987.

7. See J.-P. Foissy, 'L'évolution de la Côte d'Ivoire (1960–85)', *Problèmes Economiques*, No 1987, 27 August 1986.

8. *The State of World Food and Agriculture*, FAO, Rome 1983. Africa's agricultural trade balance witnessed 'a switch from a small surplus [in 1981] to a deficit of over $2,000 million'. A. Basler, 'Exportations agricoles et déficit alimentaire en Afrique', *Economie rurale*, No 173, May–June 1986. 'In 1975 it took 200 kg of cotton seeds for one plough, by 1980 it took twice as much.'

9. In 1985, sweeteners made from maize represented half the total caloric sweeteners consumed in the USA. Sugar has been almost eliminated in the production of drinks. Protectionism to ensure a high price for sugar has encouraged the use of isoglucose. IFRI (1985).

10. M. Marloie, L'Internationalisation de l'agriculture française, *Economie et Humanisme*, Paris 1984.

11. 'Did not the exorbitant cost of servicing the Ivorian external debt of 380 million FCFA for 1983, equal to 36% of export receipts, have its origin in paying for the sugar plan?' See S. Michailof, Les apprentis sorciers du développement, *Economica*, 1984.

12. Africa is the continent with the lowest industrial production despite the relative industrial advance of some countries. While the share of developing countries in world industrial production was some 11.9% in 1984, for Africa it was only 1% for a population accounting for 10% of the world total.

13. 'When incomes rise following a sharp rise in exports of primary products, a large proportion of it will be spent, not on industrial goods but on food, especially in poor countries.' A. Hirschman, *Vers une économie politique élargie*, Editions de Minuit, Paris 1986, p. 43.

14. A. Basler, 'L'agriculture d'éxportation . . .' op. cit.

15. Land rent set at 65 cents per hectare (1979), wide access to subsidized credit, financing of large farms by the surplus obtained.

16. For smallholdings see Uma Lele, Clara Else, Hailu Mekonnen, 'Pays d'Afrique socialistes et à économie de marché: différence entre les politiques en matière de prix agricoles et la commercialisation des produits agricoles', mimeo document for the World Bank Seminar on Economic Reforms, Paris, 2 August 1985.

17. See Joseph Casas, 'La stratégie agro-alimentaire de Cuba depuis 1959 et ses résultats', in 'Politiques et stratégies alimentaires', *Economie et société*, Cahiers de l'ISMEA, No 18, July 1985, PUF, Grenoble.

18. To use P. de Bernis' words: 'L'économie algérienne depuis l'indépendance', *Annuaire de l'Afrique du Nord, 1972*.

19. Thomas G. Rawski, *Croissance et emploi en Chine*, World Bank, Economica 1979.

20. Criticisms of industrialization in Algeria have been particularly sharp and numerous, in contrast to the paucity of relatively well-documented studies and objective criteria to assess the results. Thus, for example, industry can be criticized simultaneously for being too capital-intensive and for depriving agriculture of manpower.

21. Celso Furtado, Non à la recession, non au chômage, *Anthropos* 1985.

22. See G. Myrdal, 'Paths of development', *New Left Review*, No 36, 1986, pp. 65–74.

23. De Bernis, op. cit., p. 20.

24. Claude Servolin, 'Les politiques agricoles', in *Traité de science politique*, Vol. 4, PUF 1985.

25. In France, for example, while over half the farms disappeared between 1892 and 1955, the rate of disappearances accelerated and there was a rapid concentration of capital after 1960. Between 1950 and 1979, the number of farms of 50 – 100 hectares rose from 75,000 to 114,000, and of those over 100 hectares from 20,000 to 35,000. In 1979, farms over 50 hectares occupied over 13 million hectares or 45% of the cultivable area.

26. G. Tapinos, *L'économie des migrations internationales*, Armand Colin 1983.

27. André Kospi, *Les Américains*, vol. 1 'Naissance et essor des Etats-Unis 1607–1945', Seuil, Paris 1986. See also Yves Henri Nouailhat, 'Evolution économique des USA du milieu du XIXe siècle à 1914', Paris Cedex 004 1982, pp. 10 – 11.

28. In Nigeria 'the traditional tenure system gradually decayed under the impact of population pressure, the exodus of young people and the fragmentation of land inherited through the patrilineal system. The increase in the amount of land leasing and selling eroded communal mechanisms of controlling and managing land. The principal criticisms of this system are made by advocates of the modernization of

agriculture: according to them the most successful farmers must be able to have access to more land and to have a right of ownership to protect their investment.' Johnny Egg, 'Agriculture du Nigéria', INRA MT, November 1985.

29. See also 'La CEA et le développement de l'Afrique', 1983 United Nations, New York April 1983. *Terres vives et population*, FAO 1983.

30. *Le Monde Diplomatique*, May 1985.

31. See International Institute for Social Studies/OAU Addis Ababa, 'Comment parvenir à l'autosuffisance: essais et difficultés au Sénégal au Ghana et en Tanzanie'; C. Feliu, 'Evolution et diversité des politiques alimentaires', in *Politique alimentaire et structures sociales en Afrique Noire*, IEDES 1985.

32. Samir Amin, *La Déconnexion*, La Découverte, Paris 1986.

3. Food Self-sufficiency: Crisis of the Collective Ideology

Bernard Founou-Tchuigoua

The 1970s was the decade when the African bourgeoisies became aware of the need to ensure their food self-sufficiency and were faced with the dual risk of the use of the food weapon by the large-surplus countries and precipitous falls in production consequent upon a cycle of drought for example. The embargo on the sale of American wheat to the USSR acted as catalyst. The World Food Conference, whose goal was to de-dramatize the situation, stressed the need for worldwide solidarity on food issues and made symbolic gestures. But gradually the idea came to be accepted that food security in Africa's conditions must be ensured through the development of national food policies. A few countries adopted national plans for food self-sufficiency. Thus, in 1976, faced with the collapse of its agriculture, Nigeria launched a programme with the slogan 'Feed the Nation'. Aid-giving institutions in the states of the Centre became interested in the development of African food agriculture.[1] The doctrines and policies of food self-sufficiency were, however, strictly national in character (the struggle for a New International Economic Order, and even the doctrine of Collective Self-reliance, were rather quiet about the area of food and agriculture). But as agriculture deteriorated and the burden of food aid and purchases of food products weighed heavily in the balance of payments, ideas inspired by the theory of unequal development and the need for autocentred development gained ground. According to that theory, development from a peripheral position implies delinking and the development of South–South co-operation; reservations about the concept of autocentred development began to dissolve. In 1980, this shift culminated in the OAU's adoption of the famous Lagos Plan of Action, at the first Economic Summit, for which the realization of food self-sufficiency was the highest priority. Simultaneously, however, the ideological crisis began. It was reflected in 1986 in the same OAU's adoption of the Priority Plan for the Economic Recovery of Africa (PPERA) which is the negation of the principles of the Lagos Plan of Action, in that it gives an excessive place to external aid.[2]

This chapter is concerned to bring out the meaning and stages of this retreat and to propose an explanation based on the agro-food policies of the capitalist states of the Centre.

The Lagos Plan of Action: A critique

Of several possible readings of the Lagos Plan of Action I shall mention three.

The first considers that it is essentially ideological in content, or the outcome of an exercise in rhetoric. It would then be necessary to oppose it with a more 'scientifically' formulated document: one with no obvious political or ideological content. Furthermore, it is alleged that the language used is too Third Worldist. This is the Western viewpoint expressed in the World Bank report, for which the quest for the autonomy of the agro-food system does not promote development, but on the contrary hampers it, since it involves using resources in a way that does not maximize 'world welfare'.

The second reading consists in considering the Lagos Action Plan as an interesting document but one that should be consigned to the archives, since there are no social forces to demand its implementation. On the contrary, the crisis is pushing governments to go deep in debt rather than to implement the World Bank's programme.

My reading consists in examining the Plan with a critical eye and considering it as a step on the road to the formulation of objectives and strategies that respond to Africa's needs. The Plan presents the achievement of food self-sufficiency as an aspect of a global strategy of autocentred development. The preamble recalls that, in Africa, the principal feature of the crisis of economic development (and not only of growth) is integration into the capitalist system as a periphery for several centuries. The priority given to agricultural development is largely justified by historical experience and by theory. This point is important; it is what led to placing such hopes in the Lagos Plan despite its gaps and contradictions. To the extent that it has now been practically abandoned, it must be asked if it has fallen victim to its own weaknesses. The drafters used the concept of the strategy of food self-sufficiency in a very narrow sense, since it excluded: gaining control of the food agro-culture system; and problems of securing autonomous financing, industrialization and the accelerated development of a technological base necessary for food agriculture. In addition, the diagnosis ignored the problem of the distribution of the product during either the colonial or the post-colonial period. In particular, the economic and political relations that, in general, make super-exploitation of the peasants and rural dwellers possible, to the benefit of a small domestic minority (urban and rural) and the nations in the Centre, and not of industrialization or of the towns in general, are not spelled out. Consequently, the means advocated to achieve recovery remained very vague; in these circumstances, it was easy to predict the achievement of self-sufficiency between 1980 and 1985. Even this objective, limited though it was, was not attained but rather became more remote. For, in addition to technical weaknesses, the Lagos Plan of Action presupposed that another condition was fulfilled – that every African state has the social capacity (historical legitimacy) and the technical capacity (institutions, well-trained, nationalist and critical intelligentsia) to carry through a policy of food self-sufficiency inspired either by the Chinese or by the Indian model. But the states whose leaders effectively enjoyed historical legitimacy did not delink enough to initiate true agricultural revolutions.

World Bank 'counter-plan'

The Lagos Plan, despite its omissions, marks an important date in the struggle of ideas in Africa. The theory of autocentred development that presupposes national control of the economy won a great victory over ultra-liberalism, which is why, in 1981, the World Bank published a sort of counter-plan.[3] Obviously, behind the Bank must be seen the leading countries of the Centre, notably the United States of America, which are laying down the path to be followed. According to the ultra-liberal thesis defended in the World Bank document, food self-sufficiency is not a scientific concept but a politico-ideological one; it derives from nationalism and not from economic analysis, which teaches that the law of comparative advantage is the best guide in food matters as it is in other areas of economic activity.

According to the Bank, it is because African economies failed to apply this principle that they are in crisis; the post-colonial states had an industrialization policy, but it was one that extracted too large a surplus from the peasantry.[4] The impact of this strategic orientation on the development crisis was seen as much greater than that of 'world market forces'. If super-exploitation of the peasantry, notably through the price mechanism, had not led to industrialization, it was due to protectionism by means of fiscal and tariff privileges, over-valuation of currencies and finally a mistrust of capital that leads the state to become a necessarily inefficient entrepreneur.

The food problem is presented exclusively in its economic form in the neo-classical sense of the term. For the Bank, each African state must specialize so that the optimum allocation of its resources procures it the highest possible level of income. This allocation consists in giving priority to producing what can be developed, first under private initiative and second without protectionism, according to the doctrine adopted by Reagan that was then currently being applied in the United States.

The Bank also exploited the second major shortcoming of the Lagos Plan: its ambiguity on the role of international official assistance. It went on to lay particular stress on the need to double this assistance in real terms between 1980 and 1990, despite elsewhere registering surprise that previous assistance had not contributed to increasing food output.[5] This invitation to Western governments to step up their assistance was to work in favour of the advocates of ultra-liberalism.

Numerous seminars were devoted to the Bank's plan, whereas the Lagos Plan of Action lacked the means to become widely known, but the African intelligentsia, while holding the Bank plan to be useful for its empirical data, rejected its approach as neo-colonial. Initially, African states also treated the Bank's plan with suspicion. The fact that it was rejected by a Council of

Ministers (but adopted by the Central Bank Governors) shows how much pressure had to be exerted (notably on states urgently needing to reschedule their external debts) to secure its acceptance. But the two problematics could not be allowed to coexist: the Lagos Plan of Action's, which cannot be put into effect without planning and hence the state playing a key role, and the World Bank's, which is incompatible with the concept of planning and presupposes no discrimination between national capital and foreign capital. On the specific level of food, the contrast was total.

The United Nations' Plan (PPERA)

Finally, the contradiction (at the level of the problematic and not reality, of course) was resolved by the OAU's adoption at the July 1985 Summit of the five-year (1986–90) programme PPERA.

According to the authors' summary of the document, it is articulated around the following five measures:

1. Implementation of the Lagos Plan of Action and Final Act in an updated form.
2. Improvement of the food situation and rehabilitation of agriculture.
3. Alleviating the external debt burden.
4. Action against the effects of the destabilization policy of South Africa on the economies of southern African States.
5. Measures for a common platform of action at sub-regional, regional, continental and international levels.

It could be portrayed as a stage in the implementation of the Lagos Plan. One may have one's doubts. It may be thought closer to the World Bank's problematic. On the one hand, industrialization is no longer considered as a priority and, on the other, a special solemnity is given to recourse to external assistance. It is, in fact, a programme for the recovery and development of *African agriculture* and not of *food agriculture*. It proposes priority for agriculture, not for food crops. It proposes raising productivity without industrialization; thus virtually all the proposed financing ($116 billion out of $120bn) is for agriculture strictly so-called (42.2% of the total), infrastructure supporting agriculture (44.1% of the total), developing associated human resources (2.1%) and finally the struggle against desertification (5%). Nothing is proposed for industry!

This distribution of resources is inevitably surprising in a plan whose successful implementation formally relies on 30% external funding (and above all Official External Aid); 'formally' since among the own resources (70%), the Plan includes aid already obtained and aid promised. It is surprising because only 5% is devoted to the fight against desertification whereas in my opinion the bulk of external resources should be channelled towards that – most of the other programmes could be carried out with the mobilization of domestic resources, particularly human ones. The naiveté in the matter of economic diplomacy is also surprising: the refusal of the 'aiders' to commit themselves solemnly at the United Nations was predictable.

In reality, it is all as if the principle of self-reliance which appeared alongside the request for aid in the Lagos Plan of Action is giving way to the principle of 'partnership'.

In these circumstances, the fact that the Programme (PPERA) puts the accelerated implementation of the updated Lagos Plan of Action as the first measure to be taken ought not to deceive anyone. There has been a move from a stage marked by a coherent voluntaristic doctrine to one marked by the coherence imposed by alleged economic laws said to operate without the intervention of nation-states endowed with unequal powers, the most powerful of which resist the action of economic laws, notably in their external relations.

In addition, does not the United Nations' PPERA threaten to act as a mechanism to divide the Third World, in that, coming after the World Bank's accelerated development programme, it can be taken up by those forces seeking to isolate Africa from the rest of the Third World? In my view, special action to help African states, and especially the poorest, can be taken in the framework of existing structures within the UN system to help the least developed countries. It must be noted that, while the PPERA formally concerns all OAU member states, in reality it deals above all with the problems of sub-Saharan Africa where 25 countries are among the 36 'least developed countries' (LDCs); and the fact is that a structure already exists for dealing with these countries' problems.

It was in 1968 that the 'international community' acknowledged that special international measures were necessary to deal with the real economic and social difficulties of the least developed countries' situation and improve their peoples' extremely low living standards.

In 1972, the Third UNCTAD Conference adopted the first resolution including the whole set of special measures in favour of these countries. UNCTAD held several meetings on this issue. 'Despite these efforts, during the 1970s, the least developed countries were lagging further and further behind and in many cases, regressing.'

The 1981 UN Conference in Paris adopted the 'Substantial New Programme of Action for the 1980s' in favour of the least developed countries for the 1980s. The key objectives were: 1) to make possible the transformation of these countries to put them on the path of self-sustaining development; 2) to enable them to meet some at least of the minimum international standards in nutrition, health, education, transport, marketing and housing, as well as employment opportunities for all citizens and, in particular, for poor peasants; 3) to induce the 'international community' to look upon it as a duty to provide substantial assistance to meet these targets and to do so to complement the national effort.[6] The approach at this Paris conference or any other organization need not have singled out Africa and would have been more interesting psychologically.[7]

In short, in the space of a few years, we have witnessed a sharp ideological shift from nationalism to neo-liberalism and the risk of a weakening of the

Southern front from Africa.

The agro-industrial and financial policies of the EC and the United States involve a degree of open anti-Third Worldism. Inevitably, their productivism at any price and the aggressiveness of trade policy have uniformly negative effects on African agriculture. The way packages are sold to African states on credit from Centre states, after quick feasibility and profitability studies by Western consultants, paid for through bilateral or multilateral gifts, is too well-known to be repeated here. Suffice it to say that since the mid-1950s, related to the technological revolution in agriculture that has obliged states in the North to think in terms not of agricultural policies but of agro-food system policies, the goals of food self-sufficiency have been rapidly achieved in Europe, thus at least partially closing-off access to that market to North American products. Competition, notably in cereals, was raging in the world market. By means of food aid, the agro-food systems carved out markets for wheat and milk in the South. Contrary to the IMF's ultra-liberal thesis, the high price policy played a less important role in agricultural policies designed to achieve self-sufficiency than did credit and subsidies. As the French example shows, the prices of agricultural products remained very stable for over 30 years, as did the prices of intermediate consumption goods for agriculture (Table 3.1), while the productivity of agricultural labour rose fivefold!

Table 3.1
France: comparison of production prices and prices of intermediate consumption goods (1970 = 100)

	1959	*1970*	*1971*	*1972*	*1973*	*1975*	*1976*	*1977*	*1978*	*1979*
Deliveries	108.3	*100*	98.8	106.1	109.1	98.3	100.8	92.2	93.5	90.3
I.C.	115.2	*100*	101.2	99.2	104.3	112.1	108.0	108.3	104.4	103.8

The fact is, that the credits and subsidies make it possible to put agriculture and agricultural enterprises more firmly under the control of big industry, the banks and big business that dominate the state. This subordination makes possible a more effective production-oriented agricultural policy than that of incentives through the price mechanism.

Food self-sufficiency strategies: problems of implementation

Such radical changes of doctrine in barely a single decade indicate a considerable ideological disarray, and contradictions between the historical necessity for the strategy of food self-sufficiency and the capacity of ruling classes to implement it. Among the factors that reduce this capacity only one – the foodstuff policy of the Centre countries – will be discussed here.

The unequal development of agriculture with a trend towards trans-nationalization of the mode of accumulation (use of techniques developed for the needs of capitalist exploitation at the monopoly stage) and models of consumption, results from the anti-South dimension of the foodstuff policies of the main Centre countries. This policy of unequal development of agricultural productive forces, combined with transnationalization, is then only one aspect of the global strategy of keeping the South underdeveloped.

That the European industrial revolution was preceded by an agricultural revolution is well-known. Since then, no country has succeeded in reversing this sequence. At most it is possible to envisage a situation of simultaneous revolutions. During this stage of agricultural revolution, the circulation of consumption goods from the peripheries towards the Centre was not insignificant,[8] even though, as Bairoch shows, high transport costs constituted a natural protection for national agricultures.[9] In fact transport costs were only part of the costs. When remuneration of the labour force and rent were negligible parts of value, food products could be transported over enormous distances and be competitive on metropolitan markets; this was the case with products originating from the colonies. (It should not be forgotten that while the industrial revolution happened in the 19th century, the colonial system and slave-trading regions had existed since the 16th century.) The fact that the periphery was a net exporter of food products practically right up to the Second World War is ample proof of this thesis. I have shown elsewhere the role that local edible oils played in accumulation in France and disaccumulation in Senegal.[10]

But demand has not followed the same pattern, despite the multinationals' unprecedented effort to encourage consumption, often misleading consumers on the quality of products. Food expenditure has fallen as a percentage of household budgets (less than 22% if beverages are excluded). It is the combined effect of the fantastic increase in productivity and the stagnation of the demand for food in the Centre, plus the unsatisfied needs in the South, that explains the accumulation policies which have led to the current agricultural surpluses (Table 3.2).

Control of accumulation through control of finance, research and development and outlets has one very important advantage over a policy built

Table 3.2
Annual average change in rate local food production covers consumption (%)

	1967–69	1970–79
World	0.5	0.6
Developed capitalist countries of which:	1.0	1.3
USA	1.4	1.9
Europe	1.2	1.3
Oceania	1.1	1.3
Developing countries of which:	0.4	0.6
Africa	−1.1	−1.4

Source: UNCTAD, *Handbook, 1980.*

on prices. On the one hand (as Keynes had predicted for wages), in the short term, the peasants are concerned more about the appearance than about the reality of transactions. The state can thus not afford to reduce nominal prices. On the other hand, control through credit and markets can extend beyond national borders towards the periphery. This policy of a fantastic growth of agricultural productivity in the Centre resulted in raising the rate of self-sufficiency in products in the Centre just when it was stagnating in the periphery as a whole and declining in Africa.

The export not only of agricultural commodities but of agro-industrial packages has become a necessity. States and TNCs combine their efforts to realize values on the Third World market. The state provides export credits, of variable duration, to realize agro-industrial projects in the South. As these are realized on the basis of credits granted to states, speculation and corruption are the order of the day. This leads to over-priced projects that often do not work. We are not thereby claiming that all projects have been catastrophes; despite the Nigerian leaders' economic errors for example, there was more accumulation in agriculture in 12 years than during 20 years of colonization, preceded by several centuries of integration into the Euro-American economy.

Eventually, the process of raising agricultural productivity in the Centre and its absolute or relative decline in Africa may eliminate the effect of unequal exchange, in the sense that, despite the super-exploitation of peasants and the environment, the cost/price ratio of food-crop production in Africa could become unfavourable compared to that of the supplying countries, and policies of food self-sufficiency inspired by the Green Revolution fail to work, while the possibilities of agrarian and agricultural revolution on the Chinese model would be increasingly problematic. This prospect of Africans wandering about and dying of hunger moves peoples, including peoples in the capitalist Centre, as the popular success of 'Ethiopia aid campaigns' shows, but it does not scare the strategists of the system on which the fate of humanity increasingly depends. Thus Senator Hubert Humphrey, later to become Vice-President of the United States, declared to the Senate in 1957: 'I have heard . . . that people may become dependent on us for food. I know this is not supposed to be good news. To me that was good news, because before people can do anything they have got to eat. And if you are looking for a way to get people to lean on you and to be dependent on you, in terms of their cooperation with you, it seems to me that food dependence would be terrific.'[11]

In fact, the Centre states are not satisfied with a policy of food self-sufficiency in commodities. They are also seeking to control the transformation of the whole agricultural foodstuff system by keeping the periphery in a situation of food and technological and/or financial dependence. In order to achieve that in the conjuncture of the deepening crisis of growth, emphasis is today put on reducing production costs by letting the law of supply and demand operate, domestically first and then externally. Application of the price principle (which results from supply and demand on a competitive market) is leading to the hardening of credit conditions, and hence bankruptcies and the concentration of agricultural capital, with, as a corollary, the reduction of agricultural workers' total wages and even the lowering of real wage rates. Efficiency is more important than accumulation.

But this New Agricultural Policy is still set in the framework of food self-sufficiency and the production of surpluses. Protectionist policies are thus still obligatory. Despite the pressures from UNCTAD, GATT and the FAO the Centre states will give it up only when the new policies have created a situation such that acceptance of free trade will not call self-sufficiency into question. Africa thus risks being increasingly submerged by these surpluses which, instead of diminishing, will rather increase.

While the capitalist Centre countries pursue food policies leading to the creation of structural food surpluses, which, as a result of the development of the world market, are increasingly threatening African food crops, the African states are dithering. Their awareness of the danger of the food weapon has not withstood the ideological counter-offensive launched by the World Bank and the IMF, in order to keep African food systems in a situation of dependence and consequently in a state of technological backwardness. Obviously, the effects of the Centre states' food policies is not the sole explanation for the turnabout by African states. There are also political factors that we have not mentioned.

Notes

1. B. Founou, 'Stratégie d'autosuffisance alimentaire au Sénégal'.

2. a) 'Over the last two decades, and at a time the African Continent is facing a rapid growth in population and urbanisation, the food and agriculture situation in Africa has undergone a drastic deterioration; food production and consumption per person has fallen below nutritional requirements . . . Over the period 1980–1985 the objective should be to bring about the immediate improvement in the food situation and to lay the foundation for the achievement of self-sufficiency in cereals and livestock and fish products.' OAU, *Lagos Plan of Action*, 1980.

    b) 'Breathing new life into the agricultural sector would make it possible to find a solution to the worsening poverty of the people and stimulate material demand: in addition, it would make receipts possible, thus giving Africans the resources that they so much need to relaunch their economic growth.' OAU *Priority Programme for the Economic Recovery of Africa*, 1980.

3. The *Accelerated Development in Sub-Saharan Africa: An Agenda for Action* (Berg Plan), presented to Africa at the Annual Meeting of the joint Board of Directors of the IMF and the World Bank was not officially adopted by States but it has become *de facto* the implicit doctrinal reference point of the 'Structural Adjustment Plans' that they have adopted one after the other, as the balance of payments crisis has continued.

4. The text effectively confirms, backed by data, that African peasants have continued to be super-exploited and that that is one of the factors in food shortages and rural malnutrition. But it 'forgets' to show that the Centre nations and their TNCs play key roles in this super-exploitation.

5. 'And while land productivity is not the decisive factor for a thinly populated

continent such as Africa, when growth of total food production is compared to that of the rural population, it suggests that labor productivity stagnated in the 1960s and fell in the 1970s.

What is significant is that this decline occurred over a period when the various governments and external sources of finance focused more strongly on food production projects than ever before. Between 1973 and 1980, about $5 billion in aid flowed into agriculture, $2.4 billion of which was from the World Bank. These projects have so far failed to boost output or have been offset by declines in other parts of the food economy.' World Bank, *Accelerated Development in Sub-Saharan Africa*, 1981.

6. UNCTAD, (*The Least Developed Countries*, 1984 and 1985, Introduction to the Reports.

7. This is a common approach at the diplomatic level. Thus we know that the ACP is made up predominantly of countries in Sub-Saharan Africa. Despite that, the EC preferred a more neutral name.

8. I. Wallerstein, *Capitalism and World Economy*.

9. P. Bairoch, *Révolution industrielle et sous-développement*.

10. B. Founou, *Les fondements de l'économie de traite au Sénégal*.

11. 'The food weapon, especially in the form of aid, would then assume vast proportions. When massive food aid assumes a structural character, it has the effect of keeping in power ruling groups that are weak and incapable of initiating the process of building an autonomous national agricultural base. Reading a statement like the one by the American Secretary of State it is necessary to be clear about the meaning: nowhere does he call for the withdrawing of aid to states that cannot organize the agricultural revolution.' Susan George in *How the Other Half Dies*, as cited in Alaux, *Crise au Nord, Faim au Sud*.

4.   Algeria: Agriculture and Industry

Hamid Aït Amara

The objective of providing full employment for the population has profoundly affected the basic options in the development of the Algerian economy. It led to stress on the rapid expansion of industry in order to create conditions for modernizing agriculture. By creating jobs in the secondary and tertiary sectors it was hoped to gradually reduce unemployment and under-employment and to have a significant impact on the size of the agricultural population in order to reduce pressure on the land.

The stress on industry, in an initial phase of development, gave ample scope to the building-up of the sectors producing the production goods necessary for the modernization of agriculture, principally machinery, chemicals and petro-chemicals. In a second phase, agriculture would become more integrated into the economy, and increase its capacity to develop its purchases from industry and its deliveries of agricultural raw materials to processing industries.

Such a pattern of autocentred development is built on the hypothesis of a growth in peasant incomes fuelled by the growth of agricultural productivity, which was necessary 1) to raise the standard of living in the rural areas; and 2) to finance agriculture's demand from industry.

To carry out such a process of growth and intensify relations between agriculture and industry requires three major conditions:

1) That the global growth of agricultural production must be more than proportional to that of the numbers employed in agriculture. In other words, there must be net growth per person employed, and this is the source of improvements in incomes, ensuring a rise in both the standard of living of agricultural workers and agriculture's demand for industrial goods.
2) It must be possible to carry through the modernization of agriculture in conditions of productivity in the employment of the factors that ensure a minimum of profitability to capital invested. In other words, agriculture must be able to pay for what it buys from industry, not artificially, through continually rising agricultural prices, or subsidies from the state, but through the advances it achieves in productivity.
3) Finally, what is produced must be at price levels sufficient to meet the needs of extended reproduction, but also compatible with consumers' purchasing power. If the opposite happens, the state is forced to act massively to keep consumer prices up at the expense of investment.

To make agriculture meet these three conditions may require phasing. Distortions may appear that must be corrected to enable agriculture gradually to adjust its relations with the rest of the economy but, in due course, agriculture must satisfy these key variables of the dynamic of its relations with industry.

The first variable is largely dependent on the pace of job creation outside agriculture, the capacity of industry and services to absorb the rural labour surplus. The quantities produced may have no effect on labour productivity if they are accompanied by a proportionate increase in the population employed in agriculture.[1]

In Algeria, the increase in output per worker cannot be obtained by increasing the area cultivated per unit of labour, as was partly the case in Europe, but must be the fruit of an improvement in the physical yields of crops and livestock farming. In that way the profitability of investment in production factors will be assured and hence that of backward-linked industrial sectors. In fact, as analysis of the Algerian case shows, in an autocentred development model, the growth of yields is the key to the whole dynamic of relations between agriculture and industry.

In the absence of advances in agricultural productivity, the rise in agricultural prices consequent upon the global stagnation of agricultural production may still fuel agriculture's demand for industrial goods, but at the price of a fall in real wages and the standard of living of the great mass of urban workers. To avoid this spiral, the state has to import food products that are in short supply on the market and subsidize producer prices for commodities in order to protect agriculture from external competition.

The evolution of agricultural productivity rests essentially on agronomic and technical advances, the improvement of animal and plant species, and the introduction of new production methods. It requires that the state not only has the capacity to develop agronomic research and agricultural education and training programmes successfully but also be able to define and establish the social forms of agricultural modernization: in short, to define a *path to the modernization of agriculture* that meets the conditions of development.

The Algerian economy: development choices

The fact that there are too many people engaged in agriculture and that it has little natural potential led to the emphasis in development choices on an initial phase of intensive industrialization. The priority thus given to industry was based on the hypothesis that no significant progress was possible in agriculture without an industrial policy to provide the motive force of the whole development dynamic. Industry was both to provide agriculture with the material means for its modernization (capital goods and intermediate products), and, over a long period, absorb the net increase in the agricultural population.[2]

The first development plans of 1967, 1969 and 1970–73 aimed at keeping, 'for as long as possible', the numbers employed in agriculture at their 1966 level of about one million workers (1966 general population census). It was estimated that the total number of work-days supplied by agriculture was equal to some 700,000 full-time jobs only, meaning an under-employment rate among the agricultural population of about 30%. The analyses concluded that in order to improve productivity and incomes it was necessary to increase the number of work-days per worker.

Low agricultural potential
With 7.5 million hectares of usable agricultural land, Algeria is poorly endowed with arable land, 0.3 hectare per inhabitant, and, given the high rate of population increase from now to the end of the current decade, the area available will not exceed 0.25 hectare per person. Much less than for Egypt in 1980, if account is taken of the double cropping in that country and bi-annual cropping in Algeria where cereal–fallow rotation occupies 80% of cultivated land. In fact 4.5 million hectares only are cultivated each year by one million workers, the remainder being rested.[3]

In assessing the productive agricultural potential, account must also be taken of the importance of natural constraints on production and the low productivity of the soils.

It is estimated that land in the plain or on slight or average slopes (less than 12.5%) with sufficient annual average rainfall, (higher than 500 mm per annum) to obtain relatively regular and satisfactory yields, occupies barely 2.7 million hectares or slightly more than one-third (36%) of cultivable areas and less than 10% of northern Algeria. Furthermore, even on this land, rainfall is both irregular from year to year and unevenly distributed over the year, control of water being generally essential to intensifying crops and ensuring regular production.[4]

As always with high population density, cropping limits are largely exceeded if account is taken of the need for good soil conservation. In numerous regions, this density is excessive and leads to heavy soil degradation. As a result of the climate and slopes, erosion, both wind- and rain-induced, is considerable and the action of man on the environment simply accentuates a process which has doubtless been developing for centuries. Soil and productivity losses due to erosion are considerable and numerous cultivated areas ought urgently to be replanted with trees. An FAO study estimates that 30% of agricultural areas need protection works. It is estimated elsewhere that three million hectares need reforesting and a total of five million hectares need tree-planting in the north, as against a current rate of less than 10%.[5]

Woodland, the other aspect of agricultural natural resources, is also seriously threatened with destruction. It covers only three million hectares of which only 2.3 are subject to forestry regulations. The reforestation programmes have so far been just sufficient to replace the areas destroyed by forest fires each year, but very much less than would be necessary to undertake to protect the most threatened areas effectively.

The quantity of sediments discharged into the sea each year amounts to 120 millicn metric tons, or the equivalent of several tens of thousands of hectares (50–60,000). Hydraulic features considerably increase the costs of bringing surface water into use, and reduce the life of dams.

In semi-arid regions where rainfall is regularly less than 500 mm, the inadequacy and irregularity of rainfall strongly influence yields, and conditions for a better economic use of land are closely dependent on irrigation. In Algeria, while potential water resources may appear relatively high, exploiting them proves to be limited and costly, as a result of the difficulties of the terrain and the narrowness of the coastal plains.[6]

The bulk of the run-off in the northern parts of the country, 12 billion m³/year, simply flows into the Mediterranean.[7] The drainage basins of the highlands (100,000km²) and the Saharan regions (100,000 km²) with 0.7 billion m³ each, run off only a little more than 10% of total rainfall. To surface water must be added exploitable subsoil resources, 1.7 billion m³/year in the north, 2 billion m³ in the Saharan regions. But these are only rather rough estimates, no complete inventory having so far been carried out and these figures probably do not reflect the real level of mobilizable resources and possibilities of exploitation, if one thinks of the reduction of available water stocks, the fall in ground water tables, the depletion of wells, and so on, observed in recent years.

Exploitation of this potential is uneven, depending on the region and the nature of the water resources.

In the northern areas, only 5% of surface water is regulated with 0.6 billion m³/year exploited, and 80% of ground water, with 1.3 billion m³ exploited. In the Sahara, 30% of ground water is mobilized, 0.7 billion m³ (50,000 hectares irrigated).[8] There is also small-scale irrigation, surface water and off-takes from rivers, amounting to 0.9 m³, but this figure seems too high.

In all, only some 3.5 billion m³/year is available, a very inadequate volume compared to other countries in the region. For example, Morocco has 10 billion m³/year (800,000 hectares irrigated) and Saudi Arabia some six or seven billion m³/year, Egypt 55 billion m³.

Agriculture receives about three-quarters of the available water, 2.6 billion m³ for 260,000 hectares irrigated (95% in Morocco). The areas of the large, irrigated perimeters have remained unchanged for the last two decades, and the increase is essentially due to cheap small-scale irrigation projects: surface wells, hillside lakes, drawing water in the Oueds; which further throws doubt on the figure for irrigated areas used in the statistics.

Drinking-water supplies (one household in two has running water) is the second biggest user with 760 billion m³. Industry consumes only 4% of the total water available, far less than agricultural and human uses.

The additional irrigation of 300,000 hectares planned by the year 2000 would require the mobilization of a further three billion m³ or the building of 60 new dams and the digging of three million linear metres of wells – the cost would thus be very high.

Agricultural natural resources are, however, not limited to cultivable land. Algeria has vast areas of land, some 15 to 20 million hectares, situated between the 100 and 300 mm *isohyets*, devoted to livestock, essentially goats, which should be included in the country's production potential.

It is of course true that degradation of pastures has by now gone very far and the average number of cattle per hectare cannot be more than one goat for five hectares (in some regions it is much lower than that – one goat for 10 hectares) with the result that the total number of goats that can be fed from the steppe's own resources is no more than four or five million head, with a net meat production in the region of 25 to 30,000 metric tons, indicating a very low productivity of soils and flocks.

Environmental degradation is the consequence of replacing the old social forms of rangeland by ranching that facilitates rapid, intensive exploitation of resources for the market, which has led to the gradual impoverishment of small herdsmen and their eviction from the pastoral areas. The evolution towards higher meat prices has led to a heavy concentration of the flocks in the hands of dealers who control the sheep market, and the decline of direct forms of exploiting flocks. The reduction of natural forage resources is leading to the clearing of the best soil for speculative barley-growing intended for feeding flocks.

Yet despite the importance of the agro-ecological constraints, scope for agricultural progress does exist. The cropping system has remained extensive, mobilizing only limited land and labour resources, for yields per hectare that are excessively low. It is estimated that by bringing fallow land into production some two million hectares, 40% of the area cultivated each year, could be cropped. In addition, mobilization of water resources could significantly increase irrigated areas, thereby creating conditions for more intensive cropping.

In the steppe, experiments have shown the possibilities of increasing forage production. Quite striking results have been achieved by setting aside areas closed to grazing animals covering 10,000 or 20,000 hectares. Forage production has thus been doubled or tripled and the number of livestock per hectare has moved in the same proportions; extending these results requires settlement of the problem of the customary use of rangelands prior to the introduction of techniques of regenerating vegetation and maintaining grazing areas.

Such a level of exploiting agricultural resources implies a heavy recourse to industrially produced factors of production to update equipment and cultivation methods.

Character and scale of industrialization

In the autocentred model of development, agriculture constitutes both a market for industrially produced capital and intermediate goods and a supplier of products for the foodstuff sector. Industrial development is thus governed by an internal dynamic and is not simply a means of maintaining the external balance or a supplement to the export economy (as in the cases of Tunisia and Morocco).

Algerian exports of manufactured or intermediate goods are in fact virtually non-existent – less than 2% of exports, comprising almost entirely hydro-

Table 4.1
Ranking of industrial projects by type

	First tranche 1965–71	Second tranche 1972–77	Estimated third tranche 1977–82
Agricultural equipment:	Tractors Agric. machinery Valves and pumps Lorries	Light construction	
Intermediate agricultural goods:	Nitrogenous fertilizers PVC tubes Steel tubes Phosphate fertilizers	Plastic film Plant protection products Drawn wire	
Equipment goods for construction & public works:	Lorries	Cranes Public works appliances	All surface vehicles
Intermediate goods for construction & public works:	Cement Bricks Steel (flat) PVC tubes Steel tubes	Paint Steel (long products) Sanitary ware Bulbs Telephones	Construction equipment
Industrial equipment:	Standard machine tools General engineering	Construction Hollow-ware Smithing Casting Cables MV LV electric	Heavy electro-mechnical equipment Applied research Process engineering Electronics
Industrial intermediate goods:	Steel (flat) Electricity Natural gas	Steel (long products) Synthetic fibres Basic chemicals	Special steels Aluminium Pig iron Gars Djebilet mines West steel mill
Manufactured consumer goods:	Textiles Clothing Shoes Schools items Foodstuffs Metal food packaging Rural electrification Natural gas network LPG School articles	Gas bottles Cookers Refrigerators Radio & TV Home furnishings Paper industry	Private vehicles Washing machines Etc.

Source: A. Thiery (J.P.) *La Crise du Système Productif Algérien*, IREP, Grenoble 1982.

carbons, which account for 98% of external receipts.

Industrialization programmes have given ample scope to sectors capable of supplying agriculture with the goods necessary to modernize its techniques and improve its productivity. As Table 4.1 shows, priority has been given to the agricultural equipment industries since the earliest phases of industrialization:

A look at the dates when industrial projects were launched shows that most of those concerned with agricultural demand were initiated during the first phase of industrialization, 1966–71: agricultural machinery, fertilizers, irrigation equipment and so on.

Agricultural demand concerns a wide variety of branches of industry: upstream, steelworks and metal processing industries, metallurgical industries and machine industries (tractors, valves, pumps, transport equipment, agricultural implements), electrical industries (motors, cables for electrification) and finally chemical industries (fertilizers, chemical products, plastic items).

Throughout the 1970s, the establishment of a wide range of industries (including hydro-carbons) took a large share of total investment: 55% for each period 1967–69 and 1970–73; 58% for 1974–77; 56.1%, 1978–79 and 32.6%, 1980–84. Agriculture's shares were: 16%, 1967–69; 14.8%, 1970–73; 11%, 1974–77; 8.5%, 1978–79; and 5.2%, 1980–84.[9]

Throughout the period, industrial investment narrowly defined amounted to approximately 28% of investments, the remainder (28–30%), more or less the same proportion, was absorbed by the hydro-carbon sector. It was thus a relatively modest percentage, compared to those of partly industrialized countries today (Yugoslavia, Mexico, Brazil).

Agricultural investment was around 10% of the total throughout the period,[10] but a considerable proportion of industrial investment in the first and second phases of industrialization was devoted to the production of goods intended for agriculture. It should also be pointed out that the fall in industrial investment in the 1980s has not necessarily meant a shift to agriculture in relative terms; agriculture's share fell back by two or three points during the period 1978–84 compared to 1967–77.

The number of large production complexes set up to produce equipment and intermediate goods for agriculture is evidence of the stress put on the priority satisfaction of the needs of the agricultural sector; the tractor factory at Constantine (8,000 tractors a year), the agricultural machinery factory at Bel Abbès, the pump and valve factory at Médéa, the diesel motor factory at Tizi Ouzou, the water pipe factory at Réghaia, and so on.

In petro-chemicals in particular, two large chemical fertilizer complexes were completed: one at Arzew (nitrogenous) and one at Annaba (phosphate), the operation of which required the building of several independent plants to manufacture intermediate products.

The Annaba complex includes a plant producing sulphuric acid with a capacity of 1,500 metric tons per day and one producing 500 metric tons per day of phosphoric acid. Two other plants producing multi-nutrient fertilizers at a rate of 500,000 metric tons per annum are in production in the same region and proposals to expand them during the period 1981–84 led to the creation of two new plants for nitric acid (400 metric tons per day) and ammonium nitrate (500 metric tons per day).

In plastics, the completion of a methanol complex in 1971 and a synthetic resin plant at Arzew, and a plastics complex at Skikda made it possible to create units producing sacks and sheets for agriculture. Production capacity is currently 100,000 metric tons per annum, with consumption for crops under plastic and packaging for irrigation pipes absorbing 31% of total production.

After a decade and a half of industrialization, the greater part of agricultural demand for equipment and intermediate goods is being met by local production. Finally, for chemical products, an average of 90% of demand is met: phosphate fertilizer, 286,000 metric tons, and ammonium nitrate 170,000 metric tons.

Agriculture's productive consumption of industrially produced goods has increased much faster than these industries' production capacities. Contrary to widespread ideas about Algeria, demand has constantly outstripped projections. As F. Yaçhir points out, this is true whichever industrial sector one looks at. Recourse to imports is still necessary because local supply is insufficient.

Projections in the 1969[11] industrial programmes on the needs of agriculture up to 1980 were easily surpassed by the consumption levels between 1970 and 1985. Agriculture more than doubled its equipment and purchases of intermediate goods between 1976 and 1985, compared to the periods 1966–75 and 1953–62. The total number of tractors in the country increased from 23,484 units in 1962 to 25,122 in 1973 and 60,000 in 1984. Fertilizer use has risen on average by 9.5% p.a. since the beginning of the 1970s: from 100,000 metric tons in 1970 to 205,000 metric tons in 1983–84.[12] The use of minor irrigation equipment, in the motor-pumps groups, also rose fivefold during the 1976–85 period, absorbing all local production.

Domestic supply is inadequate not only in terms of quantity, but agricultural equipment is often unsuitable and there is little variety of supporting equipment. Fertilizers and pest control products too, are not quite what the crops need.

Investments in sectors producing agricultural goods have thus been insufficient, judging from the high level of additional imports and the potential demand that programmes to step up agricultural production will create. In fact, despite the marked increase in intermediate consumption, the quantity of industrial inputs used falls far short of the technical norms deemed *necessary*.

The use of industrial inputs, especially fertilizers and agricultural machinery, compared to those of countries with intensive agriculture in the North, or a country such as China, is still relatively low. In Algeria, there is one tractor (60 hp) for 182 hectares and one combine harvester for 500 hectares.

The Ministry of Agriculture estimates that the use of fertilizers is only 44% of the quantities recommended to secure a marked increase in yields. The supply of agricultural equipment has grown by 6% to 8% p.a., but shortfalls are estimated to be 43% for tractors, 38% for combine harvesters and 65% for ploughing equipment.

Those responsible for agricultural development emphasize the important role of chemical fertilizers, mechanization, selected seeds and irrigation in raising yields, but this introduction of modern means requires changes in cropping methods and action by engineers and skilled workers to promote the use of *new interdependent production factors.*

The objectives of the four-year plans were to spread the use of herbicides on cereals and pulses, develop soil disinfection and intensify treatment with insecticides and fungicides in fruit-tree growing, but use of these products has reached only 40% of the recommended amounts.

To meet the demand from agriculture thus requires increased production of agricultural machinery, particularly low-powered tractors for smallholdings in the mountainous areas, and the diversification in supply of equipment and intermediate goods to meet the needs of diverse agricultural conditions.

Industrialization: Effects on agriculture

The sustained growth of non-agricultural employment and the transfer of part of the rural labour force to the towns have made it possible to stabilize the number of agricultural workers and halt the growth of population pressure on the land, thus creating the conditions for improved labour productivity and peasant incomes. Industrialization has been accompanied by a rapid rise in the demand for food and in agricultural prices, creating profitable outlets for agriculture and thus increasing purchases of industrially produced goods.

Reducing pressure on the land

In spite of a particularly high population growth rate, 3.4% p.a., employment targets were practically attained in the 1970s and first half of the 1980s.

Between 1967 and 1984, the working population increased at an annual rate of 4.3% or 1,602,000 persons. Between 1966 and 1980, according to the Ministry of Planning, some 1.5 million new jobs were created, which meant that everyone coming on to the labour market could be offered a job.

Table 4.2
Growth in the Working and Employed Populations ('000)[12]

	1967	1977	1983
Working population	2,598	3,059	4,200
Employed population	1,724	2,336	3,632

Sources: Algeria, Ministère de la Planification and Office National des Statistiques.

Thus, the sustained economic growth was able to meet the social demand for employment and begin to reduce the pre-existing volume of unemployment. The number of new jobs rose by about 6% p.a., absorbing all the annual growth in the labour force.

In 1966, the population census gave 610,000 unemployed: 433,100 in the rural areas (65% of the total) and 177,000 in the urban areas, plus 262,900 people seeking their first job, making a total of 873,000 unemployed, or an unemployment rate of almost 30%. By January 1983, the number of job-seekers was 563,948, as against a total employed figure of 3,632,594. Thus, between 1966 and 1983, the number of unemployed had fallen in absolute terms. Despite the increase in the working-age population over the same period the unemployment rate had fallen from 30% to 13.4%.

Interestingly, the employment situation had been reversed in favour of the rural sector, the percentage of unemployed falling from 65% in 1966 to 18% in 1983 due (as indicated below) to the high demand of the building and public works sector, the bulk of whose labour force originates from the rural areas. Industry's share in total job creation was small: an average of 20,000 jobs p.a. between 1966 and 1984, or approximately one job in six. Services (that is, all activities other than material ones) provided the highest percentage, rising from 31% in 1966 to 38% in 1984. The greatest number of jobs in services were created between 1980 and 1984, which explains the relative fall in industrial employment from 17.2% in 1977 to 13.8% in 1984 and the fall in the number of people in the material production sectors.[14]

Table 4.3
Employment by Sector, 1966–1984

	1966	%	1977	%	1984	%
Agriculture	852,300	49.4	692,000	29.6	854,077	23
Industry	172,000	10	401,462	17.2	513,523	13.8
Building & public works	90,900	5.4	345,816	14.8	698,726	18.8
Transport	75,500	4.4	132,420	5.6	239,365	6.4
Sub-total	1,190,700	69	1,571,698	67.25	2,305,691	62
Total employed	*1,724,900*	*100*	*2,336,972*	*100*	3,713,803	*100*

Sources: RGPH 1966–77; Algeria, Office National des Statistiques, *Enquête emploi 1984*.

Despite a relatively high annual growth of 11% p.a., industrial employment is well below that of partly industrialized countries where it accounts for between 20% and 30% of the total working population. Industrial production, apart from hydro-carbons, rose at a similar rate, some 10% p.a.

These data indicate the limited character of industrialization during the 1970s and should go some way towards dispelling the oft-repeated suggestions that industry received too much attention at the expense of agriculture – when agricultural stagnation is not blamed on the growth of industry. Neither can the capital intensity of industrial investment explain the low volume of industrial employment. The average cost per job in industry was 380,000 AD (US$70 to 80,000), varying from 600,000 AD in the ISMME to 110,000 AD for the textile industries (Confère Etude de l'Agence Nationale pour l'Aménagement du Territoire, 1985).

Table 4.4
Employment by Manufacturing Sector (1985)

		%			%
Mining	150,516	5	Foodstuffs	153,726	18
ISMME	619,634	37	Textiles	109,296	5
Construction materials	411,667	11	Leather .	79,254	3
Chemicals	577,659	5	Wood	251,124	7
Sub-total	*2,352,876*	*62*	**Total**	**3,811,987**	**100**

Source: Algeria, Ministère de la Planification; Agence Nationale pour l'Aménagement du Territoire, 1985.

In reality, the rate of investment in industry was much less than it seems. Hydro-carbons were in first position, totalling some 30% of the financial resources invested over the 1970s as a whole. This was due partly to the function of financing development assigned to hydro-carbons which constitute the sole source of external receipts. Hydro-carbon and natural gas resources have been used to sustain the programmes for importing capital goods needed for industrialization and other sectors of the economy.

In fact, the principal phase of industrialization – the construction of a capital goods sector – has not yet even begun and has so far received less than 10% of industrial investment. The first core of industries, set up during the 1970s, still requires a significant volume of imports of intermediate and capital goods in order to function. According to Algeria's Ministère du Commerce, of total imports for 1979, 1980, 1983 and 1984, capital goods' share was 43%, 38%, 37% and 33% respectively. For the same years, raw materials and semi-finished products' share was 35%, 36%, 38% and 39% respectively. Combined totals for both types of goods were: 1979, 78%; 1980, 74%; 1983, 75% and 1984, 72%. This situation considerably limits the local productive system's autonomy from the outside world.

The experience of countries that have embarked on accelerated industrialization shows that three or four decades is needed to crystallize all the investments into an integrated industrial system. Poland, an underdeveloped European country before the Second World War, in three decades reached tenth place among the industrialized countries of the world. In Yugoslavia, between 1950 and 1980 industry grew at an annual average rate of 8.6%; and in China, 10% for three decades.

The number of non-agricultural jobs was enough to absorb virtually all the natural population growth, both urban and rural, but it did not lead to an absolute decline in the number employed in agriculture. (In Europe, this began to decline at the end of the 19th century (c. 1880), thus making possible an increase in area per worker and helping to fuel rises in labour productivity.) Despite a sharp relative decline in the agricultural population, from 49.6% in 1966 to 22% in 1983, the number employed in agriculture changed little over the period 1966–85 (852,000 in 1966; 692,000 in 1977; 854,000 in 1983; and 1,010,000 in 1985).

But non-agricultural activities' soaking-up of the demand for jobs did make it possible to stabilize agricultural population numbers and prevented increased pressure on the arable area.

This apparent stability in terms of population and land, however, does not account for the same socio-economic reality. Rather than many farmers abandoning agricultural activity and the land being concentrated in the hands of middle peasants, as has been observed in a number of countries, there has been a gradual shift of the agricultural population towards holding two jobs or part-time employment. A degree of industrial and administrative decentralization helped the creation of non-agricultural jobs in the rural areas to such an extent that by 1977, only some 51% of the population was engaged in agriculture, and by 1984 only 37.7% – barely one employed worker in three – as the percentages according to the Office National des Statisques show: 1977, 51%; 1982, 46.2%, 1984, 37.7%. In the same document, percentages of rural population engaged in building and public works were: 1977, 16.06%; 1982, 19.1%; 1984, 21.54%; and in the same years, the rural population employed in industry was: 10.6%, 8.4% and 9.1% respectively.

In fact, more generally, rather than farmers doing two jobs it would be more accurate to speak of a variety of sources of jobs and income among members of farming households. Given the limited available arable areas and population density, 70% of holdings are less than 10 hectares, and the majority of peasants cannot produce enough for their own subsistence. In other words, production is lower than the cost of maintaining the worker and his family. The potential number of those who would migrate from the rural areas and agricultural employment if non-agricultural employment were to grow rapidly is thus extremely high. It is well-known that it is the top of the economic cycle, with the growth of employment opportunities outside agriculture, that promotes this movement of the working-age population.

The spread into the rural areas of industrial activities associated with the development of social and economic infrastructure, and administrative, communication and socio-cultural facilities, has made it possible so far to keep the bulk of the non-agricultural population outside the big urban centres.

The rural population grew on average by about 2% p.a. over the period 1966–84 which, given the land situation, shows that there was a moderate amount of rural out-migration, probably less than half the natural population increase, which is estimated at 3.2%, slightly less than 1966 when it was 3.4%.

There was more social and geographical mobility among casual agricultural workers, landless peasants, the total number of whom fell from 622,500 in 1966 to 114,000 in 1977, while the number of permanent workers in the public agricultural sector rose from 187,800 in 1966 to 192,604 in 1977. The fall in the number of rural workers in the 1970s also affected family workers, the number of whom fell from 214,000 in 1966 to 52,768 in 1977. In percentage terms, the urban/rural distribution of the population for the years 1966, 1977, and 1984 was, urban: 32%, 41.2% and 43% respectively; and for the same years, rural:

68%, 58.8% and 57% respectively.

The spatial distribution of industries, and of public investment more generally, has proved an effective means of fighting against the rural exodus. While the import-substitution industries of the first phase of industrialization (textiles, leather) were labour-intensive and created to mop-up pockets of unemployment that had built up in the large and medium-sized towns, the programme of small and medium industries scattered all over the country affected virtually all the largest provincial towns. This policy had the effect of keeping the bulk of the surplus agricultural population in place by offering it employment outside agriculture. The agricultural exodus[15] was achieved without migration or involved only short-distance migration.

Relations between industrialized towns and the rural areas have restructured the regional space to favour agriculture by keeping the population on farms and increasing the incomes of peasant–worker groups. Conversely, as Prenant notes, urban growth around tertiary activities has tended to be parasitical on the rural areas.

As the Second Four-year Plan (1974–77) got underway, most urban centres were in a position to fill the increased number of job vacancies from their own natural increase. As early as 1974, Prenant observed a more rapid growth of towns in the hinterland and the fact that numerous small centres were taking on urban functions. He could thus observe that:

> The urban growth currently underway in Algeria seems to be marked less by the mushrooming of the big towns than by many small centres taking on urban functions. Sometimes the functions lead to the demographic growth of localities that previously had small populations, perhaps even villages created to receive these functions, sometimes on the contrary they urbanize already existing large settlements of the rural population and give them, or restore to them, an urban character.

Food demands and price increases

The rapid expansion of wage work among the economically active population – 70% of the total employed population – put strong pressure on the demand for food. It is estimated that this rose by 4–5% p.a. throughout the 1970s.

In common with all the oil-producing countries, revenues from hydrocarbons made it possible to improve the level of the population's food consumption. The daily calorie intake, scarcely more than 2,000 (2,100) in the 1960s, had risen to 2,500 per day by the late 1970s, with a very marked reduction in the differences between rural and urban areas. The improvement in per capita daily calorie intake was both quantitative and qualitative since meat and dairy products, eggs, fruit and vegetables account for a high proportion of food consumed. Thus, per capita meat consumption rose from 8.2 kg to 15 kg over the period, and milk consumption from 34 to 61.3 kg; such a rapid rise in demand necessitated increasing quantities of imports.

The proportion of local production in total consumption has diminished continuously since the 1970s. For the principal basic staples, agriculture supplies only a small proportion of needs: as statistics for 1982 show, the basic daily intake was largely covered by imports: 75% for wheat; 70% for pulses; 80% for vegetable oils; 50% for milk products and eggs; 100% for sugar.

The quantity of imports rose on average by 8% per annum, reaching a total value of 9,200 billion Algerian dinars in 1983, equal to slightly less than US$ 2 billion, as against receipts from hydro-carbons of some 13 billion dollars in the same year.

Contrary to what has happened in many countries, however, these imports have not been an obstacle to the growth of total production. Measures were taken to protect domestic agriculture from the effects of world markets and to *increase peasant incomes*.

Imports were limited to basic products (wheat, vegetable oils, dairy products and sugar) which account for most of the calorie and protein intake of the bulk of the population and for 80% by value of imports. Leaving aside this group of products, and some additional imports of beef, mutton and lamb, local production has not had to face competition from imported products, total supply exceeding demand.

Protection of local agriculture from world markets is also assured by delinking consumer prices from producer prices. For some products producer prices are higher than both the prices of imported commodities and consumer prices. This is the case for wheats and pulses, vegetable oils (olive oil), milk, eggs and potatoes. The state subsidizes both production and consumption, production subsidies tending increasingly to replace consumer subsidies following the increases introduced in 1983-84.

The fact there are two sources of supply – imports and local production – and two price systems – fixed prices and market prices – has led to the establishment of a dual organization of markets and circuits for distributing food products.

There is a relatively integrated state network that includes firms importing, processing and packaging products, and a chain of distribution outlets; and a network of private businesses, made up of several tens of thousands of wholesalers and retailers. State trading, conducted essentially in the cities and main provincial towns, distributes basic commodities that fall into the category of products whose prices are fixed administratively: cereal products, pulses, vegetable oils and sugar purchased by the state on the local market or imported. Private trade distributes the bulk of the products of domestic agriculture, particularly red meat, fruit and vegetables, at market prices.

More than the producer price policy, however, it is the global weakness of supply compared to demand that gives local production its most secure advantage. Imports are not quantitatively sufficient to affect the prices of domestic products. This limited availability, or relative shortage, which often takes the form of interruptions of supply, makes it possible to market all local products at market prices, which are distinctly higher than the prices fixed by the state. It also has the consequence of limiting the consumption of certain basic imported products such as cereals, eggs, pulses and potatoes.

Given the structure of relative prices and wages, households ought to have consumed more milk, eggs, cereal products and pulses than they do today.

Thus, in the event of a price rise, when one product is replaced by another, the replacement cannot always be the cheapest but a product that is available even at higher prices. As a result, there is no competition between imported products and local commodities and the price level is fixed independently on the two markets – state and private. Depending on its origin and the distribution network involved, the same product can be available simultaneously at different prices; imported red meat is sold at 35 dinars/kg, local meat at 100 dinars; imported potatoes at 2.5 to 3.0 dinars, local potatoes at 5.00 dinars; reconstituted milk at 1.30 dinars, local fresh milk at 5.00 dinars.

This structure of supply has so far made it possible to sell local products at very high prices, and facilitated a major transfer of the social surplus, mainly to the benefit of private agriculture which holds control of some 15,000,000 hectares of pasture and grazing devoted to rearing sheep and cattle, almost 65% of the irrigated areas are devoted to the production of vegetables and fruits.

While these measures as a whole acted as an effective protection for local production, they nevertheless led to an even closer integration of the system of production and consumption into world markets.

High demand, at high price levels, for fruits, vegetables and red meat, led peasants to turn away from such basic staples as wheat, pulses, and oilseeds, because relative prices, as a result of strong demand emanating from high income groups, made it more profitable to produce fruits, animal, and market-garden crops. The rapid rise of agricultural prices has also slowed down improvement in the population's real consumption, increasing the relative share of the household budget devoted to foodstuffs at the expense of other consumer items.

In 1980, households had to devote a larger share of their expenditure (57%) to foodstuffs than in 1968 (41.6%) for a still inadequate nutritional level. Consumption has not yet reached the level (3,000 calories) beyond which there is a relative decline in the share of food expenditure in the household budget.[16]

The continuous rise in the relative share of food expenditure reflects the effect of the inflation of food prices rather than any rise in real consumption. For an equal food level, about 2,500 calories, Tunisian households spend only 41% of their expenditure on food. The consumer price index in Algeria rose on average by 15% p.a. between 1968 and 1980 (6% in Tunisia over the same period) whereas household incomes rose by about 12% p.a. (at current prices). Compared to the evolution of per capita expenditure which makes it possible to eliminate the effect of household size, the elasticity coefficient of food demand rose from 0.944 in 1967 to 0.999 in 1980, which reflects a high and rising average propensity to consume.

With 2,500 calories, the quantitative limit has not yet been reached, since it can be observed that all groups' consumption of foodstuffs is rising, whatever the income band considered. The demand for food remains largely unsatisfied and consumption continues to rise faster than production.

Agriculture and industry: interaction

The rise in the demand for food and in agricultural prices has stimulated the development of agriculture, its capacity to increase its purchases from industry and its deliveries of products to the market. Increased consumption of producer goods has been sustained by increased agricultural prices and state subsidies for the purchase of equipment more than by advances in agricultural productivity; the growth in agricultural production has been obtained by extending crops rather than by increased yields.

Agriculture's demand for industrial goods
Over the past decade there has been striking growth of agriculture's demand for industrially produced goods. Between 1965 and 1985 the number of tractors has more than doubled, from 24,510 to over 50,000; the number of combine harvesters increased from 2,450 to 4,800. Consumption of fertilizers and other chemical products has risen more slowly.

The greatest growth has been of goods and inputs, use of which ensures high production: mechanization, irrigation equipment, fertilizers and plant protection products for growing fruit and vegetables, and so on.

The public agricultural sector still absorbs the largest share of capital goods and intermediate products, but in the 1980s, the private sector has rapidly reduced the gap with consumption of some goods (irrigation equipment, building materials and means of transport) exceeding that of the public sector.[17] Between 1980 and 1983, the private sector acquired 27,000 tractors, 4,000 hand ploughs, 10,000 transport vans, 2,000 lorries and 30,000 motor-driven pumps.

Table 4.5
Consumption of Agricultural Equipment: Private Sector

	Total consumption	Private sector	%
Haulage equipment	49,651	24,435	49
Harvesting equipment	43,524	15,835	36
Ploughing equipment	67,993	26,351	33
Motor-driven pumps	60,611	47,734	79
Fertilizers (metric tons)	226,320	56,700	25
Plant protection products (quintals)	170,620	36,075	28

Source: Algeria, Ministère de l'Agriculture.

Most private sector purchases are for livestock (transport, drinking water equipment), market-garden crops (irrigation equipment, fertilizers, pesticides) and cash crops, whose prices have risen strongly and continuously since 1980.

Fertilizer and pesticide use is, for example, almost wholly limited to market-gardening and to a much lesser extent to cereals; only the public sector is developing the use of mineral fertilizer on cereals and pulses along with a more intensive use of mechanization and improved seeds.

In the private sector cereal farming, where topographical conditions are favourable. machines have replaced animal power and human labour, but without updating cultivation techniques to promote more intensive soil-use. Instead, there has been mechanization of traditional techniques, whose effects on soil conservation are negative.[18] Private producers' use of mechanization is to reduce growing costs rather than as a means of intensification of production.

Unlike the demand for machines, which is potentially high following the reduction of the number of milch cows and the rise in wages, the use of fertilizers and chemical products seems to have stagnated for several years. Consumption levels are less than half the norms recommended by the crop intensification targets set by the Ministry of Agriculture. (For example, 203,951 metric tons in 1984, as against a target of 459,000, or only 44%.) This is because in years of inadequate rainfall, or in areas where annual rainfall is less than 400 mm, fertilizers have little effect on productivity.

Generally, despite more widespread use of chemical products and machines, yields for all crops and livestock have remained excessively low: six or seven quintals on average per hectare for cereals, 18 quintals for forage crops, 60 to 80 quintals for vegetables and fruit, 2,500 litres of milk per cow.

State policy during the period 1973–83 was to promote agriculture's use of industrially produced goods. Large subsidies were given for agricultural machinery, chemical products and irrigation equipment. In particular, it attempted, through the relationship between cereal and fertilizer prices, to increase the demand for fertilizers and plant protection products. As Table 4.6 shows, the wheat–fertilizer price ratio went from 1.15 to 1974 to 2.90 in 1985.

Table 4.6
Prices: wheat/fertilizer compared

	Producer price: wheat	Producer price: fertilizers (NPK 12.18.18)	Ratio: cereal/ fertilizers prices	Yield per hectare
1974	67.70	55.2	1.15	5.8
1980	125.00	55.2	2.26	6.4
1985	200.00	69.0	2.90	6.09

Sources: Adapted from various issues of *Statistiques Agricoles.*

Until 1982, industries had to directly subsidize agriculture for the acquisition of equipment and products, selling prices being imposed by the state and frozen at their 1973 level. Since 1983, when the government took over direct aid to agriculture as a charge on the budget, it has begun gradually to reduce the amount of subsidies and align selling prices on acquisition (import) and/or manufacturing costs. To balance this, it has agreed to large increases in agricultural producer prices in order to maintain demand. For example, the price of one quintal of hard wheat in 1980 and 1981 was AD 125, in 1986 AD 220; soft wheat at AD 115 per quintal in 1980 and 1981 rose to AD 210 in 1986;

milk, 1980 and 1981, AD 1.75 per litre, 1986 AD 4.00. Potatoes, beans and lentils showed similar increases between 1980 and 1986.

Prices of fertilizers and mechanical traction also rose. Thus the rise in the prices of agricultural commodities (partly borne by consumers) more than compensated for the elimination of subsidies for purchasing agricultural producer goods.

The transfer of incomes, in the Algerian case of a fraction of oil sales, to agriculture through raising agricultural prices and wages can be justified by the high proportion of the population that agriculture must still retain. It avoids or slows down the transfer of workers when sufficient non-agricultural jobs have not yet been created. It also makes possible the equipment of farms to a higher level and, when the conditions are created, the modification of production methods. Increased agricultural productivity will enable the self-financing of agricultural development, enlarging the demand for industrially made goods and providing the dynamic force in relations between agriculture and industry.

Stagnation of agricultural productivity may of course call into question the validity of this pattern of financing. Intensification through enhanced use of industrial inputs without advances in production would simply increase the waste of resources and encourage the substitution of capital for labour.

The volume of investment in agriculture depends heavily on agronomic and technical advances which condition advances in production and the level of profitability of investments realized. In Europe, for example, after the Second World War, with the implementation of a new model of production, mechanization, chemical fertilizers, and production specialization, the proportion of intermediate consumption in gross agricultural product rose from 27% in 1950 to 50% during the 1970s. Over the same period, agricultural productivity was rising by 4% p.a.

It should be noted that, ill-considered use of intensification techniques can, however, have a permanent negative effect on the conditions of production through destruction of the natural environment and acceleration of soil erosion, due to ill-adapted mechanization, and salting of soils when irrigation techniques are inadequate.

Agricultural production and productivity
It is premature to conclude that there is now a permanent tendency for agricultural production and yields to rise consequent upon a wider use of new inputs. Statistics published by the Ministry of Agriculture for 1985 and 1986 reveal a significant increase in final agricultural production compared to the average of the results obtained during the first half of the 1980s.

Agricultural production has been marked by the two very good cereal harvests, in 1985 and 1986, which substantially raised the average of the previous five years. Climatic conditions were particularly favourable but the results were partly owing to the effect of the Ministry of Agriculture's crop intensification programmes. The year 1985 even saw record production, with three million metric tons of cereals harvested; the ten-year average since the beginning of the present century has been around 1.8 million metric tons.

Compared to the best three harvests of the 1970s (1971, 2,362 million metric tons; 1974, 2,680; and 1975, 2,313 million metric tons), the 1985 and 1986 harvests registered an increase of 15%. These production volumes were obtained on slightly fewer sown areas (2,600,000 hectares) than the average for the 1970s (3,000,000 hectares) which indicates a major improvement in yields.

The pattern for other products, both vegetable and animal, was more varied. Vegetable production rose from 1.43 million metric tons in 1980 to 2.54 million in 1986, an increase of 77%. For animal products, poultry meat rose sharply, 12% p.a., beef and mutton 3% and 1% respectively, while milk production rose only 1% p.a. In total, increased production was markedly more for vegetables, fruit, white meats and eggs than for cereals, milk or other animal products.

It should be noted that private farmers have put more stress on market-gardening (+45%), forage crops (+35%), and barley (+36.7%) intended for animal feed and meat production. The big state enterprises, the socialist agricultural estates, increased the areas under pulses, wheats, and forage crops for milk production. The state sector's policy thus attempts to correct the effects of the market and price system that favour the production of vegetables and meat over that of pulses, cereals or milk.

It must, however, be again stressed that increased production of some crops results more from an extension of areas cultivated than from improvements in yields. Areas devoted to market-gardening rose from 132,160 hectares in 1976 to some 260,381 in 1986 (+97%), those of forage from 239,330 (1975) to 468,840 (1984) and vegetables from 125,726 to 152,627 hectares (+21.3%). A partial substitution of barley for wheats should be noted, since barley, which accounted for about 26% of the cereals total in 1976, accounted for 37% in 1984 and 40% in 1985. The same applies to the relative growth in animal products, which is mostly owing to imports of soyabean cake, maize and barley, rather than development of forage crops.

Theoretically, the extension of forage crops, pulses, vegetables and fruit was achieved by the bringing into use of part of fallow land, which totalled on average three million hectares during the 1970s, 40% of the land under annual crops. By 1985–86 fallow land occupied only two million hectares and was expected to decline to 1,600,000 hectares in 1986–87.[21] There is thus considerable potential for extending crops since it is estimated that some two million hectares, with good rainfall (more than 350mm) remain fallow. But these figures are only indicative of a trend, more marked in the public sector, towards improving crop rotation and developing forage crops to replace fallow.

Deliveries of manufactured goods have enabled agriculture to improve its equipment, extend the areas cultivated – forage crops and pulses, market-gardening – and intensify some crops (cereals), but their impact on yields is not yet clear.

Average yields, measured since the 1980s, have remained low both for cereals and for livestock: 7.35 quintals per hectare for cereals, 18 to 20 for forage crops, 80 quintals for vegetables and fruit, 3.6 for pulses. The only significant rise in yields was recorded as a result of the two very good harvests of 1985 and 1986.

It is, however, difficult to be sure that this is a permanent result of an advance achieved following the successful mastery of a technical change.

The increase in fertilizer consumption, for example, has not had all the effects expected on yields in the public sector, where they were most used. Similarly, the extension of mechanization, notably the widespread practice of mechanized ploughing (deliveries of equipment have doubled in the 1980s), has not much improved yields in the private sector. Thus, the process of agricultural intensification initiated by the agricultural services in the public sector, on the basis of a marked increase in consumption of capital, agricultural equipment, fertilizers and pest control products[22] was achieved at very low levels of technical and economic efficiency.

The fact that the new technical methods were not adapted to local conditions, and that there has been no genetic renewal of seeds, together with the acute lack of trained manpower on farms, considerably limit the profitability of capital committed to increasing yields. The generalization of intensified rotation (cereals – pulses – forage replacing cereals – fallow rotation) makes the production units in the state sector bear the financial risks of insufficiently tested technical and agronomic choices. Production, for a majority of farms, does not cover growing costs and workers' wages, and each year the state has to balance the budget of cereal-growing.

Private farmers have limited the use of mechanization, seeking instead to develop sheep-raising to compensate for the losses recorded by cereal-growing. They have increased the consumption of inputs only for those irrigated crops (vegetables) that fetch the best prices on the market. In short, they prefer to maintain a more extensive productive system, using less fertilizers and then only in years with good rainfall, keeping more fallow and reducing their growing practices to limit expenditure on mechanization.

These observations demonstrate that the question of the productivity of inputs precedes that of the volume of investment to be devoted to increasing agricultural production. Opening up access to credit for farm equipment and running costs, and increasing public investment in agriculture can, indeed, make possible marked advances in production. But the costs are such that, even if they are borne by the state budget, it is legitimate to question the economic and social utility of a policy directed essentially at enhanced use of the material factors of agricultural intensification.

Numerous authors have shown the relationship between the growth of the consumption of capital and technical change in agriculture.[23] While usually technical change cannot occur without an increase in capital, this does not automatically lead to the adoption of new, more efficient farming methods, especially if, for example, they are not yet available. The volume of investment should depend on the margin of agronomic and technical progress available that condition the level of profitability of funds committed in the production process. In other words, the volume of investment can be increased, especially when it is realized partly in foreign exchange,[24] and imported equipment, fertilizers and other intermediate products, and yet lead to a decreasing yield.

In fact, the agronomic and technical conditions for a greater use of machinery and chemicals in agriculture have not been created concomitantly with the construction of an industrial sector oriented towards the needs of agriculture.

In Europe, the development of modern industry after the 1950s went hand in hand with the achievement of decisive results in the selection and improvement of vegetable and animal varieties and new methods of farming and animal husbandry. The increase in purchases by agriculture occurred along with an improvement in yields and labour productivity. The share of intermediate consumption as a percentage of the gross agricultural product rose from 27% in 1950 to some 50% an average in the 1970s. Over the same period, agricultural productivity improved 2.5 times.

Numerous studies have stressed the decisive importance of technical change in the global growth of production, and especially of the chain of agricultural progress constituted by the link between research, training and development.[25]

Agronomic research

So far, in the area of biology and technology, Algeria has mainly sought to adapt the species and techniques of the North to its own less favourable natural conditions. Rather than adopting an autonomous approach agronomic research has opted for the idea of the *transfer of technology*, of the advances realized by developed agricultures. It has thus proceeded to import animal and vegetable varieties and equipment that are the product of selection in different ecological, economic and social contexts.

In the semi-arid regions, soil and rainfall conditions make any adaptation very difficult, and resort to imported technologies has proved to have little effect on improving productivity. It has, however, had the effect of deepening dependence on the industrialized countries, and increasingly placing agricultural reproduction in thrall to growing and costly imports.

In the North, for example, animal selection and research on livestock feeding have been carried out on the basis of large cereal surpluses, particularly in the USA.[26] Transfer of the industrialized or semi-industrialized model of animal husbandry, aviculture and dairy cattle, has forced Algeria to import increasing quantities of animals and secondary cereals (maize, barley, soya-cake, for example) which it cannot produce in sufficient quantities.

Imports of barley (2.1 million quintals) and maize (1.8 million quintals) in 1977, rose to seven million quintals in 1983 and ten million in 1985 (in addition to the 30 million quintals of wheat intended for human consumption). The original proposal was to develop milk production through the exploitation of genetically improved livestock imported from France, Germany and Holland. The growth of herds from this imported cattle has been extremely slow. The number of milch cows increased from 10,000 head in 1966 to fewer than 100,000 in 1985, as against a local breed herd of 700,000 head.

Genetically improved animals require a rich and balanced diet, and environmental conditions that cannot be found locally. The animal, therefore, has to adapt to a type of diet, made up of poor quality hay plus imported concentrated feeds, which underuses its genetic potential.[27] Milk yields are low, between 2,000 and 2,500 litres per annum, as against a potential of 4,000 or 5,000 litres. Despite major investments in the import of cattle, the building of modern cattle sheds, the veterinary network, for example, this type of livestock rearing accounts for only 12% of total production and 6% of consumption. Compared to local cattle, reared by peasant methods, milk yields have barely doubled on average. Stock breeding has totally ignored the potentialities of local cattle, certain breeds of which, for example the Guelmoise, had been improved during the colonial period. Local cattle, like local sheep, have thus not benefited from any effort at selection and improvement, whereas a productivity gain of 10% would have been enough to make up for the milk production realized from imported cattle.

The development model for aviculture, for the production of chicken meat and eggs, relies on the importation of genetically improved strains and feed purchased abroad. Dependence is total, since strains, feed, veterinary products and certain equipment have all to be replenished from time to time.

Other factors of agricultural reproduction have to be imported which reduce the autonomy of local agriculture. Imports of potato plants rose sixfold, from 13,000 metric tons in 1971 to 83,000 metric tons in 1981, equal to 80% of the country's plant requirements. The same applies for forage seeds (86%) and kitchen garden plants (60%). Potato productivity is very low: production is equal to only three or four times the quantity of plants used, 0.3m mt of plants for fewer than 1m mt of potatoes for consumption.

In addition to the difficulties of mastering the techniques of cropping methods, are the factors associated with plant health and the timing of imports. Essential products still depend on the quantity and quality of external supplies of intermediate goods, and shortages of foreign exchange can generate supply problems here.

The Ministry of Agriculture has embarked on so-called development research, that is, research that seeks to apply the biological techniques and advances achieved by industrial countries. This approach has led to the establishment of eleven development institutes, running programmes arranged by broad categories of crops and dismantling the system of agricultural research set up during the colonial period, which was better attuned to local resources.

By 1980, in its 15 research stations, the Institut National de la Recherche Agronomique (INRA) had only about 20 engineers and 30 technicians who, in principle, covered every area of agricultural research.

For the six experimental research stations of the most important development institute (concerned with cereal crops, pulses and forage crops, which are grown on 87% of the usable arable area), there were only 17 engineers and 50 technicians; the institute for market-gardening had nine engineers and six technicians; the institute for fruit tree research only five engineers and 18 technicians. In total, the research apparatus has only a few dozen experienced researchers for vast programmes, and they generally work in isolation from one another. The financial resources available for research are less than 0.5% of GNP.[28]

The education and training system has suffered from a similar approach, based on the idea that agricultural modernization can be achieved only by exogenous methods. The engineers and technicians who graduate from the schools of agriculture are theoretically responsible for disseminating new technical knowledge to replace old techniques. But the agricultural education system has developed independently of local research and the potential demand of peasant society.

In 1982, there were 50 teaching establishments, and the levels and possibilities of training have been gradually increased and diversified. Between 1973 and 1983, some 4,800 applied engineers and 1,000 state engineers completed their training course in the various schools of agriculture.

Despite the increase in the number of persons trained, however, the education system's impact on technical and social change in agriculture has been almost imperceptible. The agricultural education system has remained external to rural society in two ways: 1) the recruitment of students; and 2) the fact that the schools themselves are situated in urban areas. Thus recruitment favours not the children of peasants or those destined to set up as farmers, but those of city-dwellers, aspiring to be civil servants. Furthermore, virtually all the products of education are absorbed by state departments or para-statal agencies involved in agriculture.

There has been direct training of producers only for the lower levels of the various teaching grades, through those adult training centre programmes aimed at agricultural workers and wage-earners in the public sector, and for short courses – usually introductory or general – of between a week and a month. Over the ten years 1974–84 they involved only 64,000 workers, compared to the working agricultural population of 1,100,000.

As Table 4.7 shows, only an insignificant proportion of the peasantry has received any specialized training at all. This external orientation of the education system in relation to rural society, which also performs functions other than those of simply advancing that society, calls into question the relationship between training and development.

Table 4.7
Employed population by qualification (%)

	General education	Specialized training	Experience	No training	Total
Farmer/herder	—	0.2	89.8	9.9	100
Full-time agricultural worker	0.6	3.0	79.6	16.8	100
Seasonal agricultural worker	0.3	2.6	46.6	50.4	100
Family helper	0.1	—	58.5	41.4	100

Source: Algeria, Office National des Statistiques, *Enquête main d'oeuvre et démographie 1984.*

Effects of structural reforms

Material advances are not the only factors in technical change in agriculture. Equipment cannot be modernized without changing the methods of cultivation, neither can new techniques be widely disseminated without implementing the necessary structural reforms. The dialectic between equipment and organization, to use De Bernis' expression,[29] is essential to an understanding of the interactions between agriculture and industry and the dynamic of the growth of agricultural production. Structural reform refers not only to the distribution of land among agricultural holdings of different sizes but also to the social forms of the organization of labour and the manner in which the peasantry is integrated socio-politically into the global society.

In the Algerian strategy, the option for an autocentred development model implied the choice of a structural policy involving exploitation of the whole potential agricultural space and full employment of the agricultural population. In other words, it involved the rejection of the colonial and/or capitalist pattern which consists in concentrating the development of agriculture on the best land and on the water resources available to them. In fact, a rejection of a process of socially excluding the majority of peasants from the conditions of agricultural modernization, leading to the destruction of soils and the deterioration of the factors of agricultural reproduction in vast areas of the country.

The conditions of long-term agricultural growth rested on nurturing a natural environment that had been destroyed by earlier modes of exploitation.

The response to agrarian dualism appeared in the 'agrarian revolution' programme initiated in November 1971, in the first phase of the take-off of the plans for industrialization. Restriction on the size of privately owned land in favour of landless peasants was the aspect that attracted most attention, at the expense of the new pattern of exploiting agricultural resources that it heralded.

It was proposed to increase the cultivable area by two or three million hectares in order to bring the total usable area to about ten million hectares through gradually putting into effect programmes of rehabilitating the soil, mobilizing water resources, planting trees and achieving full employment of all the available agricultural labour force. This option had the advantage of considerably increasing the amount of agrarian reform land by adding areas of soil rehabilitation so as to assign them to landless peasants and those whose farms were too small.

Finally, it was intended that the 'groupments de mise en valeur' (development groups), a form of work co-operative and a means of the organization of collective labour, by landless and small peasants, to carry out soil improvement programmes, should eventually be transformed into agricultural production co-operatives which the state would provide with enough land and equipment for them to function.

The implementation of the agrarian programme during the 1970s showed the limited and largely formal character of the measures put into effect to accompany the industrialization process. While the nationalization of settler estates in 1963 had enabled the state to build up a sizeable agricultural domain of two million hectares, 27% of the usable agricultural area, the impact of the 1971 agrarian reform on private land ownership was very slight. The national agrarian reform domain had only some one million hectares, of which only 438,774 had been taken from private ownership, a little less than 10% of the total amount of land cultivated by individual farmers. The total number of collective assignees did not exceed 7% or 8% of the total number of agricultural workers, or 90,000 beneficiaries, organized, from above, into production co-operatives. Public ownership thus increased from 2,084,000 hectares to 3,206,580, 45% of the total usable agricultural area (7,710,810 hectares, leaving 4,504,230 in private hands).

By the end of the 1970s, about one-third (330,000) of the agricultural labour force was employed in the collective work sector, the other two-thirds (600, to 650,000) were individually farm holdings of various sizes, most of which were too small to support the households.

There was no real impetus to encourage small peasants to accept the new structures and collective forms of mutual assistance and co-operation, which were at the very heart of the strategy of agrarian modernization. The 'groupements de mise en valeur', the centrepiece of the plan to mobilize and organize the landless and small peasants, have a total of only 5,650 members settled on slightly under 100,000 hectares. Under other legal forms – peasant mutual assistance co-operatives – 16,000 other peasants have formed producers' associations based essentially on shared use of equipment.

In fact, the emphasis has principally been upon building-up a public agricultural sector and expanding state control over production and distribution. As in many African countries, the co-operatives have served more as a means of state control over the peasantry than as a democratic structure for organizing the peasantry and enabling their participation in the process of transforming agriculture.

Disaffection towards the agrarian reform and the co-operatives soon appeared among the peasants, especially as, without political and technical back-up, they had to face the inherent difficulties of introducing collective labour discipline and managing an agricultural enterprise.

In 1982–83, the formal policy of agrarian reform was abandoned in favour of a conception of the development of agriculture based more on market forces and activity by individual producers. In the general framework of restructuring the economy, the agrarian reform co-operatives were dissolved as they had been formed: without consulting the peasants who belonged to them. The public domain was split almost equally between the 'socialist agricultural estates', new names for self-managed agricultural enterprises, the area of which thus rose from 2,084,580 to 2,800,000 hectares or 36.03% of the usable agricultural area, and the individual sector – whose relative share grew – with 63.7% of the cultivated area. The service co-operative agencies (set up in each commune) were also dissolved; these had previously given assistance to the agrarian reform sector and small peasants, especially in the area of mechanization. This last measure was immediately followed by a sharp rise in charges for hiring agricultural equipment on the market.

The experience of agrarian reorganization shows that the strategy of agrarian modernization in Algeria has been largely frustrated by the desire to keep the agrarian reform within limits that retain the general balance of class relations within the rural areas. State action was presented as a measure to preserve social order in favour of the poor population in the countryside. Even so, it did not disarm the fractions of the middle and well-off peasantry, hostile to the agrarian reform process, whose positions might be threatened by any extensive democratization of social relations in the rural areas.

Slowing down the process of social differentiation, limiting the size of holdings and redistributing land, as has been observed in many countries, rather consolidated the position of middle peasants in whose favour the new agricultural policy has been implemented since 1982.

Abandoning the programme of assigning the potential agricultural labour force to extending the exploitation of agricultural resources based on control of the natural environment has, however, resulted in limiting agricultural growth and the role of agriculture in meeting the food needs of the population. It has also accentuated earlier trends towards soil deterioration, particularly in livestock farming and mountainous areas, further reducing the possibilities of agricultural reproduction in the long term.

The global dynamic of employment was thus sufficient to orient the rural labour force to other non-agricultural activities throughout the 1970s and the early 1980s and, through employment and mixed incomes, to keep a large number of small peasants on the land. But, today, it seems that with the fall in the growth rate of the economy and the concomitant fall in external receipts, the problem of employment is again leading to the question of which path the development of agriculture should take.

Notes

1. Meaning productivity per worker per annum. In China, for example, a stagnation of the value of the working day per employed worker but an increase in the number of days worked in the year, and hence an increase in production per worker and per annum can be observed. See Thomas G. Rawski, *Growth and Employment in China*, World Bank, 1978.

2. As Mahmoud Ourabah stresses, the clichés peddled about the Algerian economy's choices are long-lived, such as 'the alleged deliberate choice to sacrifice agriculture in favour of industry, industry allegedly sought more as an end than as a means, or again the option for heavy industry over light industry . . .' *Les transformations économiques de l'Algérie*, ENAP, Publisud 1982.

3. If the cultivated areas appear to have remained at 7.5 million hectares *for several decades*, presumably there must have been an extension of crops in the least favourable regions, notably in the steppe, to make up for the good land in the plain overtaken by urbanization. The stability of the usable agricultural area contradicts what can be observed and thus conceals a deterioration in the quality of the land being cultivated.

On the distribution of usable agricultural land by country see *Terres vives et population*, FAO 1984.

4. According to Monjauze, 'Exposé de doctrine sur la rénovation rurale en Algérie', Direction de l'Agriculture et des Forêts, Algiers 1959.

5. See *Le Maghreb, Hommes et Espaces*, Armand Colin, Paris 1985; Jean Dresch, *Géographie des Régions Arides*, PUF, Paris 1982.

6. 'The Algerian Tell is very disadvantaged, not only because it has few real plains, [and] a good part of them are in the rain shadow of the littoral chains, but also because their geological structure does not really lend itself to the mass infiltration and retention of the water that flows there. Most . . . simply runs into the sea.' See Monjauze, 'Le sol et l'homme', *Algérie Agricole*, Algiers 1966.

7. By comparison, in Morocco, surface water is estimated at 16 billion m^3 and underground water at five billion m^3 for a total of 21 billion m^3 as against 17 in Algeria.

8. D. Dubost, 'Notes pour une nouvelle stratégie de développement agricole des régions sahariennes', *Bulletin d'Agronomie Saharienne*, No. 5, July 1983, Ministère de l'Agriculture, Algiers.

9. Ministère de la Planification et de l'Aménagement du Territoire, Algeria.

10. For the period 1978–79 and 1980–84, investment in irrigation is not included in agricultural investment. With two-thirds of water resources used by agriculture, it is logical to increase the figure for agricultural investment by the same proportion.

11. See the IREP/Ministère de l'Industrie study on the needs of the agricultural sector for industrial goods, 1970.

12. Compared to the norms recommended by the technical services, the use of fertilizers is less than 41% of prescribed needs in the public sector and 18% in the private sector; the quantity prescribed for the whole of agriculture totals 500,000 metric tons.

13. The economically active population includes the employed population plus those seeking work and women working part-time. The employed population includes the population working at the time of the census or who worked at least six consecutive days in the month preceding the census.

14. In Egypt, the share of material production in the employed labour force was 66% in 1978–80. See Dowidar, 'La politique économique de l'Infitah et la construction industrielle', *L'Egypte Contemporaine*, No. 397, July 1984.

15. A. Prenant, 'Aspects de la croissance relative des petits centres urbains en Algérie', *Tours*, November 1973.

16. See ONS No. 7, April–June 1985, 'La loi d'Engels de la baisse relative des dépenses alimentaires par rapport au budget est-elle vérifiable en Algérie?'.

17. The rise in agricultural prices led to an explosion of private sector demand in the areas of construction (cement, concrete, iron, bricks etc.) goods intended for replacing dwellings and, more rarely, speculative buildings.

18. In the private sector, soil is generally prepared for sowing by two treatments with an offset disc harrow; seeds from the previous harvest are hand sown. The recovery of seed is also done with the harrow. Exclusive use of the offset disc harrow for soil preparation frequently forms a ploughing shield that resists rainwater infiltration and root penetration. Use of the same implement for covering seeds also leads to a random lifting followed by poor development and bad tilling after the lifting.

19. These prices must be seen as floor prices applicable to the public sector which

delivers its production of cereals, pulses and milk to state marketing and processing agencies. Market prices valid for the private sector are much higher.

20. There were two successive rises in the prices of semolina bread and cereal derivatives: 20% in 1985 and 20% in 1986.

21. See interviews with the Minister of Agriculture in *El Moudjahid*, 24 June 1986.

22. The budget head 'supply of so-called "intensification" factors' rose from AD 1,500 million in 1982 to AD 2,250 million in 1986.

23. See Keith Griffin, *The Political Economy of Agrarian Change*, Cambridge, Mass., Harvard University Press 1974.

24. The foreign exchange cost of production for some staples can reach 90% for battery eggs; in Morocco, it is approximately 60% for cereals.

25. Yamada and Hayami assert that in Japan 40% of global agricultural growth is due to an increase in inputs and 60% to technological change. Griliches' analysis of the growth of total productivity in US agriculture demonstrates that farmers' educational level accounted for 13.5% and extension and research 27.4%. J. P. Wampach, 'La croissance de la productivité agricole', *Développement Economique et Agriculture – Cahiers de l'ISEA*, Vol. IV, No. 2, 1970.

26. See Revel and Ribond, *Les Etats-Unis et la stratégie alimentaire mondiale*, Paris, Calmann-Lévy 1981.

27. See K. Hadjait, 'Dépendance alimentaire et modèles de développement de l'élevage', in *L'Evolution de la Consomation Alimentaire en Afrique*, Geneva, Editions Sociales.

28. FAO, *Rapport sur la recherche agricole en Algérie*, Rome 1985.

29. 'De l'existence de points de passage obligatoire pour une politique de développement', *Cahier de l'ISMEA*, Vol. XVII, No. 2, February 1983.

5. Mauritania: Nomadism and Peripheral Capital

Abdel Wedoud Ould Cheikh

North-western Africa, known today as the Sahel, has always been an area particularly suited to animal husbandry. From the 1,000 head of zebu that Askia Ishaq II used as a protective cover ahead of his troops in March 1591 (Kati 1964, 264) when the Songhai Empire collapsed under the blows of the men of Djouder, to the vast herds all over this area today, there is ample evidence of enormous wealth in livestock of the countries of the Sahel. Before 1972 this was represented by a total of 21 million head of cattle (Gallais 1977, 268).

It was not this wealth of livestock that attracted the Moroccan conquerors. Nor does it appear to have motivated more recent onslaughts, notably the French colonial occupation. But, inevitably, the organization of the pastoral societies of the Sahel, largely centred on cattle and their resources, was profoundly and permanently affected by this occupation. Other factors, such as the recent drought of the 1970s, have contributed to a dangerous acceleration of the process of disarticulation of the Sahelian pastoral systems, but the major factor in the evolution of these systems remains their marginal integration into a monetary economy centred in towns, which themselves are experiencing accelerated and disorganized growth. For Mauritania, which is examined here in order to provide an illustration of recent transformations of Sahelian pastoralism, two figures are enough to indicate the scale of changes that have occurred in recent years: whereas in 1965, nomads made up some 65% of the Mauritanian population, by 1976, they represented only 36%. Over the same period, the urban population grew threefold, rising from 90,000 in 1961 to 300,000 in 1977.

Leaving aside the terminological problems – the relationship between 'pastoralism', 'nomadism' and 'semi-nomadism' (Salzman 1980) – this chapter first presents a short outline of the factors of pastoral production, and then examines the forms and effects of the integration of pastoral society into an economy dominated by commodity relations. Finally, the social and political aspects of this integration will be considered in order to attempt clarification of the specific forms taken by the contradictions – of clans, groups, classes – within a pastoral society undergoing massive upheavals.

Pastoral production

The original complex constituted by the symbiosis of agriculture and animal husbandry in the prehistory of human societies (Leroi-Gourhan, I, 227–37) developed and survived at the cost of a specialization often involving violence. This complex and the more or less voluntary association between agriculturalists and herders constituted a permanent feature of the organization of Sahelian societies, and especially of Moorish society.

The environment and its resources

The key features of the Mauritanian climate are high aridity and extreme variations of temperature. It is dominated by dry winds (the maritime alize from the Azores anticyclone and the continental alize, the *Irivi* in the Moorish dialect) often laden with sand.

In July–August the monsoon winds from the high pressure zones in the South Atlantic provide the bulk of the rainfall, which barely exceeds 600mm in the best watered regions of the country (the far south). Further north rainfall declines to less than 100mm above a Nouakchott–Atar–Oualata line and to less than 50mm along the coast in the far north.

The influence of the maritime and continental alizes and the monsoon winds, combined with distance from the ocean, makes it possible to distinguish two broad climatic zones, each with a coastal and a continental aspect: the Sahara and the Sahel. North of Nouakchott, the coast, which has constant humidity, low rainfall and relatively low temperatures in winter, is a 'tropical coastal desert'.

The Saharan climate properly so-called, covering the vast bulk of the country, is marked by large variations in temperature, low rainfall and high evaporation.

The northern limit of Sahelian Mauritania is usually placed along the 150mm isohyet. Temperature variations in the coastal parts of this Sahelian zone are small and, on average, temperatures are lower than in the continental Sahelian climate.

Naturally, the types of vegetation and grazing land vary, depending on the climatic situation. The plant cycle also depends on the latitude and the nature of the soils. From north to south we can distinguish:

1) A vast desert zone stretching over mineral-poor soils, with sparse vegetation generally concentrated in areas with many streams (steep slopes in the mountains, *oued* courses and so on). Tree cover consists mainly of *Acacia Raddiana* and herbaceous plants, mainly of hardy graminaceae (*Stipagrostis Pungens*), making it possible, apart from short periods when the very irregular rainfall produces fresh pasture, to engage in animal husbandry (camels, sheep, goats) that sometimes requires movement over only short distances.

Apart from these areas of greater or lesser concentrations of plants (in the Saharan context, of course!) the sporadic grazing areas in the Saharan regions and notably the salty grasses (*Cornulaca Monacantha*) constitute excellent winter pastures for camels, virtually the only animals able to get any nourishment from them, given the distances to be travelled and the scarcity of watering points (in cool weather, camels feeding on these grasses can survive without drinking for over two months).[1]

2) A Sahelian zone with pastures renewed each year by relatively regular rainfall. The vegetation becomes denser and more varied as one moves south. Alongside a scattering of large trees (*Adansonia Digitata* and *Combretum Glutinosum*) that herald the Sudanic savanna, more or less dense copses of various varieties of acacia (*Acacia Senegal*; *Acacia Flava*; *Acacia Nilotica*, among others) as well as trees or shrubs (notably *Commiphora Africana* and *Zizyphus Mauritania*) of lesser forage value, dominate a bushy vegetation in which the typical Sahelian graminacea (*Cenchrus Biflorus*) occupies a preponderant place in the rainy season. This zone is mainly a cattle area, but there are sheep and goats too. Dromedaries, on the other hand, can stay there only in the dry season; in the wet season there is an abundance of tsetse flies carrying the very dangerous camel sleeping-sickness (*tàburit*).

Mauritanian livestock

The adaptation of Sahelian animal species to these harsh, natural conditions, the result of a long process of selection, has been stressed by several observers (Charles Toupet 1975, 227 and 29). The mediocre results so far obtained by attempts to acclimatize exotic species or by the few attempts at cross-breeding them with indigenous breeds, suggest that the Sahelian–Saharan species, with their qualities of resistance and moderate food and water needs, are not about to be replaced by new breeds, despite their low yields.

Goats, sheep, camels and cattle are the predominant animals reared in these areas. The so-called 'Sahelian' goats are the most widespread. These are of varying colours, high on the hoof and quite light when they reach maturity (averaging between 15–20 and 40 kg); females produce 70 litres of milk annually for a lactation period of 120 days, and adults are estimated to produce 10–15 kg of meat.

There are two kinds of Mauritanian sheep: the 'Fulani' sheep, quite large, with a short, white or black and white coat, and an adult weight of 30 to 50 kg, producing up to 30 kg of meat, excellent for human consumption; and the smaller, longer haired 'Moorish' sheep, which provides the main raw material of nomad tents – and produces more milk than the Fulani: 1.5 to 2 litres per day in the rainy season.

All the camels raised in Mauritania are the single-humped *Camelus Dromedarius*. Used for transport, and for milk production, the camel is also used as a draught animal and as a source of meat for human consumption. Its hair, especially that of young animals, provides a valuable supplementary raw material for making Moorish tents. The adults weigh on average 450 to 550 kg, and can provide 150 kg of meat. Females produce an estimated average of 400 litres of milk per head per year for a lactation period of 270–360 days.

The cattle in Mauritania – *Bos ludicus* – are distinguished as 'Moorish' zebu and 'Fulani' zebu. The Moorish variety, with an average adult weight of between 320 and 360 kg, provides 500 litres of milk annually for a lactation period of 180–200 days. The heavier Fulani zebu (up to 400 kg on average in adulthood) produces less milk (some 300 litres for a lactation period of 180–200 days). Average meat production from adult males can reach 150–250 kg.

The low productivity of Sahelian livestock reflected in these figures is somewhat compensated for by the large size of flocks and herds that some observers consider to be excessive compared to the meagre resources available. The load capacity of Sahelian pastures will be assessed later.

There are great disparities in the quantity of livestock owned by individuals and families. These disparities confirm a hierarchical stratification marked by a longstanding system of pseudo-castes which has been considerably accentuated by recent imbalances consequent upon the urban commercial sector's domination of the pastoral economy that has developed in the wake of the colonial and post-colonial administration.

Particularly since 1968 (the beginning of the recent wave of droughts in the Sahel) as a result of the steep fall in cattle prices (in 1968 a milch cow was selling at Francs CFA 1.500 at Boutilimit, whereas two years earlier it had been worth 20 or 25.000) there has been a massive transfer of cattle from traditional herders to traders and bureaucrats in the towns. This development and its economic and social significance will be discussed later.

Regarding the average size of traditional-type family herds, no established estimates exist, but from a limited empirical knowledge of Mauritanian and especially Moorish pastoralism it can be said that for large ruminants, herds bigger than 100 head are exceptional. For many families of herders, livestock resources are limited to a few dozen sheep and goats, and rarely to more than 20 head of cattle or camels.

Charles Toupet, citing pre-drought estimates, suggests for 1968, 1.9 cattle per inhabitant for a total Mauritanian population then estimated at 1.091,500 (Toupet 1975, 240). The author stresses that compared to the FAO's figure (0.31) at the same time for the whole planet, this is very high. The annual growth rate of Mauritanian livestock was recently estimated at 8% for a population growing annually by some 2.5%, which testifies to the devastating effects of the drought in the Sahelian region since the beginning of the 1970s.

Table 5.1
Livestock numbers 1969–80
('000)

	1969	1970	1971	1972	1973	1974	1975	1980
Cattle	2,000	1,850	1,550	1,500	1,115	1,150	1,135	1,400
Sheep and goats	7,000	6,750	6,500	6,500	5,850	6,300	6,800	6,500
Camels	710	705	700	670	680	680	685	750

More significant for the management of family flocks and herds, particularly for a proper assessment based on what some observers consider to be an excessive accumulation of redundant and useless livestock (for example, a large number of young males and old animals) would have been a precise assessment of the average composition of flocks and herds.

The scattered figures that can be found. which must be accepted warily– fear of the 'evil eye'. and of heavy taxes, mean that statements made by herders are not entirely trustworthy– and which relate almost exclusively to cattle rearing, are, due to their very imprecision, difficult to interpret. A few are. however, given below.

In the early 1960s. the following distribution was suggested for the cattle herds in the Moudjéria region (central Sahelian Mauritania) made up on average of 120 head (Toupet, op. cit.. 249): 5 bulls; 10 bullocks; 67 cows and heifers; 38 calves of both sexes.

The livestock department's official estimates for the same period suggest a much higher proportion of males: males 4 years old and above, 8%; females 4 years old and above. 38.5%; males aged 1 to 3 years. 18%; male calves. 7.5%; female calves. 7.5%.

Following are more recent figures for the Mauritanian region of Tagant. the same region that was the focus of Toupet's surveys (Grosser and Ba. 1980. 30). Bearing females: sheep and goats 40%; cattle 40%; camels 30%. Adult males: sheep and goats 10%; cattle 10%; camels 20%. For young growing animals, 50% in each category; and for numbers of births per female per annum: sheep and goats. 2%; cattle 0.6%; and camels 0.4%.

In order to explain the 'rationality' or 'irrationality' of the economic behaviour of Sahelian herders these figures must be put in the overall socio-economic context. Changes in this context since colonization and the gradual integration of Sahelian pastoral societies into a dependent and dominated market economy will be discussed later.

Rather than any individual Sahelian herder's desire to accumulate cattle. the reasons for the growth in numbers of livestock supported with increasing difficulty by the poor pastures of the Sahelian region must also be examined in the socio-economic context. The pre-colonial pastoral system's relative functionality is generally recognized today, involving as it did building up a stock for food and trading purposes adapted to environmental conditions and periodically readjusted to these conditions by razzias and natural disasters. But it did not withstand the growing grip of commodity relations, which the economic crises of capitalism and local climatic crises have helped accelerate. The emergence of a market for cattle, and the enhanced dependence that the development of an essentially unequal exchange signified for herders, were processes contemporary with the transformation of political and social conditions (notably replacement of the disorganized razzia violence by the 'rational' violence of what was called 'pacification') that affected political control of the pastoral space. These factors, combined with the establishment of an embryonic modern health and water infrastructure. helped increase demands on the grazing areas of the Sudan and the Sahel.

Examination of the 1938 figures– even judged by the colonial administrator Beyriès. who reported them. to be one-third short of reality – shows, in comparison to Table 5.1. how big this increased burden was: in that year, less than five years after the final stabilization of colonial rule, the Governor of Mauritania's annual report (the Hodh circle was not yet part) gave the following figures for the whole country: 75,871 camels; 212,175 cattle; 1,713,631 sheep and goats.[2]

Compared to current estimates of the forage resources of Mauritania, figures in Table 5.1 show the first phase of a saturation process which, according to some forecasts, will become total and effective by the year 2000. In fact according to a recent study for the Mauritanian Ministry of the Economy and Finance (RAMS, 'Livestock subsector study'), the load capacity of the 55 million hectares in Mauritania that can be grazed (one unit of tropical cattle requiring between 4 and 70 hectares depending on the state of the biomass) will, if current trends continue, be reached by the year 2000.

This type of assessment must be treated with caution since, while the volume of cattle/useful area ratio is convenient to give a rough assessment, it glosses over many parameters whose complex interaction can alone provide the bases for a well-founded forecast. Independent of the strictly geographical factors, social and technical constraints decisively alter this ratio, which is also heavily dependent on the forms of state intervention (forage policy, reserve policy, and so on) and its regional and sectoral economic choices (Gallais, 1979, 121).

In the space available here it is not possible to survey all of these factors. The changes in the system of pastoral production, the various techniques of acquiring and processing livestock products, all of which directly affect herders' consumption and incomes,[3] are of relevance, but here only one crucial aspect for the future of pastoralism will be highlighted. This is mobility, which constitutes both the distinguishing feature of pastoral life and a permanent means of adjusting human and animal occupation to the precarious and unevenly distributed resources of the natural environment of the Sahel and the Sahara.

Mobility and herding

Aside from its cultural significance as a focal element of pastoral civilization the nomadics' life-style aims, above all, to procure access to basically rare and precarious resources. It is the decisive role of mobility, that constitutes both the form and the major means of subsistence of the pastoral community.

Nomadic movements show a degree of permanence in to where, how, and when they take place. These movements are tightly conditioned by the seasonal character of the rainfall, although the distance covered by herders annually has markedly decreased, reflecting the weakening of large- in favour of small-scale nomadism, a tendency that is often the prelude to sedentarization.

Mauritanian and more generally Sahelian–Saharan nomads move back-and-forth from north to south, following the annual rainfall pattern. From the first tornadoes over the southern regions of the country (June–July) a slow movement northwards gets underway and continues until the end of the cold season. A movement in the opposite direction then begins, taking large numbers of nomads as far as the banks of the river Senegal and the Niger bend by the end of the dry season.

In contrast to this regular north–south movement, a second, much more diffuse and irregular form of nomadic movement corresponds to the development of exceptional grazing areas in the beds of *oueds* or in the *gràyar* (areas into which water runs off mountainous regions). This form, typical of the Saharan part of the country, generally involves small-scale movements.

The annual range of north–south migration, which varies for both full and semi-nomads, depending on the volume and distribution of rainfall, reaches its maximum among camel-keeping nomads who may cover over 1,000 km annually (UNESCO, 1965). For example, the *Hmu dnnāt* of the Dhar of Oualata spend the winter around Agweylīl Nmādi, over 200 km north-east of Oualata on the saline *ḥàṭ* pastures, often several days from the nearest watering point; their dry season and early winter stay is generally on the Tāgurārut cliffs, near to the well of the same name some 260 km south-eat of Agweylīl. In winter, the camels are sometimes left to roam freely, moving much further north than their owners who meet up with them at the beginning of the hot season at watering points where they are accustomed to drink. Occasionally some cattle thief – rustling is still quite common in this region – upsets this almost automatic mechanism.

In bad years, such as have been the case since 1968, much greater distances are covered. In March 1980, at the watering-place at 'Weynāt r-ražžat, about 10 km south-east of Néma, we met a young *ḥmu nni* shepherd (from the *ḥmu nnāt*, a D-dlākne 'fraction'), who had come down with his family from the remote regions of the *dhar* where they had spent the winter and who, when we met them, had already travelled 400 km southwards. Given that there had been almost no rain in the Oualata region in 1979, they had only a very vague idea of how far south they would go. Perhaps, they said, as far as Ras el Me (lake Faguibine, in Mali). Their quest for grazing lands in the south would then have taken them over 800 km, which they would have to retrace in the opposite direction as soon as the rains started in order to save the camels from contracting *taburit* (trypanosomiasis).

The movement of semi-nomadic cattle herders and shepherds has the same seasonal characteristics as that of camel herders (acceleration in the rainy season, slowing down in the dry season) it generally extends, barring a major climatic disaster, over much smaller areas.

For example, in January 1980, we encountered a camp of S-sxaymàt cattle herders 75 km south-east of Magta Lajar. Usually, when rainfall was more or less normal, they moved throughout the year between el Wàd Lebya in the south-east and Wàd Leyrdi in the north-west. When we met them, as in the previous year, they were just beginning a journey southwards, due to the catastrophic failure of the rains in 1979. Only two men and a paid Fulani shepherd were accompanying the herd, on a journey that would take them 300 km to the Selibaby region. These were full nomads whose sole activity was herding and who, in order to save what was almost their only resource, were capable of a great burst of large-scale nomadism. With the increase of agriculture in their activities the capacity to undertake this sort of move is becoming lost.

As some Ideggmolle agriculturalists explained, since the construction of the Magta Lajar dam (1,400 hectares flooded) in the late 1940s they have tended to settle alongside the fields, thus creating a large village with 3,821 inhabitants by 1977. 'In the beginning,' a notable belonging to this group told us in January 1980, 'we used to send a lot of people with the herds and very few to the fields, but today almost everybody is farming and only a few people are sent with the animals.' The correlation between nomads' practice of agriculture and the increasingly lesser distance they cover each year is obvious.

Recent data from the 'Provisional Results of the General Population Census' conducted in January 1977 by the Mauritanian Ministry of Planning show that almost 30% of nomad households practise agriculture, with a low percentage in the north and far east (regions of large-scale camel-herding nomadism) and a much higher percentage in the southern regions.

A high percentage can be observed in the Adrar (46.1%) and Tagant (32%) despite the relative aridity of these regions. This is linked to the presence of a large number of palm groves which, without any loss of pride, the nomads can cultivate freely (palm growing is more 'noble' than working in the fields, which is generally poorly regarded and even despised).

The 1977 census figures show a relatively small proportion of large-scale nomads among the non-sedentary population. Only 17% of those counted make annual moves of more than 200 km; these are mainly in the camel-herding regions of the far north-west and south-east of the country.

The importance of semi-nomadism and transhumance compared to long-distance nomadism indicated in Table 5.2 is only the most striking manifestation of an erosion affecting every aspect of Mauritanian pastoralism, principally the conditions and forms of mobility, the key feature of pastoral life.

It has been noted that the relative abundance of cattle, periodically controlled before colonization by natural disasters and razzias, might appear to be a compensation for the mediocre productivity of these Sahelian–Saharan breeds. The rapid growth in numbers, especially from the 1950s,[4] in which some observers claim to see a process of saturation beginning, and as both cause and effect of desertification, the consequences of which became particularly dramatic after 1968, resulted in fact from the complex interaction of numerous factors in which the hegemonic extension of commodity relations played a central role. Mobility itself, the key factor of pastoral production and the reproduction of pastoral society, was profoundly affected by changes that gradually increased semi-nomadism and transhumance compared to large-scale nomadism, and often led to nomads settling in rural villages or on the outskirts of the new urban agglomerations.

Integration of the pastoral world into the market economy

It scarcely needs stressing that there are internal sociological, cultural and economic reasons for these changes and the vulnerability of Sahelian pastoral societies, enclosed as they had been for several centuries in the poverty and

Table 5.2
Distances travelled by region (%) and camp sizes (numbers)

Region	Households present	Households in permanent camps	Households moving over 200 km		Average camp size (numbers of persons)
			Total	Those moving	
Eastern Hodh	54.6	0.6	27.2	27.4	25.6
Western Hodh	51.6	6.4	31.3	33.4	21.8
Assaba	33.5	15.8	6	7.1	25
Gorgol & Guidimakha	11.1	11.3	4.3	4.9	30.2
Brakna	33.7	4.5	7.4	7.8	26.5
Trarza	49.3	3.2	6.4	6.6	12.8
Adrar	32.1	0.6	14.2	14.3	14.1
Tagant	57.6	2.9	23.2	23.9	25.3
Nouadhibou & Inchiri and the two Tirises					
El Gharbia	12.4	1.8	70	71.3	11.9
National total	33	29.8	16.7	17.6	21.4

Note: There seems also to be some correlation between the scale of annual migration and the size of the nomad units even if the gaps shown by this latter variable in all regions remain rather small: in the north-west where the proportion of nomads annually moving over 200 km is 71.3% the camps have an average of 11.9 persons, or more or less two-tent households (average size of nomad households: 4.84), whereas in Gorgol-Guidimakha where the lowest regional proportion of large-scale nomads is recorded (4.9%) the size of camps rises to an average of 30.2 persons, or six-to-seven-tent households.

monotony of a particularly Spartan way of life. It is equally obvious that these changes and their recent manifestations were related to the effects of colonization and the unification of a 'world-economy', to use the terms of Wallerstein and Braudel, centred on the capitalist West.

The major consequence of colonization – and possibly its essential vocation – was the creation and development of a dominant commodity sector in the pastoral societies of the Sahel and the Sahara whose production, organization and values had been hitherto based upon pre- or non-capitalist structures even though commodity exchanges, including with European traders, frequently occupied a not insignificant place within these societies.

The various historical stages of the establishment of the hegemony of commodity and monetary economy in Mauritania will not be detailed here, but simply a brief overview to clarify the present situation to be followed by an examination of that situation.

The establishment of a market in cattle

Commercial activities have always represented a significant proportion of the economic life of the western Sahara regions which, since the Middle Ages, have been crossed by caravans taking the products of the Sudan and the Sahel (gold, slaves, ivory, even cereals) northwards in exchange for the products of the Sahara and the Maghreb (salt, metals, weapons, fabrics and so forth). The role of gum Arabic in the Moorish world's external trade from the eighteenth century onwards is also well known, as are the effects of this 'long-distance trade' on the economic, social and political structures of the groups most immediately in contact with it, the emirates of Trarza and Brakna, 'controlling' the 'trading posts' of the river Senegal in particular (Hamès 1977).

But neither trans-Saharan nor river trade (on the Senegal) or the Atlantic trade led directly to the widespread establishment of a dominant commodity and monetary sphere within Moorish pastoral society. Not until the completion of colonization (1902–34) was there substantial progress in the incorporation of the pastoral economy into the market economy. This progress can be seen particularly in the establishment and development of a market in cattle.

Here some results of Pierre Bonte's research on this topic are summarized (Bonte 1981). He writes: 'The formation of a market in cattle was the essential – and almost immediate – consequence of colonization.'

Leaving aside France's political and military interest in securing control of Mauritania, that territory was, at the beginning of the twentieth century, seen as a food crop and commercial appendage to the economic development represented for the regional colonial authorities by the groundnut zone of neighbouring Senegal.

Without neglecting the development – or rather the exploitation – of Mauritania, [they] gave it as a result two main functions: 1) to supply the labour force for the rural and urban sectors of groundnut production (that involved essentially the Black Africans along the Senegal valley who migrated southwards in large numbers); 2) to supply cheap food and especially meat to the groundnut producers and to the wage-earners in Senegalese towns. (Bonte, 1981)

It was this second function that affected the evolution of pastoralism more directly since it contributed to the rapid emergence of a market in cattle that more specifically concerns us here. Two main reasons explain the rapidity with which this market was established.

The first relates to the central role of animal ownership among the nomads' resources. They turned increasingly to livestock husbandry to meet the needs for cash that colonization helped shape and extend (role of colonial 'security', markets, improved communications, consumption patterns diffused, however modestly, by the colonial schools and those close to the 'commandant', in short what Hamid El Mauritanyi (1975) called the 'colonial boyarchy'). The second reason seems to be directly linked to the accelerated growth of urban demand, arising particularly from the large Senegalese agglomerations, which experienced continuous demographic growth. By the beginning of the 1920s, the market at Louga was channelling the bulk of Mauritanian cattle exports on the hoof far ahead of the market at Goulimine (southern Morocco) where camels were the main, if not only, item of trade, cattle being unable to go into the desert regions of northern Mauritania.

But 'economic' reasons alone are not responsible for the increase in Moorish cattle sales during the first 30 years of the twentieth century: Pierre Bonte rightly stresses the role of pressures from the colonial administration. These pressures might take the form of commandeering animals for human consumption, paid for (when they were) at the official rate. As early as 1909, the 1,000-man-strong 'Guiraud column', about to conquer the Adrar, collected a heavy levy in cattle from those regions where an economic and military lesson was seen as necessary to help staunch any spirit of resistance. Colonel Guiraud was simply extending, in very disturbed circumstances, an administrative razzia that had been institutionalized in the conquered area of southern Mauritania after 1902. Despite the heavy burdens for the nomads, especially in bad years, such requisitions, open or covert, continued virtually until independence in 1960, and even beyond – as a tax.

In 1926, in the Adrar, the requisitions were for 1,500 camels (out of 9,000). The administrator himself noted that this burden was too heavy and was contributing to the famine then raging in the Adrar. Each fraction in turn had to provide transport animals (one-fifth of animals levied), at least 55 camels per month for administrative transport; these animals had to be maintained near the posts, even if there were no grazing areas! In addition, they had to provide animals for the annual transport of supplies to the Adrar from Rosso and Podor. (Bonte 1981, 8)

As the free market developed, the requisitions, whose unpopularity is easy to imagine, tended to diminish.

The small-scale development of motorized transport saw the first regular commercial links between Atar and Rosso made by lorries belonging to the Lacombe company in 1935. On this route, Lacombe's 35 lorries had a virtual monopoly and transported 2,770 metric tons of freight and 4,782 passengers in 1950, as against 2,500 metric tons of freight and 3,990 passengers in 1947 (Brechignac, 1952).

During the Second World War, however, there was a temporary return to camel transport, both for the needs of internal Mauritanian traffic for which requisitions reached 8,000 camels per year, and for transport to Senegal which required 11,000 camels. In addition to the administration's requisitions there was the cattle tax, opportunistically named *zakat* (Muslim religious tithe) by the colonial authorities.

This tax was levied on a lump sum basis for each tribe or fraction of a tribe. Tribal chiefs, sometimes accompanied by guards, collected *zakat* and received a percentage of what they collected as payment; an arrangement that gave rise to countless abuses. For the most prosperous herders payment was relatively easy (helped by a great deal of under-declaration), but it was a heavy burden on the livestock resources of smallholders, especially in bad years. Nevertheless, the combination of administrative 'incentives' and economic motivation resulted in bringing growing quantities of stock on to local and foreign markets.

The figures available, quoted below, cannot claim to be other than notional. In 1940, when the effects of the long crisis of 1933–36, which had contributed to a sharp fall in cattle prices, were beginning to diminish and as an era of lasting market disturbances associated with the War was about to begin, the archives provide the following figures for exports of Mauritanian livestock to the Senegal markets (Saint-Louis, Louga and Dakar): 9,723 camels, 9,853 cattle, 126,765 goats and sheep.

It is equally difficult to estimate the recent development of these exports. The lack of strict border control, of controllable marketing structures and administrative means of control, and the fluctuations of official policies for livestock exports, are factors that explain the inevitable imprecision marking any effort to quantify recent exports.

As regards official policies, a belated realization of the danger to national animal resources in the continuation of massive exports of cattle on the hoof began to emerge in the late 1960s. Thus, in 1969, a Mauritanian meat marketing company (COVIMA) was set up, with the Mauritanian state taking a major stake in it. The COVIMA, thanks to the cold stores at Kaedi (3,000 metric tons of frozen meat per annum), was the first step towards replacing exports of cattle on the hoof by marketing meat, at a time when annual sales outside Mauritania were estimated (for 1968) at 52,000 cattle and 330,000 sheep and goats. Financial difficulties, partly associated with transport problems and – as this was the beginning of the drought that has been affecting the Sahel for over ten years – the poor quality of the meat it had been hoped to sell on the open markets in the Canaries and Libya, rapidly immobilized the company. In 1975 it was completely nationalized, becoming the Société Nationale pour l'Industrialisation et la Commercialisation du Bétail, SONICOB, but this did little to improve its situation, and today, it works – at a loss – simply to meet the local needs of Kaedi.

Placing a quota on exports of cattle on the hoof, instituted as a counterpart to the measures aiming to gradually replace them with the export of meat, has since been abandoned, in the framework of ECOWAS agreements. Quite clearly, exporters had not waited for these measures to end before resuming and intensifying a trade encouraged by price differentials with neighbouring countries and doubtless, indirectly, by the creation, in June 1973, of an inconvertible Mauritanian national currency (the *ouguiya*) that further accentuated and bureaucratized the monopoly of import–export activities in the hands of a handful of Nouackchott middlemen. The Mauritanian cattle export networks that were the source of leading Moorish fortunes thus continue, on the back of a movement largely begun in the colonial period, to fuel the ever-expanding regional markets.

The creation of a meat marketing company was also designed to act as a means to regulate a domestic market rendered particularly unstable by regional geographical disparities (variations in rainfall), considerable distances between the producing areas (especially the south-east) and the importing towns along the Atlantic coast (Nouakchott, Nouadhibou, the mining region) and finally the inadequacy of means of transport. Before dealing with meat consumption and how it has evolved, it is necessary to look at commodity circulation for cattle on the hoof within the Mauritanian market.

As already stressed above, the distribution of Mauritanian livestock resources, and the circulation of these resources before colonization was carried on mainly in a non-monetary framework. The global significance of livestock and its products and circulation will be dealt with later, as part of social (family, hierarchical, clientage) relations within the Moorish pastoral community.

The role of *razzias* in the circulation of Mauritanian cattle in the pre-colonial period is well known. Usually, much less stress is put on the role of other forms of more 'voluntary' distribution – which indeed were more or less associated with the permanent insecurity engendered by the institutionalization of the *razzia* – such as the *mniha*. This loan on the usufruct – *manaha* means supplying the products of an animal lent – offered the double advantage of consolidating kinship and clientage relations while ensuring a prudent dispersal of the herds which were never safe from some unforeseeable occurrence or some enzootic disease.

Alongside these forms of circulation, plus gifts associated with matrimony (before colonization dowries were predominantly settled in cattle) or status (payment of tribute, for example), or particular ceremonial circumstances (births, deaths, festivals, marriages and so on) commodity exchanges in the internal circulation of Mauritanian livestock in the pre-colonial period were marginal.

The role of economic incentives (the rising monetary needs of herders) and administrative coercion in the establishment of a 'free' domestic market in cattle in Mauritania, has already been noted. While this market's needs, notably for meat for human consumption, remained relatively modest throughout the colonial period (urbanization did not take off until after Mauritania's independence in the early 1960s) the continuous growth of supply combined with a relative fall in the cattle prices, compared to imported products (sugar, Guinea fabrics, among others), gradually put traditional herders at the mercy of administrative or commercial middlemen, who themselves had relatively stable monetary incomes. There were sharp upsurges of this process during local climatic crises (1917, 1942–43 and so on) and during economic or political crises in the dominant capitalist system, and well as when there was a catastrophic conjunction of the two as in 1940–43 or since 1970. On the basis of an index of 100 in 1940, Pierre Bonte (1981, 20) calculated that the price of one kilo of millet officially reached 433 in 1942 (1,333 on the black market), on kilo of sugar from an index of 100 in 1939 increased to 1,500 in 1942, the price of one metre of Guinea cloth (the Moorish people's traditional clothing) rose from 100 in 1939 to 737 in 1946, and a kilo of imported rice rose from an index of 100 in 1939 to 2,533 in 1942. Over that period livestock prices tended to stagnate and not until 1948 did these price curves begin a significant recovery.

Recently, in the areas most affected as a consequence of the cycle of drought that began in the late 1960s, livestock prices have fallen sharply: in some localities of Trarza, in 1968, impoverished nomads who had been forced to settle were selling milch cows for 1,500 Francs CFA; two years earlier the selling price would have been 20,000.

But conditions in periods of crisis cannot form a basis for deriving conclusions about some unilinear or continual deterioration of the trade terms between the Mauritanian pastoral economy and the commodity system of world capitalism. A comparison of prices of local products (notably of livestock) and imported goods, from the beginning of colonization to the present day, shows a succession of movements that are far from uniformly unfavourable to herders. But the weakening of the herders' position as they became integrated into the commodity economy cannot be measured solely by the relative market prices between their products and imported ones. This is only one element in an overall situation marked by a global erosion that affects both the system of production and exchange and the cultural models and social relations that govern reproduction in nomad society.

The move of more and more livestock from traditional herders to bureaucrats and traders in the towns in the wake of crises – especially that which has continued since 1969 – is not due simply to a difference in incomes between the two groups but also to a whole range of different attitudes towards livestock and its upkeep.

An essential condition of this transfer lies in the 'liberation' of the labour force (servile or tributary) from traditional leaders. This is a vital prerequisite to the extension of wage-earning that has become the dominant relation of production in the sector we have called elsewhere (Bonte and Ould Cheikh, 1981) 'second herds'. After the damage to Mauritanian livestock caused by the drought, and given the apparent recovery of rainfall over the last three years, it is clear that the increase in stock maintained in this ('second herd') way, sold at the right time, can bring in considerable profits. Unfortunately, there are no statistics to facilitate an appreciation of the scale of this livestock transfer into the hands of the new (and not so new) rich in the towns which, in our opinion, is destined to play a key role in the future of Mauritanian pastoralism.

Another aspect of internal commodity circulation is linked to the local market's need for meat. Here, too, precise data are lacking, largely because most slaughtering is done privately, even in the large towns where wealthy families prefer to buy a whole sheep to be consumed as required, rather than to buy meat from butchers. It is also well known that traditional herders rarely eat animals they themselves have reared.

Compared to other Sahel countries, Mauritania's high level of meat consumption (according to some estimates) is probably a recent phenomenon. Estimates for annual per capita meat consumption according to the FAO's *Annual Report on Production and Trade* for 1977[6] are: Mauritania, 26.8 kg; Mali, 13.8 kg; Senegal, 14 kg. The reason for this increased meat consumption since the early 1960s is, above all, the development of urban areas, for example, in 1961 the inhabitants of Nouakchott consumed 70 kg of meat per head (Lacrouts et al., 1962).

At this time the building of Nouakchott and other mining towns in the north, such as Zouérate and its port of Nouadhibou, were underway, and together (with Akjoujt after 1967) accounted for virtually all the modern sector jobs in the Mauritanian economy. Consequently they experienced extremely rapid population growth, sometimes to the detriment of older rural centres.

The big (in the Mauritanian context) towns in the west and north attract large quantities of cattle from the livestock regions of south-east Mauritania. Facilitated by the tarred road, which will soon link Néma and Nouakchott, this movement, especially for sheep and goats, will doubtless grow in size. Already, on the Nouakchott–Kiffa stretch, articulated lorries regularly carry cargoes of livestock to the capital for slaughter; some of them are then carried northward.

It is not possible to provide figures on the full extent of this trade or to accurately quantify Mauritanian domestic meat consumption, but, as an example, Table 5.3 shows the number of controlled slaughterings in Nouakchott in 1980.

Whatever the precise volume of meat consumption, the estimates, rough though they are, suggest that, given the rate of population growth in Mauritania and the limits on the load-bearing capacity of the grazing areas, it cannot be maintained at its present level over the next 20 years. A recent study (Ministère de l'Economie et des Finances, *RAMS Project*) suggests that the Mauritanian authorities should immediately reduce the population's consumption of red meat in order to preserve the number of livestock still recovering from the depletion caused by the drought in the early 1970s. Moreover, the author of this advice assumed that the traditional system of livestock organization and management, extensive nomadic herding, would be maintained, it being considered that this was the form of land-use best adapted to the scarcity and fragility of natural resources in the Sahelian–Saharan environment.

Table 5.3
Livestock slaughtered in Nouakchott, by month (1980)

Month	Cattle	Sheep	Goats	Camels	Total
January	1,286	457	493	171	2,407
February	1,226	489	480	212	2,407
March	1,252	376	383	308	2,319
April	1,184	286	298	326	2,094
May	1,128	216	207	418	1,969
June	604	199	236	599	1,638
July	486	253	145	894	1,778
August	540	385	393	983	2,301
September	1,140	869	577	527	3,113
October	1,219	990	597	242	3,048
November	1,558	1,186	624	293	3,661
December	1,650	1,532	387	244	3,813
Total	*13,273*	*7,238*	*4,820*	*5,217*	*30,548*
Average	1,106	603	402	434	2,545

But this system, as has been stressed several times, was centred on spatial mobility and dispersion, and involved a set of technical, economic and ideological behaviour patterns: in short, it derived from a *culture* which, since the advent of colonial occupation and particularly since the upheavals engendered by the latest cycle of drought, has shown signs of ever-more widespread erosion. The transformations suffered by the Mauritanian nomadic way of life in relation to the advances of the dominant commodity sector can be seen particularly in an examination of the incomes and expenditure of nomad households.

Recent changes of nomads' incomes and expenditure
Surveys in which we took part were carried out in 1979 and 1980 in the framework of a project aimed at providing basic data and defining possible scenarios for the principal projects of the Fourth Mauritanian Economic and Social Development Plan, especially in the rural sector. Part of these surveys concerned the structures of the income and expenditure of rural people, including the nomads with whom we are particularly concerned here. For many reasons, both material and methodological considerations (for example, the small sample surveyed, shortness of time, lack of training of those involved) and the obstacles inherent in any survey among nomads (dispersion and mobility of the target populations, mistrust of the 'administration', fear of the 'evil eye', among others), the figures emerging from these surveys cannot be regarded as a faithful reflection of the socio-economic reality of nomad life. Even if they were shown to be absolutely accurate, they would still be a partial image of a nomad milieu heavily marked by community and hierarchical values that further limit the scope of the key concept – 'family budget' or 'budgetary unit' – of the survey a few results of which follow.

For the sedentary rural population, monetary income was derived from: wages 26%; gifts 17%; trade 17%; herding 14%; agriculture 6%; pensions and family allowances 5%; fishing 2%; loans 4%; handicrafts 1%; other 8%.

Nomads' monetary income was derived from: herding 60%; handicrafts 7%; agriculture 2%; trade 7%; wages 4%; gifts 16%; loans 4%.

This research revealed how small is the annual monetary income of nomads compared to that of sedentary rural dwellers: rising to 9,280 MU (US$ 206) per capita for nomads, and to 13,494 MU (US$ 300) for sedentary rural dwellers. A nomad's annual monetary income thus represents only 65% of that of a settled rural dweller.

Herding continues to be the essential means of meeting nomads' domestic needs and the principal source (60%) of monetary income. Wage-earning (4% of monetary income), as indicated here, is less than had been previously supposed given the development of wage-earning in herding, nevertheless, it reflects a significant change in the traditional relations of production. While the stress given here to the transfer of livestock into the hands of pseudo-managers from the bureaucratic and commercial sector has some foundation, if this transfer is accompanied by an extension of wage-earning, the fact that the percentage of wage-earnings in herders' monetary income is so small might be due to a low *monetary portion* of the wage paid by owners to shepherds; the shepherds themselves are often small herders, preferring payment in kind in the framework of traditional-type contracts such as: usufruct of herd, right to a new-born calf when an animal gives birth to twins, right to one animal of a given age and sex each year fixed on the basis of the number of animals herded, for example.

Gifts in kind from relatives or clients resident in or working in towns (16% of herders' income in kind) testify to nomads' growing dependence on temporarily migrant or permanently settled kin. But it only partly reflects the scale of the rural–urban drift and of sedentarization, which over the years 1964–76 was responsible for a decrease in the proportion of nomads in the population from 64% to 36%.

The insignificant monetary profit accruing to herders from agriculture (2%) does not fully reflect the nomads' role in agricultural labour; a relatively high proportion (29.8% overall) of nomads engage in some agricultural activity.

This figure is the outcome of a change that became apparent from especially the late 1940s. The vertiginous rise in cereal prices (30 times higher in 1949 than in 1940!), the support of the colonial administration, which saw the development of agriculture as a means to make good the food deficit and facilitate the settlement of tax payments, and the gradual emancipation of the former slaves of Moorish herders, large numbers of whom settled in independent villages (*àdwàba*) and devoted themselves to agriculture, are all factors that explain the development of nomads' agricultural activities. The repercussions of these events on herders' mobility has already been underlined. Combined with other factors transforming the economic and social environment of nomadism they led to large-scale and disorderly sedentarization of nomads.

It is, however, hardly surprising that the current monetary contribution from this agricultural activity appears marginal in the herders' annual accounts. The best lands (courses of *oueds*, in particular) are still sometimes the object of violent disputes, associated with the demands of newly sedentarized groups, but they have long since been divided up. Nomads anxious to diversify their food resources are left with only the very unreliable product of rain-fed cropping, yielding barely 300 kg of millet per annum, thus to secure a marketable surplus requires exceptional circumstances. Harvests can, therefore, for the most part provide no more than a little extra food for subsistence. This is why the bulk of the expenditure of nomad budgetary units is devoted to food.

The 1980 RAMS survey puts the annual individual consumption level of nomads at 13,778 MU, distributed in the following proportions: cereals 15%; fruit and vegetables 6%; meat 11%; milk products 57%; tea and sugar 9%; other 2%.

The movement towards monetarization of nomad consumption continues to be very uneven (only 49% passes through the monetary circuit), in so far as regional disparities reflect the uneven penetration of commodity relations. This is itself a function of how close an area is to the centres from which these relations are diffused (the strip along the river Senegal and the Atlantic coast since the 18th century, the capital and the mining towns since 1960) or of the particular role of a regional community: in the Eastern Hodh, the most useful inland region of the country, and where pastoralism has remained most vigorous, only 17% of the nomad consumption involves monetary exchanges; while in Tagant, the homeland of the most active trading tribe in Mauritania (the Idawa'li) 78% involves money.

Among the non-food expenditure of nomads, clothes come first for the modest sum of 245 MU (barely 25 French Francs) per capita per annum. In this area, old habits – since the eighteenth century, the so-called 'Guinea' cloth and percale have remained the undisputed leading choice for Moorish veils and *boubous* – limit the needs of nomad households to one or two purchases a year.

Some expenditure on leisure or toiletries, which is sometimes an extension of old practices – the purchase of glassware and other 'trade' goods in the slave trade period – completes this picture of the consumption of nomad households whose energy needs (estimated at 445 kg of wood per capita per annum) are met in the framework of traditional gathering methods.

According to the most recent data, these are some essential features of consumption and incomes of nomad households in Mauritania. We have no illusions about the real significance of the figures provided by the survey on highly mobile populations, traditionally suspicious of anything that they see as deriving from central government, and living in a system still heavily marked by communal values that are hardly compatible with the individualization of budgetary units practising rigorously autonomous accounting. But despite these reservations, the estimates obtained do throw a significant light on the socio-economic evolution of the Mauritanian nomad milieu. The major feature of this evolution is identified as a growing monetarization associated with colonization and the postcolonial heritage. The gradual emergence of a market in cattle, sustained by the growth of nomads' monetary needs, administrative requisitions and, more recently, the development of urban centres and the beginnings of a modern transport infrastructure, has been the driving force in a profound change in Mauritanian pastoral society which climatic and/or political and economic crises have helped to speed up. The social and political implications of this change demonstrate the contradictory character of a transformation which has all the appearances of a crisis.

Evolution of the social and political framework of nomadism

Claude Lévi-Strauss wrote of functionalism: 'to say that something functions in a society is a truism, to say that everything is functional is an absurdity'. A statement with which I agree, and grant the structures of nomad society only a relative functionality, expressing in various domains (economic, technological, institutional, ideological and so on) the adjustment of a necessarily discontinuous human and animal occupation to the scattered and often ephemeral resources of a poor natural environment. I have earlier stressed the role and influence of the natural and economic constraints in the evolution of Mauritanian pastoralism. In the following pages the evolution of the political organization of pastoralism will be examined, and an attempt made to determine the role of the social and political structures of nomadism in the contradictions of present-day Mauritanian society which, in turn, has diverse effects on the structures of nomadism.

Women, herds and capital
Numerous observers have stressed the uniqueness of the social and political structures of pre-colonial Moorish society in which the apparent rigidity of status and hierarchical positions both confirmed and cut across the political control of a territorial space with ill-defined boundaries. What was the nature of this hierarchy and political control? How has the evolution described above of the economic context, and particularly the extension of commodity relations, affected this organization? What do the changes in the institutional, juridical and ideological framework of nomadization that have occurred since colonization mean for the future of pastoralism?

One of the most prominent characteristics of African pastoral societies in general and those of the Sahel in particular, and one that has engaged the interest of numerous ethnologists,[7] is the close and many-sided relationship between pastoralists and their herds. These bonds largely conditioned the social and political structures of Moorish pastoralists, in which the necessary mobility of livestock and the hierarchical circulation of animals and their products (gifts, loans, tributes) played a central role. But other considerations must be taken into account, notably those concerning meeting nomads' cereal and agricultural needs and the specialization that they required, or specific features peculiar to the constitution of the ideological and political arena of this pastoral society.

The works of many anthropologists (Bonte, Stenning, Hopen, Asad, Galaty and others) who have observed nomad societies stress, over and beyond the immediate functions of livestock as a means of meeting elementary needs, the place occupied by livestock in the reproduction of the nomad community itself. The privileged role of livestock in the social relations and community life of nomads that ethnologists designate as a 'cattle complex', even 'boolatrie' (cattle worship) is thought by some observers to be essentially the obstacle to a 'rationalization' of the exploitation of the herds.

We have already mentioned the role played by *mniha*, the loan on the use of animals, especially milch cows, in the creation and consolidation of bonds of reciprocity and clientage in a society in which agnatic solidarity and its clientelist extensions represented the principal recourse against the constant threat of a *razzia*. The forms of *mniha*, the nature and number of animals it involved, the period of loans and the relations between givers and receivers naturally varied a great deal. A *hartàni* (former slave) with a flock of ewes may loan a former master, or some needy marabout or notable, one or two milkers for as long as they are giving milk, although he may well be concerned for their kids, which generally benefit very little from their mother's milk and may even simply have their throats cut before the mothers are returned. The religious benefit (receiving the marabout's *baraka*) or the political one, in the widest sense, or sometimes simply the inequality in power would usually be enough for such an 'irregularity' to be disregarded. A wealthier dependent or client would grant the loan of a herd for a long or even indeterminate period, contenting himself with a periodic inspection or occasionally collecting dues. Between kin too, great disparities in the distribution of animal wealth may be the source of *mnayah* (pl. of *mniha*) helping both to affirm kin solidarity and establish a hierarchy between givers and receivers.

In addition to the practice of loaning, tributes, ranging from a few kilograms of wool or a goatskin of rancid butter, to one or more head of cattle per adult male, contributed to ensuring that the circulation of livestock and its products had permanent role in maintaining and reproducing the social relations peculiar to the nomad group. Such tributes continued to be collected until 1951, when, under the aegis of the colonial administration, tribute-payers settled their last dues, partly in livestock, partly in cash.[8] Finally, while in Moorish society, Islamized from a very early date, gifts, and ceremonial and ritual sacrifices were on a smaller scale than among other groups of pastoralists, they still made a significant contribution to the reproduction of the social order.

In this connection, the fundamental role of livestock in the payment of bridewealth (the dowry in the pre-colonial period was almost wholly settled in livestock) points to a very clear conjunction between the renewal of the pastoral society and the growth of herds. Summarizing generally the meaning of the reproduction and circulation of livestock as a privileged vehicle of social relations within Sahelian pastoral communities, Pierre Bonte writes:

It is in so far as the reproduction of domestic groups appears simultaneously as the reproduction of the communal conditions of pastoral production within domestic units that it requires the existence of a large surplus over and beyond the immediate needs of reproduction of labour and is integrated into a wider cycle of livestock circulation, resting on successive changes in the value of livestock. It is the moment when this livestock circulates as a social value that appears as determining of other moments of production because these are moments when it makes possible the simultaneous reproduction of the domestic groups as a whole and the community as such. (Bonte 1977, p. 49)

The reproduction of pastoral society and its chief means of subsistence was effected in an institutional and territorial framework that has been largely undermined by the changes that began with the colonial occupation.

First, at the level of the social hierarchy, was the apparent rigidity of a structure that fixed the heredity status of each Moor, thus assigning him by virtue of his descent to one of the following groups: warriors, marabouts, tributaries (servant group), artisans, griots, former slaves and slaves. While this distribution of the Moorish population does not directly reflect a division of pastoral labour itself[9] (only those tributaries specialized in animal husbandry appear to have been directly affected), the links between this structure and livestock, the focus and principal weapon of all social competition, may be clearly distinguished in almost every aspect of Moorish nomad life and activity.

This summary of the hierarchical and ceremonial circulation of livestock will not here be dealt with in detail nor will the role of the *razzia*, the activity that formed the base of the warrior aristocracy's power. It should be stressed that the work of artisans, paid for by the products of herding was, obviously, aimed at meeting needs associated with pastoral life (saddlery, tent equipment, milking equipment, shearing equipment, veterinary equipment etc).

The status of former slaves, many of whom were agricultural workers in the oases and in the more watered regions in southern Mauritania, was largely instrumental to maintaining the necessary complementarity between pastoral production and agricultural production referred to at the beginning of this chapter. This specialization of former slaves was, of course, maintained and reproduced to the advantage of the dominant groups who could thereby ensure for themselves a monopoly of political control of the land. Here, it is necessary to digress briefly in order to comment on the political control of the land, in which the changes over the last 50 years have had a crucial effect on pastoral mobility.

The apparent simplicity of what survives today of pre-colonial Moorish land tenure institutions – a tribal-type collective appropriation of the land – should not permit the earlier complex control of the area of pastoralism, in which use-rights and ownership rights were associated and interwoven with status and personal ties, to be forgotten.

First, it must be emphasized that appropriation of land, claimed to be operative over a territorial area with more or less recognized and acknowledged boundaries, actually concerned only the most useful parts of the territory appropriated: watering places and growing areas. Control of watering places, which largely commanded control of transhumance circuits, was itself subject to varied and contradictory norms.

Apart from during exceptional circumstances and notably in the event of armed conflict, permanent water sources (lined wells, natural springs, large winter ponds and so on), while deemed to belong to this or that 'tribe' or tribal 'fraction', were freely accessible to all nomads. Cases of enclosing a winter pond in order to restrict its use to a particular group were rare and often hotly disputed. The realization of seasonal draining wells, where adequate surface water made this possible, was not a problem, since this did not justify any permanent appropriation of the land.

The relationship between watering places and grazing areas explains the nomad tribes' resolute opposition should elements external to the tribe propose to dig a permanent well on 'their' land. Beyond an expression of tribal nationalism (the tribe being, above all, a political unit) this opposition obviously reflects the nomads' fear of restrictions that might affect the free availability of grazing areas.

In pre-colonial Mauritania, possession of watering places formed part of the complex game of status relations and marked out the institutional framework of control of the pastoral space rather than did the fluid territorial boundaries.

Wells, for example, were mostly in the hands of marabout groups, the leading organizers of the pastoral economy, but they generally had to take account of the political hegemony of the warriors who were prepared to use their weapons to ensure permanent access to forage and water resources for themselves, unless established privileges enshrining their hegemony in this area were institutionalized.[10]

Control of the use of grazing areas often assumed its most stable form in the payment of individual or collective dues that, in principle, were part of a contract for protection in a society which was constantly prey to *razzias*.

Despite the precarious nature of their authority, only the emirates (Trarza, Brakna, Adrar, Tagant), which emerged in the seventeenth and eighteenth centuries, tried, within often indeterminate boundaries, to provide a precise territorial framework to the political and hierarchical system whose unity they both expressed and guaranteed. There too, imposing a tax on nomads from outside the emirate, a sort of entry tax in exchange for their (relative) security, was a means of regulating the use of grazing areas as well as an instrument to affirm the hierarchical power of warriors within the emirate since only they were able to impose and collect this sort of due. The instability of the political power of the emirates, not only in the sense of a chronic precariousness of the leaders' personal positions but also in the sense of uncertainty as to the legitimacy and effectiveness of its ideological and hierarchical foundations (the real or supposed power of some great marabout, reputed to act on occult forces might, in some cases, effectively oppose that of the emir) in addition to the absence of fixed and recognized borders in fact left herders a freedom of movement limited mainly by the extent of their alliance network or their capacities to defend themselves against possible aggressors.

Such are the broad outlines of the situation before the French colonization of Mauritania. The upheavals that have since occurred, affecting the territorial and political organization, and hierarchical structures of Moorish pastoralism, have profoundly transformed a nomad social milieu made increasingly vulnerable to the vicissitudes occasioned by an unpredictable climate.

Pastoralism and the Mauritanian state
With colonization, the web of relations that was the key characteristic of any group or category: caste, tribe, religious brotherhood, rank, status, and so on, and the power relations it underpinned which, as we have noted, were closely linked to the political organization of the pastoral space, came under the direct control of the French administration. The overall movement of nomadism in a now unified territorial area – with the disorderly violence of the *razzia* supplanted by the violence of colonial rule – as well as local population movements, were considerably changed by this new situation. Nomad society itself was integrated into a larger territorial and political grouping embracing communities of sedentary black agriculturalists and suffered the levelling effects of the market economy. Its reproduction became increasingly difficult. Since independence (1960) pastoralism was generally only indirectly affected by the official options of the Mauritanian authorities but these, nevertheless, helped accelerate what has in recent years become a pronounced trend towards the sedentarization of nomads.

The 'security' inaugurated by colonial peace and the 'freedom of grazing' decreed by the colonizer created major obstacles to the free movement of men and livestock. Through those close to the 'commandant' (petty administrative staff, guards, servants, and so on) the creation of administrative centres and the opening of a few schools favoured the diffusion of modes and models that underpinned the extension of the commodity relations.

This extension itself precipitated and required, if not a dissolution, at least a profound weakening of traditional social relations that was essential to the 'freeing' of labour mentioned above. This meant at least a partial 'loosening' of the hierarchical relations that provided the framework for the production and reproduction of pastoral society. Some progress, though ambiguous, has been made in this direction in recent years.

In the past, as today, the principal issue in 'freeing' labour is the status of dominated groups in Moorish society (probably over half the total Moorish population) and the nature of their relations with the groups that dominate them.

With colonization, as already remarked, the warriors' autonomous military power ceased. But by adapting to the new situation, the power of the marabouts, whose essential vocation lies in the production of what Weber called 'the goods of salvation', tended to be maintained and even to grow, in order to handle the diffusion of the ideological negotiations of a society in crisis.

The colonial administration claimed that one motive for its action was to eliminate marabouts' and warriors' exploitation of groups whose support it hoped to win over. But it soon adopted an attitude of compromise with the ruling classes of Moorish society, once their military resistance had ended (Coppolani and Gouraud columns in 1902–5 and 1908–9). The 'Patey instructions' (from the name of the then Governor of Mauritania) of February 1910 set out the broad outlines of the policy to be followed in reestablishing a now loyal tribal chieftaincy. By taking on tribal notables, or recruiting them as functionaries after a brief spell in the a 'School for the Sons of Chiefs', a system of 'collaboration', which offered the advantage of maintaining the traditional social hierarchy apparently intact, was rapidly established. These were the first steps in the formation of the post-colonial bureaucratic class in which elements from the traditionally dominant groups or families have retained much of their hegemony.[11]

The same 'prudence' was observed by the colonial administration in its attitude towards the dominated groups in Moorish society. Under colonial rule, tribute-payers continued for a long time to pay dues to their lords and, only belatedly, after 1946, was the redemption of tributes by the payers themselves speeded up under the auspices of the administration; the last transactions took place in 1951.

Slavery, although officially abolished, was – and still is – widely tolerated by the authorities.[12] Contrary to widespread belief, Moorish slavery, an institution probably as old as the Moors themselves, does not, for the most part, derive from the isolated kidnapping of blacks by raiders. Doubtless there were many such cases and the insecurity maintained by Moorish *razzias* among the sedentary black peasants in neighbouring areas left memories that are still very much alive. But our few brief surveys show that over 80% of Moorish slaves who still remember where they or their ancestors were enslaved (only a minority of those we questioned) were from Bambara country where they were bought in the nineteenth century. Slaves were used as herders and shepherds, and as well-diggers in agriculture, or generally as share-croppers – in which case they were usually former slaves paying dues that might range from a symbolic quantity of seeds to virtually the whole harvest. At the time of the slave trade, they were also used to collect gum. Moorish slaves were not a servile mass employed in heavy communal labour, as in Graeco-Roman antiquity or on the American plantations, but 'house' (or rather 'tent') slaves whose status and personal living conditions varied, depending on the master's status, from beast of burden to confidant and personal adviser.

While officially abolishing slavery, the colonial administration did not embark on any systematic action to make such a measure a reality. There were even frequent cases of complicity between some local representatives of the authorities and owners who had come to claim slaves who had run away. It should be noted, however, that fear of a possible repression and the support that maroons could sometimes count upon, particularly among the black auxiliaries of the colonial administration, tended to make administrative centres places of refuge. Since the end of European slave trading, and given how little traffic in slaves there was across the western Sahara, sales of slaves in

Mauritania which had only ever involved small quantitites of human merchandise, or even just individuals, became rarer. Isolated cases of sales (some are still reported today) thus increasingly took on an exceptional and more or less clandestine nature.

In addition to these factors, the advance of agriculture, encouraged by the colonial administration which supervised the building of a few small dams such as that at Magta Lajar in the late 1940s, accompanied and reflected advances in the sedentarization of slaves and former slaves that signified not only an abandonment of the pastoral way of life but also the beginning of an emancipation movement still continuing today.

The recent stepping-up of this movement towards sedentarization, which of course does not involve only former dependents, has helped accentuate the imbalances and contradictions of a pastoral society no longer able to control its mechanisms of reproduction.

The drought affecting the whole of the Sahel since the late 1960s; the development of an urban wage-earning sector associated in particular with mining activities and currently totalling some 25,000 jobs; insecurity in the countryside associated with the war in the Sahara, which began in 1975; the development of road transport, notably the building of the Nouakchott–Néma road (begun in 1974), which more or less coincides with the track now used by nomads, who previously frequented the now desertified areas further north; are all factors that explain the scale of sedentarization and migratory movements directly affecting the organization, values, and the very existence of pastoral society.

Resort to agriculture as a substitute for or supplement to the severely reduced income from herding (herd losses due to drought have been very high, over 80% for many families) is not problem-free. The scale of the population pressure engendered by sedentarization on the few cultivable areas is leading to an exacerbation of land disputes. In some places, given the overall contradictions of Mauritanian society and the clientage and 'racial' nature of the available ideological models, these disputes are taking on more a tribal and ethnic, rather than a strictly class character.

Moorish slaves' and former slaves' challenge, encouraged in the towns by their growing importance in some sectors of the Mauritanian state apparatus, especially in the other ranks of the army, and helped or supported by the few of their number who occupy a position of some prominence in this apparatus, is thus itself set in the tribal and ethnic framework that gives it its specific features and limits. A number of contradictory aspects of a development, highly significant not only for the future of pastoralism but also for the whole of Mauritanian society, need to be stressed here.

Dominant groups in nomad society, ruined by the drought and hardly enthusiastic about agricultural work, settle close to land, often for long cultivated by their former dependents, and attempt to impose a share-cropping system upon them on lands that both parties agree belong to the tribe collectively. Previously, the nomad groups would have been satisfied, with more irregular and tolerable contributions in exchange for a few products of herding. Like their former masters, the former slaves, faced with the claims of other former slaves, justify their possession of the land on the basis that they belong to the tribe that owns the land. But the tribal juridical framework, covering the hierarchical stratification already detailed (warriors, marabouts and so on) with the former slaves and slaves at the bottom, implies the exclusion of this group from ownership. The former slaves' class aspirations and demands, and their desire to appropriate the land, thus conflicts with the tribal framework that integrates them into pastoral society as agricultural labourers but excludes them from ownership of the land, exclusive enjoyment of which is based on the political power of the dominant groups that, in turn, it contributes to establish and reproduce.

The hierarchical structures of pre-colonial pastoral society have thus been largely transferred into the present Mauritanian state order (marabouts and warriors occupy bureaucratic and commercial jobs, former slaves and slaves the lowliest and worst paid – labourers, domestics and so on). This helps to maintain, even perpetuate, a brutally hierarchical social order, involving collection of tribute, unpaid labour and corporal punishment. This order is gradually giving way to a clientelist and pseudo-philanthropic practice in which yesterday's masters who have become today's bureaucratic inter-mediaries, pose as protectors – or even as victims of clients who sometimes have to be lodged and fed in the urban areas.

The tribal political model's perpetuation through its clientelist extensions also partly explains the ambiguity of the political expression of the movement to emancipate former slaves. This ambiguity reflects both the continuing significance of the model according to the logic of the pre-eminence of the dominant class' ideology and the sociological heterogeneity of a rural- and 'tribal'-based movement under an urban leadership from the middle bureaucracy aspiring to convert clientelism in such a way as to legitimize what otherwise would not be fully operative. Social identity, measured in terms of the tribal system that based prestige and legitimacy on a genealogical (re)construction that excluded slaves and former slaves was not practicable for the latter, but within the range of available communal identifications there remained that of ethnicity. This was all the more tempting because it enabled their 'representatives' to play on the existing ethnic rivalries (a fundamental feature of the Mauritanian political scene) by integrating and (re)emphasizing an ethnic origin (former slaves and slaves are black Africans) that was a permanent mark of their inferiority within the tribal order. Thus, following the *coup d'état* of July 1978 there were tracts calling for a division of power on an ethnic base.

These observations upon former slaves and their efforts to secure emancipation (the Moorish slaves have just been solemnly 'freed' for the third time in half a century by government decree), and the integration of this phenomenon into a wider field of clientelist-type (tribal or ethnic) political contradictions and rivalries that run through present-day Mauritanian society, have only apparently taken us away from pastoralism and its future. These rivalries and contradictions are, it is true, over-determined by a regional and international context marked by competition between local micro-hegemonisms and between the commercial and strategic interests of the great powers which, inevitably, are concerned about the Sahara war and its possible 'tribal–ethnic' fall-out. But what, in reality, is at stake in this interweaving of alliances and oppositions between various social strata of pastoral society, between 'tribes', 'ethnic groups', and between sedentary people and nomads, is the future of pastoralism. Here, a particular and decisive aspect of the network of contradictions that encloses and moves Mauritanian society – the condition of servitude and quasi-servitude – has been stressed. This is because within it are articulated and expressed, in the dominant political idiom, the language of a clientelism with 'tribal' and 'ethnic' overtones, the problems and contradictions of a pastoral society profoundly transformed by colonial and commercial domination.

Conclusion

First, we must correct the impression of a possibly over-inflated contrast in presentation between the 'functionality' of the pre-colonial order and the dysfunctionality of the order that has replaced it, in short the opposition between the 'good poverty' of the past and the 'bad poverty' of the present. To exalt either the *razzia* or slavery, or the epidemics that periodically scarred a nomad society, which always led an extremely precarious existence, was not intended. It was, however, necessary to stress the striking resistance of a way of life resting on a fragile balance between a bio-climatic threshold marked by scarcity of water and grazing land and a set of technical, economic, institutional, ideological and other behaviours.

The devastating role of the last 15 years of drought in unleashing the exodus from rural areas, and the massive sedentarization of nomads has, justifiably, been stressed. But droughts and famines are not new in the countries of the Sahara and the Sahel. The Oualata Chronicle, for example, mentions no fewer than five great famines between 1249 AH (1830–31) and 1311 AH (1893–94) plus half a dozen epidemics (especially the serious one in 1286 AH (1869–70) that carried off over 300 people), not to mention countless *razzias*.[13] The Tichitt Chronicle[14] records the same recurrence of the cycle of drought–*razzia*–famine–epidemic that seems to have marked the whole history of this locality. But these disturbances, serious as they may have been, never occasioned a real break-up in the pastoral way of life comparable to that we have been witnessing for the last 15 years. Before colonization, the vagaries of the climate never led to the formation of a town; nor did they contribute significantly to a rise in the population of the caravan camps which the increasing number of tributes and *razzias* made particularly inhospitable in times of crisis. But once the economic and ideological wellsprings of pastoral societies had been broken in a process in which violence and coercion combined with the effects of commodity relations, conditions were ripe for such a climatic catastrophe as that the Sahel has recently been experiencing, to have mortal consequences for pastoralism.

The role of the state – a mechanism to administer legitimate violence, as Weber defined it – in this process cannot go unmentioned.

The role of political control of the pastoral space in the mobility that is a key part of the nomad way of life and mode of production has been demonstrated. Some argue that this control was exercised solely through segmentary tribal structures governed by kinship and excluding the appearance of any centralized political authority, or a state. This is notably the opinion of C. C. Stewart[15] who takes up the functionalist theory of segmentarism developed by Evans-Pritchard and his followers, and considers pre-colonial Moorish society to have been 'anarchic', 'acephalous', 'stateless', and in which the emir, like any other tribal chief, was simply a 'primus inter pares' with no real authority. According to Evans-Pritchard, the opposition (both antagonistic and complementary)[16] between equivalent lineage segments, conceived as a correlate of the genealogical structure of unilineal descent groups ('Arab' marriage with the patrilateral parallel cousin) which leads to strong agnatic solidarity[17] and to an equally strong tendency to fission, obstructs the emergence of autonomous political structures within segmentary tribal societies that are perpetually condemned to 'anarchy' and war. While this representation undeniably contains features that portray part of Moorish social and historical reality, it has the disadvantage of being unable to explain the emergence, even in an embryonic form, of political structures that were becoming autonomous: those of the emirates. For even though these structures suffered the effects of the segmentary system and kinship they nevertheless represent the beginnings of a political power, a state in the process of being constituted. Neither does it seem that the emergence of those proto-state emirate forms associated with social stratification, which cannot be explained solely in the framework of the functionalist problematic of the theory of segmentarity, can be explained within the framework of social contract theorists (Locke, Hobbes, Rousseau) and their modern descendants, solely by the desire to legitimize a domination derived from a differentiation and polarization between wealth and poverty, exploited and exploiters of which the infant state is seen as simply the scarcely veiled instrument.

Beyond this alternative, which contrasts the impossibility of the state emerging in segmentary tribal societies governed by kinship with an exclusively instrumentalist theory (the state as the tool of class domination) there is the outline of an intermediate reality: a transitional area where kinship and politics combine in a complex articulation in which the ideology and language of kinship continue to provide a body of representation to political structures that express as much domination by a class (the warrior and marabout aristocrats) as perpetuation of the genealogical principle that supposedly governs tribal unity. In the situation inherited from the slave trade period and colonization, and whatever misunderstandings may have surrounded the real nature of tribal and emirate power at that time, the effects of kinship structures on the distribution and exercise of political power have continued to operate through new forms of *clientelism*.

Whether under the regime of freedom of political competition (in fact a very tightly controlled freedom) in the late 1950s (the period of the 'loi-cadre'), or under the post-colonial regime that today, has culminated in a militarization hardly concerned with political representation associated with elections (National Assembly, regional councils, local government and so on), Mauritanian politics has continued to draw on kinship networks for the establishment of a legitimacy that has been unable to find sufficiently credible roots elsewhere.

Clientelism here, indicates the process of converting bureaucratically accumulated economic capital – payments made to local political middlemen – or 'economically' – through the mechanism ('sole agency', trading commission, for example) of local distribution of central capitalism's industrial or agricultural products – into political capital ('representativeness'), without which the expansion of wealth and prestige would rapidly cease.

The close relationship of private economic prosperity and the bureaucratic, state management of dependency, even leaving aside what Hamid El Mauritanyi calls bureaucracy's 'illegal tranche of income'[18] (the product of corruption, diversion of public funds, and so forth) appears in the reciprocal circulation of money and men in both directions. Every concessionaire[19] must, in fact, have connections in the state marketing commission and parastatals, the sole national clients of any significance, and every politician who 'retires' almost inevitably ends up with an 'agency'.

What is thus emerging is a necessary reciprocity between 'representation' in the commercial sense of the word and 'representativeness' in the political and social sense. In a society still strongly marked by its tribal structures and in which the bureaucratic–capitalist sector employs barely 2% of the labour force, they inevitably meet in the domain of kinship.

To ensure the fruitfulness and survival of their capital stock of 'representativeness', a man who becomes rich, a professional politician or aspirant to the position, must keep the broadest possible clientele happy, first, his close kin, then dependent groups and people of the same tribe. Their solidarity, generated as much by the redistribution of economic benefits as by kinship bonds, will in turn form the basis of the representatives' (politicians or concessionaires) 'representativeness' in the state and capitalist sector of the national society and economy.

Does this imply, to use Samir Amin's expression, that in common with other African states dominated by central capitalism the Mauritanian state is becoming 'transnationalized'? If this expression means the massively dominant role of managing dependency, then it cannot be denied.

Such a viewpoint can, however, be criticized as excessively reductionist if it leads to a perception of the state in dependent African countries as simply an instrument of imperialist domination. This view is strictly in line with that which Lenin, quoting Marx and Engels, helped popularize: the state as the tool of a class dictatorship culminating, according to the authors of *State and Revolution*, in the 'withering away' of the state in the communist society of the future. The Mauritanian situation, marked by a profound interpenetration of kinship bonds, will in turn form the basis of the representatives' (politicians or religious factors exercise a decisive influence,[20] does not accord with this theory.

The Mauritanian states expresses both the present dualism of the economy and the relevance of the ancient economic, ideological and symbolic structures of kinship. It is thus a hybrid, both an instrument of centralization and a central stake in centrifugal strategies. It cannot be reduced to the role of administrator or manager of dependency.

It is tempting to see in the Mauritanian state only an instrument in the service of multinational domination combined with a sort of cannibalism in which the administration of poverty-stricken indigenous populations and organization of the aid intended for them enrich the most unscrupulous sectors of the bureaucracy. In Haiti, some *tontons macoutes* allegedly sell the *blood* of their compatriots to the USA – Africa has not descended to this level. But we should beware of a cannibalism that might be an essential part of any state, for is not governing necessarily 'devouring the substance of others'?[21]

Notes

1. On all aspects of grazing and herding among the Moors, see the following works: Francart, 'Le pâturage en Haut Adrar', *Bull. IFAN*, 1940, II, 3–4, 285–78; and 'Note sur le vocabulare camelin en Haute Mauritanie', *Bull. IFAN*, 1941, III, 45–52; V. Monteil, *Essai sur le chameau au Sahara Occidental. Bull. IFAN*, Saint-Louis-du-Sénégal, 1952; and *Contribution à l'étude de la flore au Sahara Occidentale*, Paris, Larose 1949; A. Leriche, 'Vocabulaire du chameau en Mauritanie', *Bull. IFAN*, 1952, XIV, 3, 985–95; and 'Coutumes maures relatives à lélevage', *Bull. IFAN*, 1953, XV, 3, 1316–20.; Leborgne, 'Vocabulaire technique du chameau en Mauritanie', *Bull. IFAN*, 1953, XV, 1, 292–380; Charles Toupet (thesis) 'Le sédentarisation des nomades dans la Mauritanie Centrale Sahélienne'. Paris, 1975.

2. 'Rapport annuel sur le commerce et l'industrie pendant l'année 1938', Colonie de la Mauritanie. Archives de la RIM, série Q No 411.

3. See also: Ould Cheikh, *Les Maures*, RAMS, 1980; P. Bonte and Ould Cheikh, *Nomadisme, sédentarisation, migrations dans la société maure*, Unesco, Population Division, 1980; J. P. Hervouet, 'Types d'adaptation sahéliens', Thèse de IIIe Cycle, University of Rouen, 1975.

4. Concerning water for grazing purposes, one of the main areas of herding where the administration has taken action, the second Mauritanian economic and social development plan (1970–73) estimated that there were 3,000 cement wells in Mauritania; 750 built by the administration between 1950 and 1968, including 600 in the 1950–60 period alone.

5. Urban wages (Nouakchott, Nouadhibou, Zouérate) of employees in the same category (domestics, labourers etc.) reach barely 3,000 *ouguiya* per month. It is quite common to see small, underpaid (a few hundred *ouguiya*) children working as domestics.

6. This is still far from the consumption levels in industrialized countries. The

annual average per person in France, for example, is 94 kg (see Jean Ziégler, 'Le scandale de la surconsommation de viande dans les pays riches', *Le Monde Diplomatique*, November 1981, p. 10.

7. See the paradigmatic role attributed by some authors (Luc de Heusch, René Girart et al) to the ritual behaviour of East African herders, and those 'sacred' kingships of the Great Lakes region that involve cattle. See also Bonte and Becquemont, 'Travail, valeur, besoins et conscience alienée: le cas des éleveurs de l'Afrique de l'Est', *La Pensée*, 1980, pp. 90–121.

8. Of 51 agreements to redeem the tribute (noted in the Mederdra archives for 1946–47) between dominant groups and tributaries, 36 involved a settlement in cash (120,475 Francs); five a 'mixed' settlement part cash (11,000 Francs), part cattle (29 sheep and two she-camels); eleven in cattle (174 sheep, seven cows, two steers, ten she-camels (including four with young), eleven male-camels, one she-ass, one *vliz* (strip woven from sheepswool for tent-making)).

9. The dominant ideology, of the marabout class in particular, claims to justify the Moorish social hierarchy by a decision of the Almoravid leader Abù Bakr Ben 'Umar (d. 1087 in Tagant). On his death-bed, he is said to have decided to distribute the men making up his army as follows: warriors, responsible for propagating Islam by force of arms; marabouts, responsible for religious teaching and education; the tributaries, responsible for maintaining the first two groups. See in particular 'Al wasit . . .', Cairo and Casablanca (2nd ed.), 1958, by Ahmad ben Al Amin Al-Sinqiti, p. 475 (in Arabic).

10. For example, the *al-me* clause at the end of the Sārr Bebbe war (second part of seventeenth century) stipulated that the defeated group would, when necessary, offer the victors and their descendants one-third of the water they drew from their own wells.

11. 'Virtually all the leaders of the Islamic Republic of Mauritania come from the traditional aristocratic orders: 162 out of 175. Men from tributary or artisan groups (ten) and servile categories (six) can almost be counted on the fingers of one hand . . . 90 out of 175 are chiefs or sons of chiefs, and 66 are from the families of notables'. F. de Chassey, in *Mauritanie, 1900–1975*, Paris, Anthropos 1978, p. 286.

12. On this we have collected numerous testimonies from the masters themselves. See also one by a Dahomeyan exile: Louis Hunkarin, *Un forfait colonial: l'esclavage en Mauritanie*, Imprimerie moderne, Privas 1931.

13. Paul Marty (trans.), 'Chronique de Oualata et de Néma', *Revue des Etudes Islamiques*, 1927, III, pp. 355–426.

14. Vincent Monteil (trans.) 'Chronique de Tichitt', *Bull. IFAN*, I, 1939, pp. 283–312.

15. C. C. Stewart, 'Political authority and social stratification in Mauritania', in E. Gellner and A. Micaud (eds), *Arabs and Berbers*, London, Duckworth 1972.

16. Evans-Pritchard wrote of the 'tribe without rulers' model of the Nuer: 'Each segment is itself segmented and there is opposition between its parts. The members of any segment unite for war against adjacent segments of the same order and unite with those adjacent segments against larger sections.' *The Nuer*, Oxford, Clarendon Press 1940, p. 142.

17. One has only to think of the *'asabiyya* of Ibn Khaldun, the wellspring of the solidarity and unity of action of groups of nomad conquerors and the key concept in the cyclical conception of history developed by the great Magrhibi writer. See *Al-Muqaddima*.

18. Hamid El Mauritanyi, *L'indépendance néo-coloniale*, op. cit.

19. Perhaps there is need to distinguish 'real concession' and 'fictional con-
session', the representatives who actually sell something (mass-consumed
foodstuffs, textiles, cars, and so on) market purveyors and other front names for
licences (fishing etc.), and those solely concessionaires, the middlemen who some
call ironically 'Messrs Tenpercenters'. Obviously, there are complex links between
the two categories.

20. For more detail see: A. W. Ould Cheikh, 'Comment prêcher dans le désert.
Fonction cléricale, fonction guerrière et émergence de l'Etat dans la société maure',
in P. Bonte and J. Galaty (eds), *African Pastoralism and the State*, London, Sage
(forthcoming).

21. A Tiv (Nigerian tribal group) saying, reported by Paul Bohannan and quoted
by G. Balandier, *Political Anthropology*, London, Allen Lane The Penguin Press
1970, p. 60.

6. Nigeria and the Ivory Coast: Commercial and Export Crops since 1960

Rigobert Oladiran Ladipo

Introduction

The notion of commercial and export crops is one that covers varying realities depending on the country and the historical period. In Africa, it was originally applied to tropical products that were impossible to grow in Europe but needed by the rapidly growing economies there, and those which had been introduced or developed in Europe's colonies, solely to supply the metropolitan countries. Some of these products, for example of the oil-palm, were known and used by the peoples of the colonial countries long before contact with Europeans; others, such as cocoa, were completely unknown.

The crops dealt with in this chapter have played a significant role in the economic life of Nigeria and the Ivory Coast since 1960. Cocoa, palm kernels, palm oil, cotton, groundnuts, rubber and sugar in both countries; coffee, bananas and pineapples in Ivory Coast only.

The Ivory Coast is little more than one-third the size of Nigeria (322,462km^2 as against 923,768 km^2),[1] with a population, according to UN 1982 estimates, one-tenth the size of Nigeria's (8,570,000 as against 82,390,000). Despite this disparity in size and population a comparative study of the two countries seemed of value in terms of providing a perspective on their performance. Additionally, an examination of the mechanisms that have underpinned the extraordinary growth of commercial and export agriculture in the Ivory Coast provides an addition to the debate on development.

Agricultural production trends in both countries

Statistics relating to commercial and export crops are highly reliable in so far as products such as rubber, or those not traditionally consumed in the countries where they are cultivated, such as cocoa or coffee, are concerned, but such products as palm oil or groundnuts, which are widely consumed by the local populations, and an increasing proportion of which does not pass through the official marketing agencies (except when these are themselves producers) are less easy to quantify with any degree of accuracy.

Extrapolating relevant figures from the abundant statistical data provided by the UN and its specialized agencies it is proposed to examine broad trends of production and their immediate consequences on the external trade and the processing industries of each country.

Cocoa

For both countries cocoa is currently the most important crop. At independence, Nigeria was second only to Ghana as world producer,[2] – reaching peak production in 1970, before beginning a decline that continued until 1982, when it was only 80% of its 1960 level and 64% of 1970 level. Despite this fall in production Nigeria is among the leading group of world producers (Ivory Coast, 25%; Brazil, 22%; Ghana, 10%; Nigeria, 8%; Cameroun 6.75%)[3] with 130,000 metric tons of cocoa (86.66% of its total production) exported in 1982.

The production pattern in the Ivory Coast has been altogether different. At independence, the figure for cocoa production was half that of Nigeria's. Thereafter, however, with production increased annually, by 1971 the Ivory Coast had more than doubled its 1960 tonnage, by 1974 it was above that of Nigeria, and in the year 1977–78, replaced Ghana as leading world producer and exporter.[4] By 1980, production had increased four times that for 1960.

Palm kernels

Between 1960 and 1966 Nigeria, with an annual production of palm kernels averaging over 400,000 metric tons, was far and away the leading world producer, supplying 50% of total world consumption.[5] But with the civil war (1967–70) mainly involving the former Eastern Region, which is the source of 65% of Nigeria's oil palm products,[6] production was halved for three consecutive years. Between 1970 and 1979, production increased significantly (except for the bad years, 1973 and 1978), reaching about 300,000 metric tons per annum. After 1979 Nigeria made up much of the shortfall suffered during the tragic years 1967–70, and in 1982 production was 81% of that in 1960, which sufficed to meet domestic needs and to deliver 15.71% on to the world market (as against 96.52% of total production in 1960–66).

Ivorian palm kernel production, insignificant compared to Nigeria's, was marked by a rapid succession of years of growth and years of decline. In good years, since 1974, however, the 1960 harvest has doubled, and a surplus for export has been available (17.8% exported in 1982).

Palm oil

As with palm kernels, Nigeria's annual palm oil production was very high during the first six years of independence: over half a million metric tons, and, during those years, the country was the biggest world producer.[7] As was the case for palm kernels, production of palm oil fell sharply in the 1967–70 period although by less than palm kernels (between –18% and –37% compared to the 1966 level). Production began to recover in 1970, with (unlike palm kernels) a significant leap forward in 1974, when all previous records were beaten, and progress was more or less continuous thereafter. The 1982 tonnage was almost

27% higher than that of 1960. Despite this progress, however, there was a serious problem. This product formed part of the daily diet of a large proportion of the Nigerian population, which had grown by almost 92% between 1960 (42,950,000) and 1982 (82,390,000), but the domestic consumption requirements had increased three-and-a-half times above the production level. After 1976, therefore, Nigeria became a net importer of palm oil and, in 1982, imports were 153,000 metric tons at a cost of US$ 92,000,000 in foreign exchange.

In 1960, the Ivory Coast produced less than 20,000 metric tons of palm oil, 30 times less than Nigeria. By 1982, however, production had risen by a factor of nine-and-a-half and already equalled one-quarter of Nigeria's production, despite the progress the latter had recorded. Thus not only was the Ivory Coast enabled to become self-sufficient by the late 1960s, but also to have substantial surpluses to export.

Cotton

Cotton, one of the commercial and export crops of the savanna and Sahel regions, is very sensitive to climatic vagaries. In Nigeria, production followed a rather capricious path, with a mediocre harvest (below 40,000 metric tons) one year in two, alternating with an adequate or more than adequate harvest. After 1978, however, the trend was downwards: the 1960 production figure was reduced by almost 27% in 1982 when imports of cotton fibre totalled 58,000 metric tons at a cost of US$ 85,000,000.

In the Ivory Coast, production grew almost continuously, so rapidly that by 1982, production was over 30 times that in 1960 and had easily overtaken Nigeria's. Additionally, in 1982, the Ivory Coast was able to export over 62% of its cotton production.

Groundnuts

Until 1971, the volume of groundnuts in shells produced in Nigeria oscillated between one and two million metric tons, making it the largest African producer, the largest world exporter and one of the largest world producers.[8] But after 1972 production fell to less than half a million metric tons, with the lowest levels recorded in 1973, 1974, 1975, 1977 and 1978 with harvests far below half a million metric tons. Since 1979, a slight recovery has been underway, but in 1982, production was only 48% of that in the 1960s. Groundnut oil, like palm oil, is widely used for the culinary needs of the Nigerian people. By 1975, one consequence of this dramatic fall in production was the lack of any exportable surplus; and most local refineries have closed or work only sporadically.

In the Ivory Coast, although between 1960 and 1982 tonnages produced rose two-and-a-half times, self-sufficiency seems not to have been achieved.

Rubber

Nigeria's rubber production since independence has varied between an annual 43,000 and 72,000 metric tons which, until 1971, was entirely exported. Today, it continues broadly to meet domestic demand and achieve large surpluses for sale on the world market – some 60% of total production in 1982.

The Ivory Coast, which embarked on rubber production only after independence, secured more than satisfactory results: starting from nil in 1960, by 1980 it was producing over 20,000 metric tons, all of which, so far, is sold to Third World countries.

Sugar

In 1960, neither Nigeria nor the Ivory Coast produced any sugar, all consumption was met by imports. Nigeria began producing sugar in 1965 and, until 1975, production rose reasonably satisfactorily, levelling until 1977, then beginning to fall. But at no point has Nigeria come anywhere near sugar self-sufficiency, and only in 1964 and 1968 did imports fall below 50,000 metric tons. Except in 1974, imports between 1971 and 1976 were invariably well above 100,000 metric tons, and since 1977, tonnages imported have risen precipitately: almost one million metric tons in 1981 and 1982, costing the nation almost a half billion US dollars in 1981, and US\$ 346 million in 1982.

The Ivory Coast began to produce sugar in 1975, ten years after Nigeria. But the country invested such massive resources in it that by 1981 it was already producing six times more sugar than Nigeria; was more than amply covering the needs of its population; and had large exportable surpluses. Unfortunately, Ivory Coast's sugar surpluses will be difficult to sell on the world market for reasons which will be mentioned below.

Coffee, bananas and pineapples

Nigeria's coffee production is insignificant and the available statistics make no mention of any production of bananas or pineapples. The Ivory Coast is easily the leading African producer and exporter of these fruits and produces and exports coffee.

Contrasting balance-sheets

The foregoing highlights the contrasting trends in the development of the commercial and export agricultures in Nigeria and the Ivory Coast. On the one hand, Nigeria, at independence, one of the largest world producers and exporters of numerous tropical products was, two decades later, no longer able to supply the international market (except for cocoa and rubber) and, in 1982, was producing quantities generally lower than those of 1960, and was no longer able to meet its domestic demand.

On the other hand, the Ivory Coast, in 1960 of average significance among world producers and exporters of agricultural raw materials from tropical countries, had become, 20 years after independence, the leading African country for commercial and export agriculture; a leading world producer and exporter of cocoa; the third world producer and exporter of coffee, and a leading African producer and exporter of bananas and pineapples, more than meeting most of its population's needs as well as those of a relatively large local manufacturing industry for most agricultural products.

Consequently, it emerges that a process of underdevelopment has occurred on the one hand, and an exceptionally vigorous process of expansion on the other.

In order to try to understand the reasons for this contrast the following pages will study the specific conditions and particular experiences of each country.

Ivory Coast: development strategy and commercial and export agriculture

Land: expropriation/appropriation strategy

At independence (1960) the Ivory Coast, with 322,462 km^2 and 3,230,000 inhabitants,[9] had just ten inhabitants per square kilometre. There was thus no shortage of land and each indigenous community – family or village – had sufficient to enable its members to practise the traditional slash-and-burn shifting agriculture with long periods of fallow. Land was governed by customary law, of which two basic principles were: that land-ownership rights were vested in the community, and not in individuals; and that land was inalienable. But in some regions, particularly in the East, the Centre-West and Baoulé country, where coffee and cocoa growing had developed, collective ownership had already begun to give way to permanent, alienable private ownership.

This mode of land appropriation, whose chief African beneficiaries were the coffee and cocoa planters, became official state policy as soon as independence offered the big planters, who controlled the government party (PDCI-RDA), and the state apparatus, the possibility of laying down the country's political strategy.

As early as 1961, the Ivorian head of state declared war on customary forms of ownership, which he described as out-dated, and proclaimed the right of Ivorian agriculture to develop without hindrances. On 20 March 1963, the National Assembly, all of whose deputies had been elected on a PDCI-RDA platform, adopted a law on land tenure, whose basic principles have been summarized thus: 'what is not developed must return to the State . . . what is developed must belong to the person who developed it'.[10] The Law can be summarized as follows:

a) Article 37 provides that 'the developer, to the exclusion of all other holders of customary rights in the land, may request registration of his title';

b) registration of title, a system instituted in the colonial period which was continued by the Law, effectively removes 'registered land from the control of customary law bringing it under the provisions of the [French-type] Civil Code'; it constituted 'the mode of verifying and confirming rights in land'.

c) members of the collectives whose rights have been affected by this registration, and, more precisely, those with rights under customary law, can ask only for compensation, but

d) compensation is not automatic and 'is not due if the customary rights that other members of the affected community could lay claim to have lapsed through non-use over a period greater than ten years'.

e) 'when compensation is due, the amount shall be set amicably between the two parties. Failing such an agreement, . . . the judicial agencies shall fix the amount in such a way that the debtor can pay off his debt within a maximum of five years'.

f) 'land and forest undeveloped as at 15 January 1962 shall be registered in the name of the State' and become its property.

g) registered land that is not developed or is in a poor state of production for at least five years 'may be the object of an expropriation procedure'.[11]

This Law of 20 March 1963 was, however, never promulgated, for fear, so it seems, of the reactions of the customary authorities. But this tactical retreat on the part of the state did not constitute a repudiation of the Law's provisions. Proof of this is the PDCI-RDA Political Bureau's decision in 1966 which lays down that: 'when land has been developed . . . the developer may, to the exclusion of all other holders of customary rights in land, request registration of that land in his name'.[12]

In addition to land-capital, one of the most important factors of production is labour-capital. In 1960, the indigenous human resources of the Ivory Coast alone could not provide this capital.

Imported manpower

The tradition of recourse to hired labour, mainly of Burkinabe origin, goes back to the time when most of Burkina Faso was part of the Ivory Coast. But after 1950, with the increasingly rapid development of export crops, the number of imported labourers grew rapidly, and was already sizeable before independence: 390,000 foreign workers in 1958 as against 2,320,000 indigenes,[13] or 17% of the total. This policy of importing foreign labour to meet the needs of its commercial and export agriculture (Ivorian planters turn to hired labour only for cash crops and use unpaid family labour for food crops)[14] was continued and even stepped up after independence. Thus, by 1965, non-Ivorian Africans already accounted for 22% of the total rural population and 35% of the rural adult male population.

> In the three areas of prosperous plantations, the East, the forested Centre-West and the Baoulé savanna areas, foreigners make up over one-third of the population . . . in the plantation areas strictly defined, they account for between half and two-thirds of the labour force. While, in some export crop growing areas local labour still represents a significant percentage of workers – notably in the West – in the East this is no longer the case: the local populations have been transformed into non-working 'proprietor' planters, the work being done almost exclusively by agricultural labourers from the north.[15]

In 1977, an official study, covering 75 modern agricultural enterprises specializing in commercial and export crops, found that their labour force, totalling 11,583 workers, included 10,427 non-Ivorian Africans, 90% of the total. The same study, extended to cover 159 modern enterprises operating throughout the rural areas, showed the 71.8% of their labourers were non-Ivorian Africans.[16]

These agricultural labourers, mainly foreigners, were relatively poorly paid. While the minimum hourly wage in the secondary sector was 37 Francs CFA in 1958, that for agricultural labourers in the plantations was 19.50 Francs, or 52.7% of the wage in the secondary sector. In 1979, for an eight-hour day, the minimum daily wage in the secondary sector was 1,264 Francs. That of the agricultural labourer, whose working day often exceeded eight hours, was only 400 Francs per day, or at most 31.64% of the wage in the secondary sector.[17] This low level of agricultural labourers' wages amply explains why the indigenous, non planter–proprietor for whom other possibilities are open, is unwilling to work as an agricultural labourer. It also helps to understand one of the essential wellsprings of Ivorian growth: an accelerated accumulation realized at the expense of a population with no means of bringing political pressure to bear, because it is made up of non-citizens who have often been driven into exile in the Ivory Coast by much more precarious living conditions in their homes in the Sahel. Finally, it makes clear why the planter-proprietors have been able to prosper, despite the large amounts deducted from their products' sale prices by the state and middlemen.

Mechanization: extending the ruling landed bourgeoisie's social base
The option in favour of a certain level of mechanization of agriculture dates back to 1966, and led to the formation of MOTORAGRI, a state company responsible for developing the mechanization of agriculture. To summarize the official viewpoint: manual agriculture is synonymous with small-scale holdings and thus with peasants' poverty and illiteracy, and drives the educated and semi-educated youth off the land. In addition, clearing land manually is unsatisfactory, as it leaves behind roots and large trees and the area is rapidly covered by bush. If, as a result of mechanization, there were to be some loss of soil quality, that would be largely compensated for by the gains resulting from large holdings and more thorough clearing.[18]

But there is also another explanation that flows from an analysis of political developments in the Ivory Coast since 1964. Until then, the state apparatus was firmly controlled by the group of big planters[19] of whom the President of the Republic himself was the undisputed leader. This group was aware that, in every other country in the sub-region, political power had passed to officials or intellectuals, and their group was unique among those of its type in having secured state leadership. It therefore did everything possible in an effort to ensure against sharing power with bureaucrats or any other social category. There was thus a preference for entrusting positions of responsibility in the administration and public enterprises to French technical assistance personnel rather than to nationals who were seen as potential rivals and in whom the ruling group reposed no confidence. This also explains the reason for the endless invective aimed at officials and intellectuals, as well as what lay behind the shadowy 'plots' that led to the elimination from Party and state leadership of those individuals, not of planter origin, who had emerged during the heroic struggle after the Second World War.[20]

But, after 1964, subsequent to the military coups that began in Africa in 1963, this group, reluctant to give way to the army, embarked on a rapprochement with the indigenous higher cadres, mostly young university graduates, and contemplated eventually sharing power with them.[21] But a precondition for this was that these young people should become planters themselves. On 13 March 1965, at a meeting with all the young cadres in the government, the National Assembly, the Economic and Social Council, heads of department and of regional organizations of the Party, the Head of State gave them the following directives: each must set up a plantation in his home region, of at least 15 hectares for a minister, ten for a deputy or member of the Economic Council and five for a head of department or secretary-general of a regional section of the PDCI-RDA. This meeting was held just five days after the announcement of the setting-up of MOTORAGRI, on 8 March 1966.[22] Such a succession of events cannot have been accidental. It seems reasonable to assume that MOTORAGRI was the instrument dreamed up by the planters in power to accelerate the numerical expansion of their own class and thus broaden their own social base.

Virtually from the day it was established, MOTORAGRI was provided with 120 caterpillar, and 72 wheeled tractors, plus 12 mechanical graders, mostly of American origin; management was provided by Israeli experts.[23] This mechanical equipment, and the assured availability of land and credit, stimulated those cadres affected by the presidential directives to carry them out with great enthusiasm. State and Party leaders and cadres competed with each other, anxious to enlarge and diversify their plantations, like the President; each dreaming of exceeding the 'peasant President's' productivity records or at least coming close to them.[24]

No record of the size of these plantations exists since, after agreeing (on 17 February 1962) in principle to the creation of a cadastral register, the planter-state decided against it, because in the opinion of Jacques Baulin, an adviser to Houphouët-Boigny from 1965 to 1969, 'a cadastral register would have made it possible to list the extent of the property of those in power', and,

> because of this gap, it is impossible today to verify whether President Houphouët-Boigny really owns 15, 20 or 50,000 hectares of rice and other plantations . . . and whether the properties of Mr Philippe Yacé, then President of the National Assembly, were larger in 1969 than those of the Head of State, as a minister well placed to know believed.[25]

Regarding the holdings of Mr Philippe Yacé's, the citation, read by the Minister of Agriculture, in December 1970, when he decorated him with the insignia of Commander of Agricultural Merit, included the statement 'if you are the second Ivorian figure in the political sphere, you also the second figure, as a planter, coming immediately after His Excellency President Houphouët-Boigny . . .' and went on to eulogize Mr Yacé as a leading planter of coconuts, selected oil palms, bananas for export, avocados, a leading stock farmer, a rice-grower and as embarking on the production of pineapples for export, coffee and cocoa.[26]

Here we can see the principle and practice of combining public office and profitable private activity being exalted in one of the highest figures in the state.

How the state intervenes

Mechanization alone, and even combined with large credit facilities and the availability of land, could not have accounted for the exceptional growth of commercial and export agriculture in the Ivory Coast since independence. A decisive role in accelerating agricultural growth was the state, which, despite Ivorian leaders' choice of a free trade and free competition system, and their oft-repeated faith in private initiative, soon became the real driving force of agriculture.

In January 1961, when Houphouët-Boigny presented his government's programme to the National Assembly, shortly after his election to the Presidency, he announced that the Ivory Coast 'proposed . . . to achieve a *State Capitalism*'. And he went on to state that, alongside private effort, there would be:

> a preponderant effort by the State which will take various forms: first, through public investment making use of both external assistance and national funds; second, through taking shares in enterprises using the country's natural resources, which shares will be in proportion to the size of these resources; lastly, through the creation of State enterprises.[27]

State intervention was of two kinds: 1) direct take-over of production activities, specifically for oil palm, coconuts, rubber and sugar cane. And 2) was limited to providing management for, and a variety of assistance to independent producers of crops already widely grown before independence, such as coffee, cocoa, bananas and pineapples, and also annual crops such as cotton, that do not need large investment and that pay-off after one season.

The first oil palm plan
This plan, the first concrete step in massive state intervention in the country's economy, had several aspects.

First, in 1963.[28] a state company, SODEPALM was formed, with the task of creating and exploiting commercial plantations of selected oil palms and, around each of its own blocks of oil palms, promoting so-called 'village' plantations, belonging to private Ivorian citizens. The SODEPALM plantations were to be sufficiently large and productive to 'ensure the profitability of the operation and a regular supply to the processing factories'. 'Village' plantations were to be situated at a maximum distance of 20 kilometres from the factories to enable their owners to benefit from the logistics, and the advice of the SODEPALM estate of which they were an extension. A dense network of roads and tracks was to serve the whole and facilitate its exploitation. Paid technical assistance was supplied by agronomists from the IRHO, the French research institute that specialized in oils and fats and supplied SODEPALM with selected seeds.[29]

By the end of 1978, SODEPALM owned outright 52,000 hectares of commercial plantations and 38,000 hectares of 'village' plantations scattered among 10,000 planters. Thereafter, the commercial plantations programme virtually ended, since, as the 1979–81 three-year programme of state actions announced, the Ivory Coast was already endowed 'with industrial plantations forming a viable agro-industrial core making possible the development of village plantations'.[30] Stress was then on building-up village plantations, which the 15-year second oil palm plan currently underway envisages extending to 33,700 hectares, against an extension of only 1,200 hectares for the state commercial plantations.[31]

In 1967, a similar model was applied to coconut plantations, for which a special section was created within SODEPALM. By 1981, this section owned 19,195 hectares of commercial plantations with an output, in that year, exceeding 92 million coconuts. The output of SODEPALM-supervised village coconut plantations in the same year was equal to almost 12% of the commercial section's.

The oil palm plan's industrial and commercial aspects consisted in the formation, in 1969, of two mixed ownership companies, PALMINDUSTRIE and PALMIVOIRE. The former was responsible for the management and exploitation of the commercial units integrated into the oil palm and coconut plantations, and the latter for marketing oil palm and coconut products, and for the creation of twelve palm oil mills and a crushing mill for the trituration of palm kernels and copra.

With the end of the large-scale commercial plantations programme, the SODEPALM–PALMINDUSTRIE–PALMIVOIRE group was reorganized. PALMIVOIRE was wound up and PALMINDUSTRIE was changed from a mixed ownership to a state company and, in 1978, was charged with the management of commercial oil palm and coconut plantations in the framework of the oil palm and coconut plan, for the collection of the production of village and industrial plantations and the industrialization of oil products'.[32]

Finally, the social aspect consisted in the creation of new villages able to receive and settle individual planters under the wing of the state company.

Alongside the state's oil palm plan, there existed a private oil palm subsidiary, whose agricultural role was insignificant (only 9,640 hectares of selected oil palms in 1982). On the industrial level, however, where it included four different companies and was dominated by the UNILEVER group, it was more important, in particular upstream from PALMINDUSTRIE, since this private sector processed raw Ivorian vegetable oils into refined oil, soaps, and so on.

The Ivorian development strategy: consequences and limits

What emerges from the oil palm case study is a division of labour that: 1) recognizes that the French research transnational, IRHO, has a monopoly on the production of high-yielding seeds and the improvement of cropping techniques to be applied: 2) gives a key role to the state in financing agricultural production and the establishment of structures for private planters; 3) organizes the sharing of preliminary industrial processing activities between the state and the foreign private sector, the dominant role again falling to the state; 4) enshrines the hegemony of the foreign private sector, in this case a transnational, at the level of the processing of the original agricultural product into a finished product. This division enables a transnational to have access to abundant raw material, usually after preliminary treatment by the state industries, delivered at the local guaranteed price. The multinational, in principle, is enabled to have relatively low production costs for its finished products, a major advantage over international competition and, finally, as a bonus, more or less captive markets within the Ivory Coast and countries associated with it. This guarantees the transnational a more than substantial share of the surplus generated by agricultural labourers, peasant-planters and factory workers. This windfall profit, made increasingly attractive by a more than generous Investment Code, was instrumental in attracting foreign businesses and transnationals to the country.

Outside the oil palm sector, agricultural activities associated with the production of coffee and cocoa had, by 1965, become a virtual monopoly in the hands of Ivorian private planters;[33] sugar is exclusively under the state company SODESUCRE; and rubber and cotton are wholly controlled by the SAPH and the CIDT, enterprises with majority public capital (state share: 60.4% of SAPH and 55% of CIDT).[34] In 1978, out of 96 productive pineapple plantations, 69 were Ivorian, nine mixed ownership and 20 were foreign owned. In the same year, Ivorians' plantations were 57% of the total; in 1981, Ivorians' share represented 66.5% of the total.[35]

Although no precise data exist, the impressive tonnages of bananas exported by the Ivory Coast or processed in its factories are, very largely, from either state or privately owned plantations. Private planters co-producing with a state company, benefit from the infrastructure and logistics made available to them by the state company. Those wholly privately owned are assisted by the state with management and organization, a variety of bonuses and advantages of which the most effective is the subsidy for the extension of plantations, introduced for cocoa, ox-drawn farming and (from March 1977) free fertilizer for cotton producers.[36]

Agricultural production activities are largely dependent on the scientific and technological capacity of transnationals, mostly French transnationals involved in applied research: sugar cane, IRAT; cotton, IRCT and CFDT; coffee and cocoa, IFCC and CAPRAL(-NESTLE); rubber, Michelin.[37]

Cotton-ginning is provided by the CIDT, in which the State holds 55% of the shares, while overseas marketing, spinning, weaving and printing are currently in the hands of private companies or companies with majority private capital.

Distribution of capital in 1977 showed French, Japanese, Dutch and American interests playing an active role, and, in 1981, included almost two-and-a-half billion Francs CFA of Ivorian private capital out of a total of 13 billion.[38] While 66.61% of coffee exports are controlled by public and private Ivorian interests.[56] private enterprises, especially Nestlé, are significantly involved in processing; this pattern similarly applies to cocoa and cocoa products.[39]

In addition to the social division of labour just described, another aspect of the Ivorian development strategy is the sectoral approach chosen by the state. The state mobilized a substantial share of its resources, made available particularly by the Stabilization Fund's reserves, for each major commercial and export crop and hence for each region, in turn, able to produce them. First, coffee and cocoa, then after 1964, oil palm, coconuts after 1967, sugar after 1974, and so on. In short, rather than attempting to synchronize development throughout the country, the state has accommodated itself, temporarily, to inter-regional imbalances, possibly to be corrected later.

Finally, unlike private companies, in which management is still dominated by expatriate staff, state companies have allowed Ivorian managers to rise to the positions they covet and to manage substantial resources. But in the Ivory Coast, as already noted, it is not unknown for public and private sector jobs to be held simultaneously even at the highest state levels, and its basic economic option favours the quest for profit. Increasingly, therefore, these cadres were soon adding to their already high licit incomes (72% higher than equivalent level cadres in the civil service),[40] resources drawn from illicit operations: commissions on purchases and investments; over-invoicing; or even plain malversation of their companies' resources. These illegal practices, existing also at the administration level, apparently were never dealt with seriously, and seem to be an accepted method enabling those newly admitted to the leading group to amass wealth.

Consequently, the production costs of agro-industrial complexes managed or controlled by state companies gradually increased, reducing the surpluses available for the state and the transnationals' profit margin. The critical threshold was crossed when, with the slow-down of economic activity in the West, the tonnages of Ivorian agricultural exports began to fall and their sale prices to collapse.[41] Consequent reduction in state revenues called into question the country's capacity to honour debts incurred on the international financial market, and IMF intervention became inevitable. Among the recovery measures announced by the Ivorian state at the PDCI Congress in September–October 1980, were the dissolution of 15 state companies, the removal of numerous allowances in kind to state companies' senior staff, and their salaries aligned with those of the civil service.[42] The IMF did not impose devaluation, which, in fact, it never imposes on franc-zone African countries. Privatization of state enterprises and closure of two of SODESUCRE's six sugar complexes were, however, included.

The privatization measures come as no surprise but those aimed at SODESUCRE merit more attention, in so far as they illustrate certain aspects of system's functioning and help highlight some of its limitations.

The Ivorian sugar programme was launched in 1974, in the framework of the development plan for the previously undeveloped North, an area haunted for some years by the spectre of drought. Launched in a period of strong expansion, when the state still had sizeable financial resources, it was the subject of quite unprecedented over-invoicing: 35 billion CFA francs at least, according to *Jeune Afrique*'s estimates, 34 billion for just three of the complexes, as Houphouët-Boigny himself confessed. The resulting scandal led, in July 1977, to the removal from government of the three ministers (Henri Konan Bédié, Abdoulaye Sawadogo and Mohammed Diawara) who had been responsible for Ivorian economic policy for over ten years. After three years in political exile Konan Bédié, at the Seventh Congress of the PDCI-RDA (autumn 1980), returned in triumph to the political stage by securing the post of President of the National Assembly and number two in the regime.[43] Mohammed Diawara went on to gain renewed notoriety by pocketing six billion CFA francs from the WAEC Solidarity Fund, and was arrested and imprisoned, in October 1984, by Captain Sankara, head of state of Burkina Faso and President in office of WAEC.[44]

When SODESUCRE came on stream in 1980 it had the six sugar complexes finally constructed 'with a total theoretical production capacity of 310,000 metric tons per annum (raw sugar equivalent)', and in 1983 actually produced 186,619 metric tons. Total Ivorian consumption in the same year was 102,000 metric tons.[45] What was to be done with the surplus? The cost of building the sugar complexes had resulted in Ivorian sugar becoming uncompetitive on the world market (according to Houphouët-Boigny, Camerounian sugar was 100 Francs CFA per kg, Ivorian was 250 Francs CFA). The traditional customers for Ivorian agricultural products (France and the European Community countries) whose businessmen had encouraged the Ivory Coast to engage in sugar production, and been entrusted with all the investments and thus been the chief beneficiaries of the operation, now refused to purchase Ivorian sugar because they themselves were beset by the burden of their own surplus production. 'The project of the century had become a nightmare!'[46]

To remedy this situation, the IMF recommended a reduction in the country's sugar production capacity by closing down two of the six complexes. The two complexes closed to be converted to food crops (rice, maize, groundnuts, yams) and cotton farms, and the factories on these two complexes to be dismantled to provide spare parts for the remaining four factories still in production.[47]

A development strategy based on exporting raw materials to the world market had thus demonstrated its limits. Significantly, it was the IMF that indicated producing food crops, intended principally for the Ivorian domestic market and possibly that of countries in the sub-region, as a possible way out.

Nigeria: commercial and export agriculture

Unlike the Ivory Coast, the state in Nigeria plays a limited role in commercial and export agriculture, and displays timidity in every initiative agreed.

A brief examination of Nigerian agricultural strategy by recalling the choices made *vis-à-vis* solving land tenure problems follows here.

Land tenure law and the Land Use Decree

Until the 1978 Land Use Decree, Nigerian land tenure law continued to be governed by legal texts inherited from the colonial period, the Land Tenure Law for the former Northern Nigeria, and the State Land Law that applied in the country's other regions.

The Land Use Decree proposals, and provisions relevant to agricultural development, were:

1) vesting ownership of all land comprising the territory of each state in the federation in that state's Governor (Article 1);

2) all land in urban areas be under the control and management of each state's Governor; all land outside these areas to be under local authorities' control and management (Article 2a and b);

3) the Land Tenure Law and the State Land Law shall continue to be applied by the Governor;

4) the Governor may grant statutory rights of occupancy to any person; local authorities may grant only customary rights of occupancy (Articles 5a and 6a);

5) no single customary right of occupancy be granted in respect of an area exceeding 500 hectares of land for agricultural purposes or 5,000 hectares for grazing purposes (Article 6(2));

6) the occupier should have exclusive rights to the land against all persons other than the Governor (Article 14);

7) during the tenure of a statutory right of occupancy the holder should have the sole right to and absolute possession of all improvements on the land and may, subject to the prior consent of the Governor, transfer, assign or mortgage any improvements on the land (Article 15);

8) no customary right of occupancy may be alienated by assignment, mortgage, transfer of possession or sub-lease without prior consent of the Governor or the local authority (Article 21);

9) a statutory right of occupancy may not be divided into two or more portions on devolution by the death of the occupier except with the consent of the Governor (Article 24b);

10) the Governor may revoke a right of occupancy for overriding public interest (Article 28(1)), and in some cases of revocation the holder be entitled to compensation for the value of improvements at the date of revocation (Article 29(1)).[48]

These provisions of the Land Use Decree differ from what obtains in the Ivory Coast in that, in Nigeria, the principle of an absolute grant of rights to land to the benefit of private persons is excluded.

The state's role in agricultural production

From 1960 to the present day, the Nigerian state's role in directly productive activities in the commercial and export agriculture sector has been extremely limited. Apart from a few government oil palm plantations during the 1960s, which were considered non-viable as early as 1967, the state has generally been content to create conditions to allow private individuals to engage in agricultural production as profitably as possible. Today, there are no large commercial and export crop plantations owned or managed by the federal government or any state; nor any plantations belonging to enterprises in which there is majority public ownership. Moreover, generally, throughout the country, large commercial plantations are rather the exception. Among the few agro-industrial complexes on a scale that approaches those of the Ivory Coast, are sugar complexes at Bacita and Numan, owned by two private companies comprising, in late 1980, a combined total of 7,000 hectares of irrigated sugar cane estates.

Pre-capitalist agricultural mode of production

In the absence of a policy of large commercial estates, responsiblity for production falls almost exclusively on agricultural smallholders with very limited resources. For example, all the cocoa produced in Nigeria in the late 1960s and early 1970s was from 300,000 smallholdings covering 1,200,000 acres, an average of three-and-a-half acres per farmer (1.4 hectares) in the western and midwest regions, which together produced 97.3% of all Nigeria's cocoa; and 17 acres per farmer (6.8 hectares) in the eastern states. '45% of these farms were then more than 26 years old and 95% more than 11 years.' Ninety per cent of palm oil and palm kernels were from natural palm groves that received little or no maintenance, and 95–98% of rubber was produced by small peasant farms; groundnuts were grown by small producers on one- or two-acre plots.[49]

Commercial and export crop production in Nigeria, before the oil boom, was thus carried on almost exclusively in the framework of small peasant farms relying chiefly on family labour, occasionally supplemented by wage labour. Regarding the period since 1973, none of the documents to which we have had access has enabled us to know, precisely, the type and size of agricultural farms devoted to commercial and export crops. The general impression, however, is that overall, the situation has changed little since 1973 (except that the area devoted to commercial and export crops is much reduced in size), that the dominant mode of production has remained the same, and that this mode can be generalized to the whole of the agricultural productive sector, in particular to the extent that the same individual will be producing commercial and export, *and* food crops, and that the areas devoted to each of these two categories are rarely distinct.

This predominant mode of agricultural production in Nigeria can, in my opinion, be seen as similar to what has been described as the 'peasant mode of production', the basic features of which are: a) it 'is based on family units of peasant workers, owners of the land, whose product is intended mainly for family consumption, although a small portion of it is sold'; b) 'the basic unit is both the unit of production and the unit of consumption, commodity trading is only marginal'; and c) the peasant 'does not seek to maximize profit from his "capital" and to accumulate but primarily to live on the land which is his by virtue of peasant social organization'.[50]

This mode of organizing production, as well as the land tenure system codified by the Land Use Decree, is also reminiscent of what Samir Amin has described as the pre-capitalist 'tributary mode of production'. In this mode, instead of two antagonistic classes as is typical of the capitalist mode of production, 'the bipolarity is between peasant producers (organized into communities) and a State-class which controls access to the land. Rights in the land of the peasant communities (and/or of their members) and of the State-class (and/or of the State and its constituent parts) are superimposed on one another . . .'[51] These two concepts accurately describe the reality of the agricultural sector in Nigeria.

Relations between state and producers
With agricultural producers organized thus the state simultaneously maintains two types of relations that are contradictory in kind but dialectically linked. On the one hand, a policy of support, and, on the other, measures of exploitation. The exploitation aspect dominated the period from 1960 to the oil boom, while the support aspect seems to have been the most obvious since 1974.

State policy during the first period has been assessed unflatteringly. According to Gray, for example, it was a policy that could be summed up as taxing agriculture to finance other sectors; he goes on to cite export taxes, producer taxes, and the marketing board surpluses, noting that as a result of these levies, the producer's shortfall per metric ton of produce sold during the period 1961–65 averaged 30.5% for cocoa, 8% for groundnuts, 2.6% for cotton, 10% for palm kernels, 17.2% for palm oil, and 19.6% for rubber.[52]

Y. A. Abdullahi's fuller and no less critical analysis of the same period describes the strategy adopted as a 'strategy for accumulation without responsibility' and accuses the governments, foreign companies and local middlemen of having indulged in excessive exploitation of peasant agriculture and its resources, of failing to reinvest in agricultural production the revenues and superprofits thus extorted, and therefore of having made no contribution to the reorganization and development of the productive system.[53]

The openly exploitative character of official policy in this period, or at least its scant sympathy toward the peasants, is illustrated by the extent to which producer purchase prices in 1973 had changed since the 1960–61 period: groundnuts, 11.2% reduction; seed cotton, 18% increase; palm kernels, 5% increase; palm oil, 8.7% reduction; and cocoa, 63% increase.[54]

Thus, during the first 13 years of independent Nigeria, only the price of cocoa was appreciably increased; prices for seed cotton and palm kernels had slightly increased over the 1960 levels, but palm oil and groundnuts fell below. These prices, measured against real purchasing power, represent a bleak prospect for all categories of producer.

Federal, regional and state governments did, however, invest a total of over £N 179 million. Quite clearly, this sum was invested in structures underpinning economic development, and did not serve to finance directly productive activities. It can also be said that they flowed from the desire not to kill the goose that laid the golden eggs, the goose whose very existence was to be seriously threatened, at least in the northern parts of the country, by the natural calamities of the early 1970s.

The years 1973 and 1974 marked a turning point in Nigeria's agricultural policy. There were two reasons for this: 1) the natural calamities mentioned above revealed the intense fragility of a technologically backward peasant agriculture, the impotent victim of calamities such as drought, disease or attacks by parasites; 2) the post-1974 oil boom meant that the state no longer had to depend on surpluses generated by agriculture; and a large proportion of the substantial revenues accruing from oil was diverted to agriculture, principally in the form of large-scale agricultural development programmes: National Accelerated Food Production Programme (NAFPP), Agricultural Development Project (ADP), Agricultural Development Area (ADA), and the River Basin Development Authority (RBDA).

In the framework of these programmes, major public resources – estimated at over 11 billion Nairas between 1975 and 1985 – were made available to individual private farmers who, because of the limited technology to which they had access and knew how to use, were allocated small plots, which many were unable to develop, precisely because of the handicaps that apply to smallholders in general. This financial assistance also took the form of large and generous loans that led to large-scale privatization of large tracts of land all over the country at the expense of peasant producers.[55] Finally, it resulted in producer price level increases year by year. Table 6.1 shows the steep rises in all producer prices between 1973 and 1983–84.

Table 6.1
Producer prices 1973 and 1983–84

Product	1973	1983–84	Comment
Groundnuts	N80 or £N40	N450 or £N225	Price increased 5.62 times
Seed cotton	N132 or £N66	N560 or £N280	Price increased 4.24 times
Palm kernels	N61 or £N30.5	N230 or £N115	Price increased 3.77 times
Palm oil	N84 or £N42	N440 or N495 or £N220.00 or £N247.5	Price increased 5.23 times
Cocoa	N354 or £N177	N1,400.00 or £N700	Price increased 3.95 times

Source: Central Bank of Nigeria. *Annual Report and Statement of Accounts.*

Paradoxically, this period of rapid producer price rises, massive investments in agriculture and a generous credit policy corresponds to the decline and then collapse of industrial and export crops. Why?

The first explanation that suggests itself is that all the resources put at the disposal of agriculture and all the development programmes had, above all, the objective of promoting food crops: the urgent need was to feed the population. But that, for example, at least two of Nigeria's main industrial and export crops, groundnuts and palm oil, are also basic foodstuffs widely consumed throughout the country by all social strata was not taken into account.

The second explanation flows from the fact that even with the means currently available for the promotion of food crops, Nigerian agriculture, which occupies such a large percentage of the population, is increasingly incapable of feeding the population.

In the urban areas the 1974 oil boom led to the creation of numerous new opportunities for paid employment as well as a sudden and substantial improvement in all wage incomes; this, obviously, led to yet more migration to the towns. With a rapidly rising urban population enjoying reasonable incomes the demand for foodstuffs rose to unprecedented levels and concomitant price increases, thus cultivation of food crops became more lucrative than growing commercial and export crops, despite the increasingly attractive prices offered to producers of these latter. Failing any significant modernization of farming techniques and a consequent increase in productive capacity, the rural working population, numerically declining and becoming physically weaker (as a result of the fittest and most active age groups' departure to urban areas), concentrated its efforts on meeting its own needs, and with any available surpluses, try to meet urban needs. Today, however, urban demands for foodstuffs are less and less met by national agricultural production. This situation might be explained in the following way:

The peasantry, as we now know, does not seek to 'maximize profits from its "capital"' and the product of its labour 'is intended principally for subsistence, only a proportion of it being marketed'. In a country dominated by a peasant-type mode of production, as long as the urban population remains small compared to the rural population, the commercial exchanges feasible for the peasantry could suffice to satisfy the urban population's needs. But once the size of the urban population grows beyond a certain threshold (a threshold, in my opinion, crossed in Nigeria after 1974) the unreliable surpluses of a weakened peasantry with an outdated technology become totally inadequate to satisfy all the needs of the urban market, and these needs are not limited to foodstuffs but also include the raw materials required by the industrial establishments.

Nigeria, despite the upheavals consequent upon the oil boom, retained an agricultural development strategy based, almost entirely, on the peasantry. Inevitably, it seems, the current serious shortages of foodstuffs and raw materials are the outcome of this strategic choice.

Conclusion

1) The commercial and export products of agricultural origin traditionally grown in Africa are for the most part as vital for the populations and industries of Africa as they were and continue to be for overseas countries' economies. Thus,

they call for the same care and attention as might be granted food crops.

2) The Ivory Coast has proved that the possibilities for African agriculture are enormous and that agriculture is an adequately solid basic starting point for the economic development of African countries. The surpluses generated by agriculture alone have enabled the Ivory Coast today to have a relatively large industry, whose contribution to GNP reached 23% in 1982, and whose products represented 55% of total Ivorian exports in 1981–82. It is also principally due to agriculture that Ivorians today enjoy the highest annual per capita income in the West African sub-region, including Nigeria.[56]

3) The origin and class position of the Ivory Coast's ruling group have played a determining role in the successes recorded by its export agriculture, but they are also responsible for the enhanced relations of dependency of the Ivory Coast on the industrialized world.

4) Since independence, the state has played the role of pioneer and motor in regard to agricultural production for commerce and export in the Ivory Coast, a role it alone was able to undertake.

5) In Nigeria, where British colonialism's system of indirect rule enabled pre-capitalist modes of production and pre-colonial administrative systems to survive and even enjoy a degree of autonomy while favouring the emergence of an embryonic urban bourgeoisie, independence did not bring to power a homogeneous ruling group such as that in the Ivory Coast in terms of class origins; perhaps as a result of this heterogeneity, clearly defined class position has been identified. One consequence of this is the contradiction between a Nigerian social formation described as capitalist, and its agriculture, almost wholly organized on the basis of a pre-capitalist mode of production.

6) The peasant basis of Nigerian agriculture had intrinsic limitations that prevented it taking up the challenges of a process of urbanization on the scale experienced by Nigeria since 1974. Limitations that must be taken into account when attempting to apportion responsibility for the current agricultural crisis.

Notes

1. *Africa South of the Sahara, 1982–1983*.
2. S. O. Olayide and Dupe Olatunbosun, *Trends and Prospects of Nigeria's Agricultural Exports*, NISER, Ibadan 1975, p. 12.
3. *Marchés Tropicaux et Méditerranéens*, 2013, 8 June 1984, p. 1429.
4. *Africa South of the Sahara 1983–1984*, p. 441.
5. Olayide and Olatunbosun, op. cit., p. 27.
6. Ibid., pp. 18 and 28.
7. Ibid., pp. 17–18.
8. Ibid., p. 29.
9. *United Nations Demographic Yearbook, 1970*.
10. Jacques Baulin, *La politique intérieure d'Houphouët-Boigny*, Eurafo-Press, Paris 1982, pp. 93–4.
11. G. A. Kouassigan, 'Propriété foncière et dévelopement. Tendances générales

et options négro-africaines', in *Le Village Piégé*, Presses Universitaires de France, Paris and Cahiers de l'IUED, Geneva 1978, pp. 303–6.

12. Baulin, op. cit., pp. 94 and 151.

13. Samir Amin, *Le Développement du Capitalisme en Côte d'Ivoire*, Editions de Minuit, Paris 1967, p. 40.

14. Claude Meillassoux, *Anthropologie Economique des Gouro de Côte d'Ivoire*, Mouton, Paris 1964, pp. 327–37.

15. Amin, op. cit., p. 43.

16. *Bulletin de l'Afrique Noire* (Ediafric–La documentation africaine, Paris), 997, 28 March 1979, p. 19365.

17. Baulin, op. cit., p. 87.

18. *Africa Contemporary Record, 1971–1972*, Africa Research Ltd., London, p. B596.

19. Baulin, op. cit., p. 112.

20. Ibid., pp. 99 and 146.

21. Ibid., pp. 149 and 154–5.

22. *Le Président Houphouët-Boigny et la Nation Ivorienne*, Les Nouvelles Editions Africaines, Abidjan and Dakar 1975, pp. 209 and 212; Baulin, op. cit., pp. 149, 150.

23. *Africa Contemporary Record*, op. cit., p. B596.

24. Paul-Henri Siriex, *Félix Houphouët-Boigny, l'homme de la paix*, Seghers, Paris and Nouvelles Editions Africaines, Dakar and Abidjan 1975, p. 238.

25. Baulin, op. cit., p. 94.

26. Ibid., p. 152.

27. *Le Président Houphouët-Boigny et la Nation Ivoirienne*, op. cit., p. 183.

28. *Africa Contemporary Record, 1969–1970*, p. B502.

29. *Europe Outremer*, 657–658, October–November 1984, pp. 36–7.

30. See *Bulletin de l'Afrique Noire*: 1006, 6 June 1979; and 1175, 17 March 1983.

31. *Europe Outremer*, 657–658, October–November 1984.

32. *Bulletin de l'Afrique Noire*, 1175, 17 March 1983, pp. 6–7 and 5.

33. Amin, op. cit., pp. 73–4.

34. *Africa South of the Sahara 1983–84*, op. cit.

35. *Bulletin de l'Afrique Noire*: 1029, 19 December 1979, p. 19896; and 1183, 19 May 1983, p. 6.

36. Ibid., 986, 10 January 1979, p. 19186; and 996, 21 March 1979, pp. 19346–7.

37. See: *Europe Outremer*, op. cit., pp. 16–7; Bonnie K. Campbell, 'Inside the miracle. Cotton in the Ivory Coast', in *The Politics of Agriculture in Tropical Africa*, Sage Publications, London & New Delhi 1984, pp. 145–50; Mohamed S. Halfani and Jonathan Barker, 'Agribusiness and agrarian change', in *The Politics of Agriculture in Tropical Africa*, op. cit., p. 49; Siriex, op. cit., p. 235.

38. *Bulletin de l'Afrique Noire*: 986, 10 January 1979; and 1183, 19 May 1983.

39. *Africa South of the Sahara 1983–1984*.

40. Gouffern, op. cit., note at foot of p. 29.

41. Ibid., pp. 22–9.

42. Ibid., p. 29; Jean-François Médard, 'Jeunes et ainés en Côte d'Ivoire. Le VII congrès du PDCI-RDA', *Politique Africaine* I, 1, January 1981, p. 104.

43. *Jeune Afrique*: 1013, 4 June 1980, p. 60; 1048, 4 February 1981, p. 29; 1013, 4 June 1980, p. 60; and *Africa Contemporary Record 1980–1981*, pp. B515–B516.

44. *Jeune Afrique*: 1267, 17 April 1985, pp. 11–15; 1263, 20 March 1985, pp. 26–7.

45. *Europe Outremer*, op. cit., pp. 10–11.

46. *Jeune Afrique*: 1048, 4 February 1981, p. 29; 1013, 4 June 1980, pp. 58–62.

47. *Europe Outremer*, op. cit., p. 11.

48. Federal Republic of Nigeria, *Supplement to the Official Gazette Extraordinary*, vol. 65, 14, 29 March 1978, Part A.

49. See: C. K. Laurent, *Investment in Nigerian Tree Crops: Smallholder production*, NISER, University of Ibadan 1968, pp. 2 and 11; Gray, op. cit., pp. 202 and 209; Olayide and Olatunbosun, op. cit., pp. 12–13, 19 and 39; Jude Ejeke Njoku, 'The Nigerian ground-nut marketing scheme; the role of licensed buying agents', M.Sc. thesis, Ahmadu Bello University, June 1981.

50. Samir Amin, 'Le capitalisme et la rente foncière (la domination du capitalisme sur l'agriculture', in *La Question paysanne et le capitalisme*, Editions Anthropos, Paris 1974, pp. 37–8.

51. Ibid., pp. 9–10.

52. Gray, op. cit., p. 85.

53. Yahaya A. Abdullahi, 'Anatomy of Nigerian agricultural crisis', *The Triumph*, Vol. 1, No. 5, 5 October 1985, pp. 11–12.

54. Central Bank of Nigeria, *Annual Report*, 1974.

55. Federal Ministry of Agriculture, Lagos, *Information Bulletin on Nigerian Agriculture*, January 1984; Yahaya A. Abdullahi, op. cit., p. 12.

56. World Bank, *Towards Sustained Development in Sub-Saharan Africa*, Washington, DC, 1984, pp. 59 and 57; *Bulletin de l'Afrique Noire*, 1198, 6 October 1983, p. 6.

7. Ivory Coast: Agricultural and Industrial Development

Aly Traoré

Introduction

In common with most development models in underdeveloped countries since their political independence, those of African countries have usually been inspired by a global development strategy based on the theory of the international specialization of labour and comparative advantage. According to this strategy, underdeveloped countries' interest lies in exporting to industrialized countries those factors of production that they possess in abundance, particularly agricultural, mineral and energy raw materials. This will enable them to obtain foreign exchange that, in turn will enable them to buy capital goods for their industrialization.

Twenty-five years after political independence this development strategy has proved to be disappointing for most African countries.[1] The Ivory Coast is, however, one of the rare exceptions. Numerous factors explain the relative success of the economic experience, and the development model, of the Ivory Coast. First, although possessing few mineral resources,[2] the Ivory Coast is favourably endowed with varied natural conditions that enable agriculture to serve as 'the basis and the motor' of its economic and social development. Secondly, the Ivorian development model is a liberal one, widely open to the outside world and 'regulated' by a presidential single-party system, with flexible planning and a major role for the state. This development model which, 'without being socialist seeks to realize a very bold social policy' aspires in the long run to establish a 'popular capitalism'.[3]

Finally, not only has this model rested on the intensive exploitation and export of the raw products of cash-crop agriculture but also it has sought, with some success, to establish relations between agriculture and industry, through an industrialization strategy based on agro-industry in general and the agricultural foodstuffs industry in particular.

This study is divided into two parts: 1) the role of agriculture in Ivorian industrial development; and 2) the industrialization strategy and the underlying significance of the relations between agriculture and industry for Ivorian economic development.

The role of agriculture in Ivorian industrial development

Historically, as at present, the supreme importance of agriculture in economic development in general and industrial development in particular, especially in the first stages of economic growth, is once again being demonstrated in the Ivorian economic experience.

The primary sector, which includes agriculture narrowly defined (livestock, fishing and forest products) can be divided into two sub-sectors: 1) food agriculture, largely left to its own devices; and 2) export agriculture, quite well organized by the government. The relations that have historically existed between these two sub-sectors can be described as 'conflictual', because, during the process of economic growth, export agriculture tends increasingly to deprive food agriculture of those factors of production – land, labour and capital – that it needs in order to attain national food self-sufficiency.[4]

Food agriculture

Clearly, agriculture's food production capacity plays a vital role in all economic development and especially in that of underdeveloped countries, because: 1) their people must be decently fed so that, among other things, production in the various sectors of the economy can be increased; 2) their people must receive adequate incomes by providing them with jobs, in this case in agriculture; 3) food agriculture must contribute to the growth of other sectors, above all, by providing the industrial sector with cheap labour, raw materials and sometimes, financial surpluses.

Most countries in sub-Saharan Africa have largely failed to grasp the key role of food agriculture in their development and, therefore, fall increasingly victim to famine. Of course, in common with many African countries[5] in the Ivory Coast too, there is a degree of malnutrition, but it has neither experienced famine, nor attained total independence in food. And, as its development proceeds, the imperative of the development of food agriculture becomes more urgent, not only because of the agricultural vocation of the country, but also because of the rapid acceleration of demographic, urban and economic growth. Since independence, the population, which includes many foreigners, has increased by an average of 4% per annum; urbanization at 10% per annum; and economic growth, in money terms at 8% per annum. Nevertheless, until 1960, Ivorian peasants engaged in food agriculture had, using only their traditional tools (the *daba* and the cutlass), provided almost all the staple foodstuffs except for rice, self-sufficiency in which has not yet been attained.

It has been estimated[6] that while the majority of self-sufficiency ratios in various staple products (rice, maize and other cereals, yams, cassava, plantains and taro) were satisfactory in 1985, they will tend to fall dangerously by the 1990s. If, however, the authorities take appropriate measures (currently being prepared) to halt this downward trend, self-sufficiency in these staples would be attained and, maintained, except for rice.

The production of animal proteins is less satisfactory. By 1986, self-sufficiency had been virtually achieved in poultry and pig-meat production, and the government was attempting to improve cattle, goat, and sheep production in order to enable the food sub-sector to play its full role in this area for the future of the economy and the industrial sector.

In addition to feeding the country's population, agriculture as a whole contributes to general economic development by providing jobs and incomes to rural workers – which thus makes it possible to stimulate the growth of GDP. The agricultural sector in the broad sense makes a considerable contribution to the formation of GDP, and food agriculture's contribution is far from insignificant: in 1980 it was virtually equivalent to half the value of total production of the primary sector.[7]

In most countries' economic development relations between agriculture and industry are marked by the reciprocal supply of 'factors' from agriculture to industry and from industry to agriculture. These 'factors' include: food products, cheap labour, raw materials to be processed and some financial surplus derived from the food sub-sector. In the Ivory Coast, however, every 'factor' supplied by food agriculture to industry comes not only from internal sources, but, for example, animal products may equally well come from neighbouring countries (Mali, Burkina Faso, among others) as from Ivorian livestock.

The Ivorian food sub-sector supplies workers in industry with all the tubers (yams, cassava, taro, sweet potatoes) and most cereals (millet, sorghum, fonio and maize); only rice (half of needs) and all the wheat are imported. With the new policy of food self-sufficiency currently being put into effect, rice imports are declining as national production rises, and there is still hope of achieving self-sufficiency in rice by the 1990s.

Self-sufficiency in the supply of poultry and pig-meat already achieved must be maintained and the production of a degree of abundance to make exports possible should be attempted. For other animal products (cattle, sheep and goats) including fish products, the food sub-sector is largely dependent (about 50%) on external sources.

Agricultural labour employed by Ivorian industrial enterprises originates in both the food and the export agriculture sub-sectors and comprises both Ivorian rural workers and those from neighbouring countries such as Mali and Burkina Faso.[8] The exodus of rural workers to Ivorian towns and industries is due principally to a desire to enjoy 'better working and living conditions' in the urban centres, rather than, as is usually the cause, lack of gainful employment in the countryside. As urban centres are increasingly overburdened with those seeking employment, and industries and services are unable to absorb them all, food needs in the towns increase, along with potential shortages of this or that foodstuff. (It should be noted that while the growth rate in industrial jobs is around only 5% per annum, urban growth has been 10% per annum and industrial growth 12% per annum.) Overall, the consequences of this rural exodus on economic development, especially industrial development, while stabilizing wages, and hence workers' purchasing power, reduces food production in the countryside and, rather than reinforcing the links between agriculture and industry, promotes economic and social decay in the urban areas. In response to this the government is considering a call for 'return of the youth to the land', which it is hoped will both 'decongest' the urban areas and step up agricultural production in the rural areas; and thus lead to an increased supply of agricultural raw materials to agro-industrial sector.

A scrutiny of agricultural supplies to industry shows that those from export agriculture (to which we shall return below) clearly exceed those from food agriculture. Food agriculture's potential production is, however, far from exhausted and so far, the quantities available are at times insufficient to satisfy domestic demand. Some food products (all tubers except cassava and all cereals except wheat) supply industrial raw materials for initial processing only, since scientific and technical mastery of stocking, canning and processing has not yet been achieved. Progress is, however, being made: the cassava processing factory at Toumodi seems to be a successful result of the much sought after technical progress.

In short, interactions between food agriculture and industry are by no means adequate. In order for food agricultural production to contribute adequately to the country's economic and social development a successful policy of food self-sufficiency and scientific, technical and economic expertise in food processing are essential.

Export agriculture

The Ivory Coast's development is still based on the strategic role of cash crops such as coffee, cocoa, bananas and even timber, which means not only that these products launched the growth of the economy, by monetizing it, but also that the incentive nature of their economic relations with food agriculture and with industry and commerce underpins that growth.

The cash crop products (coffee, cocoa and timber) that have formed the core of this development strategy were later reinforced in their role by such secondary agricultural export crops as bananas, pineapples and, post-1965, commercial crops embarked upon by the crop diversification policy.

The agricultural sub-sector that produces the main export crops (coffee, cocoa, timber) has to provide industry with manpower, financial flows and raw materials for processing.

In order to contribute to the country's economic and industrial development the food agriculture sub-sector is fundamentally dependent on export agriculture in that, as the economy develops, the food sub-sector provides factors of production to the export sub-sector, in particular land and labour, as well as food. In exchange, the food sub-sector receives a financial return that contributes to its monetization and integration into the national capitalist system. But, because the economy undervalues and underpays the food sub-sector for these factors of production – owing to the deterioration of domestic trade terms and exorbitant levies extorted by commercial middlemen – it generates little surplus, even for essential self-financing.

But agricultural sub-sectors contribute to the transfer of workers to the urban areas and their industries. It is the economic and social consequences of a haphazard rural–urban move that have led the Ivorian government to attempt to organize a return of the youth to the land, in the hopes of establishing a possible long-term rationalization of labour use both in the rural and urban areas.

Cocoa, coffee and timber export earnings, for the economy in general and industry in particular, have risen as follows: 1) cocoa: from Francs CFA 226.6 billion in 1980 to 319.7 billion in 1983; 2) coffee: from Francs CFA 134.49 billion in 1980 to 179.83 billion in 1983; 3) timber (logs and sawn): from Francs CFA 123.7 billion in 1980 to 96.9 billion in 1983. In total, the three products have provided the Ivorian economy with export receipts that have increased from Frances CFA 493.79 billion in 1980 to 496.43 billion in 1983.

A not insignificant proportion of these receipts – difficult to estimate precisely – contributes to Ivorian industrial development in the form of state shareholding in the 'social capital' of state companies or mixed state–private companies, state investments, the Stabilization Fund and investments by a number of Ivorians including some big coffee and cocoa planters and forest developers. Small Ivorian planters' participation in the investments is indirect, through state levies (the Stabilization Fund) on the international prices of coffee and cocoa.

These three products also supply raw materials to the industrial sector. The average percentage of unroasted coffee processed is 5% per annum of total coffee sold, that of cocoa, which is much larger, averages 25% per annum of total beans marketed. But it must be noted that whereas coffee is completely processed to the final product: Nescafé, cocoa beans undergo only preliminary processing to obtain cocoa paste and cocoa butter for export to the developed countries.

Crop diversification

The crop diversification policy, launched after 1965, was intended to attain three essential objectives:[9]

(1) to reduce regional disparities, which had been aggravated above all by the promotion of export crops in the southern forest at the expense of the northern savanna locked into subsistence production;

(2) to increase total export receipts, as the Ivory Coast is increasingly confronted with the effects of climatic variations and the deterioration of the terms of trade;

(3) to promote a dynamic agro-industrial sector, which would have as its driving force the agricultural foodstuffs industries and mainly use raw materials from local commercial crops.

The crop diversification policy led to the introduction of new crops such as soya beans and cashew nuts, and to the transfer of some crops from one region to another in order to improve the quality and productivity of commercial crops already in production: pineapples and rubber, amongst others. Finally, other commercial crops were to play a vitally important role in the economic development strategy and the struggle against regional disparities: cotton in the north; and oil palm and coconuts in the south.

In the north three crops were launched to enable the peoples of the area to increase their monetary incomes: paddy rice, sugar-cane and cotton.

The cultivation of seed cotton enabled the producers and the various producing regions to procure not insignificant receipts, as Table 7.1A and B shows.

Table 7.1A
Output and producer incomes

Season	Total production (metric tons)	Prices per kg (Francs CFA)	Total producer incomes (million Francs CFA)
1980–81	136,603	80	10,928
1981–82	135,370	80	10,829
1982–83	156,981	80	12,559
1983–84	142,283	100	14,228

Table 7.1B
Production by region
(metric tons)

Season	North	West	Centre
1980–81	62,136	43,604	30,863
1981–82	68,945	38,048	28,377
1982–83	69,476	48,507	38,999
1983–84	72,822	43,709	25,752
1983–84 value in million Francs CFA	7,282.2	4,370.9	2,575.2

Source: Bulletin de l'Afrique Noire, 1257, 24 January 1985, p. 8.

Of total production of seed cotton, once ginned, 25% went to local industries and 75% for export, the value of exports increasing from 14,593 million CFA Francs in 1980 to 31,929 in 1983.[10]

In the south oil palm and coconuts play a key role in the Ivory Coast's agro-industrial policy. The oil palm programme, launched by the government in 1963, was entrusted to the 'Société pour le développement et l'exploitation du palmier à l'huile' (Oil palm development and exploitation company) which subsequently became a state company, Palmindustrie, with outside participation. Major investments in the oil palm and coconut programme, totalling 83.4 billion Francs CFA, were financed by the Ivorian state, the World Bank, the EEC and a few smaller bodies.[11] In 1981–82 turnover reached 30 billion Francs CFA, due to bringing large areas of oil palms and coconuts into production.

This programme aimed to create industrial plantations with a very high technical level, around which Palmindustrie would develop and supervise village plantations to enable small peasants to increase their money incomes. Also, the possibilities of forage growing beneath the palms would be exploited in order to carry on livestock farming. This programme made it possible to bring large areas of land into cultivation: for oil palms; 52,000 hectares of industrial plantations and 38.000 hectares of village plantations; and for coconut palms 19,000 hectares, and 10,000 hectares respectively.[12] In Table 7.2A and B the respective productions of palm aggregates and copra may be seen in context.

Table 7.2A
Production of palm aggregates
('000 metric tons)

	1981–82	*1982–83*	*1983–84*
Industrial plantations (Palmindustrie)	500.8	514.6	503.3
Village plantations	197.1	176.7	176.1
Other industrial plantations	81.6	78.1	76.6
*Total**	*785.5*	*769.2*	*756.0*

Table 7.2B.
Production of copra
('000 metric tons)

	1981–82	*1982–83*	*1983–84*
Industrial plantations (Palmindustrie)	15.83	20.10	21.79
Family plantations	13.16	13.82	6.69
Others 12T, SICOR, various	5.52	6.16	6.17
Total	*34.51*	*40.08*	*34.65*

* The total does not include natural palm groves' production.
Source: Bulletin de l'Afrique Noire, 1257, 24 January 1985, pp. 10 and 11.

Virtually all the fruit produced in the oil palm and coconut plantations is processed locally, and today, the Ivory Coast is the leading African exporter and the third world exporter of palm oil.

The industrialization strategy

Generally, relations between agriculture and industry exist in a framework either of an industrialization strategy with an internal dynamic directed toward economic self-development, or a strategy with an external dynamic, tending to integrate the economy into the international capitalist system.

For African countries, Gérard Destanne de Bernis,[13] Samir Amin and Albert Tévoedjrè among others, favour the former strategy. Thus, de Bernis starts from the basic idea that after political independence, industrialization is vital for development of a Third World country. But because these countries are predominantly agricultural, especially Africa, 'the essential issue is thus to increase agricultural income which is linked to raising the productivity of agricultural labour'. Agricultural productivity can be increased in two ways: 1) by improving already existing structures thus increasing production and incomes by economic, administrative and social advances in organization: 2) through the creation upstream from the agricultural sector of basic industries such as steel-making, chemicals, cement and so on, in order to supply agriculture with the production tools necessary for increased productivity, implying increased agricultural incomes, partly for the purchase of industrial goods.

For mini-states, however, the application of de Bernis' model poses major difficulties. In such cases he proposes planning and co-operation among, or regroupings of states: states that seek to apply the model individually must have substantial economic and human potentials.

Algeria has opted for this type of internally driven industrialization but it is, perhaps, too soon to assess its performance.[14] Nevertheless, it seems that the country has been enabled to: 1) develop a production goods industrial sector supplying agriculture with 60% of its machinery; 2) create a large number of jobs for both rural and urban populations; and 3) substantially increase rural wages and peasant incomes.

This strategy has not, however, been problem free. The Algerian state successfully equipped, even over-equipped the rural areas by heavily subsidizing agricultural production goods, but it has failed either to avoid substituting machines (and hence capital) for labour or to adequately increase agricultural productivity, because production techniques have remained more or less unchanged. The priority given to industry has been partly responsible for massive food shortages and imports and, finally, the high cost of this strategy has, despite its oil wealth, put Algeria among the world's biggest debtors.[15]

Some African countries, including the Ivory Coast, have opted for a 'light industrialization' strategy based on both a policy of import substitution and adding value to natural resources for export.

> In fact, it is generally thought that for most underdeveloped countries: light consumer industries require less capital than heavy industries; by producing for domestic demand goods that can replace previously imported goods, light industries enable our countries to save foreign exchange while helping to mop up under-employment in the urban areas; by establishing links with agriculture, these light industries can accelerate agricultural development since they provide the peasants with consumer goods and some production goods such as pipes, irrigation pumps and sprayers.[16]

Once properly established and well organized in African countries, it is thought that light industries can yield an abundant surplus both for self-financing and for national economic development. Most light industries in underdeveloped countries, however, do not achieve these objectives. Investments are smaller than for heavy industry, but underdeveloped countries are obliged to resort to external capital, technology and senior staff, which leads to the repatriation of a substantial proportion of any surplus these enterprises may yield. Furthermore, in their import-substitution form, light industries are soon confronted with the problem of the market open to them being too small: the population, especially the working population, is small, incomes are low and usually unequally distributed, and imports from developed countries compete with locally manufactured goods.

Light industries' effect on agriculture is limited because agricultural production goods are not manufactured locally, and import costs are excessively high for underdeveloped countries. Finally, the articulation between agriculture and industry which seeks knock-on effects through an external dynamic not only makes modernization of agriculture impossible but may also lead to incomes stagnating and the transfer abroad of most of the surplus.

But what has been the practical experience of such industrialization in the Ivory Coast, a country with an obvious agricultural vocation, which has exploited its numerous food and agricultural export resources to promote import-substitution industries and industries to add value to natural resources for export? Such a strategy has been facilitated by the existence of a variety of raw materials, and an abundant labour force comprising both nationals and immigrants from neighbouring African countries. The development strategy's liberal character favoured the import of Western capital, technology and senior expatriate staff. Consequently, as we have already noted, the Ivory Coast has experienced exceptionally rapid industrial growth, reaching a rate of 12% per annum despite the negative effects of the world economic crisis since the early 1970s.

We have already looked at the degree of local processing of raw agricultural products and noted that some advances have been made in the 1980s, but what would be the possibility of exporting these products if the Ivory Coast succeeded in locally processing larger quantities? These possibilities are, in principle, rather limited for processed cocoa and coffee products, as the developed capitalist countries, which have a monopoly of processing, will ensure that their market is protected, and additionally will seek to control the creation of processing structures in underdeveloped countries, especially in Africa. Thus, currently the processing of 5% of the Ivory Coast's production of unroasted coffee into Nescafé is undertaken by CAPRAL (Compagnie Africaine de Produits Alimentaires), a subsidiary of the Nestlé group. The primary and secondary processings of undergrade cocoa beans, representing 25% of the country's production, are carried out by three subsidiaries of the Cacao-Barry group and a subsidiary of the Swiss group Interfood.[17] Consequently, that the Western multinationals have a monopoly of the industrial processing, the marketing, and demand for coffee and cocoa, leaves little scope for the Ivory Coast to seek to secure most of the economic surplus of its coffee and cocoa production, especially as the African market for these products is limited (average consumption of chocolate per person in the Ivory Coast, for example, is 100g per annum; in Switzerland it is 10 kg).

A significant potential does exist in the Ivory Coast for processing timber and cotton, particularly as there is the possibility of local and wider African demand, owing to co-operation agreements between such bodies as ECOWAS (Economic Community of West African States).

The processing of such products as bananas, pineapples, oil palm and copra, for example, as has already been noted, is carried out by enterprises in which most of the shares belong to either the Ivorian state (Palmindustrie), Ivorian private interests (pineapples) or foreign interests (bananas), and the packaged and processed products are almost all exported to the West; and, as Western countries provide much of the investment, senior personnel and the technology of agricultural holdings and processing industries, their socio-economic grasp is strong.

Without the necessary technological input the autonomous capacity of underdeveloped countries for local production of capital goods to modernize their industry and agriculture is seriously limited. The Ivory Coast is, in fact, obliged to import most of its industrial and agricultural capital goods. It, nevertheless, has units producing cement and concrete, iron rods, fertilizers,[18] and cutlasses for the agricultural sector.

In producing cement, however, Ivorian industry exercises very little dynamic effect on agriculture. The country's peasants cannot afford to use cement to build either rural shops or housing, and if they buy cutlasses and *daba*s, it is to maintain their traditional farming techniques rather than to increase their productivity. Some peasants do use fertilizers, at prices, long subsidized by government, they can afford. To encourage cotton production the government used to give fertilizers to peasants, but this policy has ended.

The government organizes the structures of incentives for agronomic research (in the hands of IDESA, Institut de la Savane), production techniques (CIMA, Centre Ivorien de Machinisme Agricole) and the use of machinery in agriculture. Thus, in order to speed up the effects of the food self-sufficiency policy, the Ministry of Rural Development, through Motor-Agri (a large stock of machinery to intervene effectively in the agricultural sector), has been carrying out free clearings to enable the peasants organized in 'groupements à vocation coopérative' (G.V.C.) to expand their production and incomes. Thus, in order to make up for the economic deficiencies of the association between agriculture and industry the Ivorian government is obliged to grant more and more costly subsidies whose effects do not seem to guarantee the expected development.

In every country and under every form of government, the relationship between industry and agriculture is economically deficient. This is especially true for developing countries. The industry that is established exercises a structural hold over agriculture. It develops only the profitable crops or those vital to its functioning. For economic reasons (technology, productivity), industry has a superiority over agriculture. The industries themselves and industry as a whole must be organized so that the dynamic effects benefit the whole population of the developing country.[19]

This statement sums up the immediate contemporary history of the principal economic and social facts of all underdeveloped countries. Temporarily, a good relationship between agriculture and industry can result in economic and social benefits for the whole population; a bad relationship may result in dependency, stagnation and impoverishment of the underdeveloped economy compared to the industrialized economies. Perroux explains that 'in the developing countries, finance is interested in activities that serve industry and, in the absence of corrections by the government, it pays far less attention to agriculture . . . and even less again to farmers'.[20] Despite certain 'corrections' made by our planners, the Ivorian development model still involves the domination of export over food agriculture and of the industrial over the agricultural sector as a whole, (as is evidenced by the priority granted to factors of industrial production by the state and external interests) although agriculture remains both 'the base and the motor' of development. In respecting this sectoral ranking of the fact that 'finance makes industry and industry makes the economy',[21] relations between agriculture and industry have a particular economic and social significance in the Ivory Coast.

As already noted, the 'factors' supplied by the agricultural to the industrial sector are agricultural labour, agricultural raw materials, and financial surplus. Initially labour was recruited by industry mainly from the rural areas and neighbouring African countries. The situation has, however, been complicated because not only has labour been made available to industry by the rural–urban migration, but also is available from the original urban population.

The majority of the economically active population in the food agriculture sub-sector is Ivorian, that in the export agriculture sub-sector is probably only half Ivorian and half Africans from neighbouring countries. In seeking better working conditions and pay, agricultural workers either opt to move from food to export agriculture, or migrate to urban areas, where the growth rate, as already observed, averages 10% per annum. The subsequent flow of job-seekers cannot be absorbed by industry with an average annual growth 12%, but only a 5% average annual increase in jobs.

At the level of population movements, the economy is increasingly experiencing distortions that militate against integration between agriculture and industry. On one hand, there is a shortage of manpower in the agricultural sector, hence the call for a 'return to the land'; on the other, at the industrial level there is competition between Ivorian and other African manpower and between Ivorian and expatriate managers. (The escalating unemployment in the Ivory Coast led an agreement with France (1985) to repatriate 2,000 French technical assistants within a few years.)

The wages of migrants (African and expatriate) are likely to be partly repatriated outside the Ivory Coast; those of Ivorians may be partly saved and hence accumulated within the country's borders. As early as 1969[22] with approximately the same ratios among the groups (63.36% Ivorians; 32.48% migrant Africans; 4.15% non-African), 5% of expatriates collected 35% of the total wage bill, a substantial part of which was repatriated by European managers and obviously unavailable for accumulation in the Ivory Coast.

Historically, agricultural development has not proceeded in the same way for all cash crops. The main agricultural export crops such as coffee and cocoa were for decades labour-intensive with minimal capital needs, and enabled agricultural workers to earn substantial incomes and the state to acquire substantial surpluses – 40% of the international prices.

But the use of more and more capital to rehabilitate old, unproductive plantations, and the worsening of the outcome of the deterioration of trade terms, mean that the reduction of surplus acquired by the state is particularly problematic since the state faces a socio-political necessity to maintain, even increase the producer purchase prices of these products each year. Virtually all the coffee and cocoa is processed in Western factories, therefore, cultivation of these major export crops is fundamentally linked to the developed capitalist countries' industries. And the relatively advanced local processing of coconut and oil palm products, pineapples and sugar-cane is even more dependent on the West because that is the source of vast amounts of vitally essential capital, personnel and sophisticated technology.

The Ivory Coast's agricultural sector has a large potential demand for industrial consumer and capital goods. But the peasants' purchasing power, and food agriculture peasants in particular, as well as that of the majority of the population, is limited, therefore, they cannot afford to purchase these goods that, locally produced or imported, carry a high price.

An analysis of the Ivory Coast's external trade tables for 1983[23] shows: 1) that for exports, over 50% of the total value of 796.8 billion Francs CFA derived from the sale to developed countries of agricultural and forest raw materials; 2) for imports, with a total value of 704.3 billion Francs CFA, were for the following items: steel products, fertilizers, mechanical, electrical, and transport equipment 173.55; cereals, milk products and fish 96.24; plastics, rubber and synthetics 34.90; chemical and pharmaceutical products 35.64; petroleum products 130.45; others 233.52.

The structure of exports, essentially of agricultural raw materials, and the structure of imports, of which the first two items particularly concern industrial development, reveal a fundamental structural disarticulation between agriculture and industry. This can be partially imputed to the agricultural sector's low productivity and the downward trend of its financial surplus, due to the deterioration of the trade terms. Nevertheless, this sector still provides sufficient 'factors' of production (especially financial surplus) not only to industry but to the whole economy, for which it still provides 'the base and motor' of development.

The same can hardly be said of the industrial sector's role in the economy. Since its creation in 1960, its average annual growth rate has been around 12%; its turnover rose from 13 billion Francs CFA in 1960 to 1,170 billion in 1983; its total wage bill rose from seven billion Francs CFA in 1960 to 105.77 billion in 1983 and so on, but it is not only handicapped by certain structural imbalances,[24] but its dependence on external sources, and growing indebtedness, militate against it becoming an active force in the development of the agricultural sector.

Industrial indebtedness, greatly increased by crude petroleum imports (72,413 million Francs CFA in 1980, 78,892 in 1983), refined in Abidjan and partly re-exported, must have been greatly reduced since the take-off in recent years of the exploitation of two petroleum deposits, 'Bélier' off Grand-Bassam, and 'Espoir' off Jacqueville,[25] which are about to give the Ivory Coast oil self-sufficiency. At the level of the economy as a whole and of the agricultural and industrial sectors in particular, the Ivorian authorities are attempting to move towards a number of reforms in order to give the development of the country a stronger impetus.

The structural nature of the difficulties encountered by the Ivory Coast over the last decade in pursuit of its development, imply that the reforms envisaged must be toward a transition from extraverted to autocentred capitalism, or auto-development: development organized and administered essentially by and for nationals. And, as formerly for the currently industrialized countries, auto-development must be based on the principle of 'self-reliance', not excluding multifaceted, fruitful co-operation with most foreign countries. For the Ivory Coast the transition to auto-development necessitates structural reforms at both the sectoral level and at the level of nationals so that expanded capital accumulation can gradually render the national economy self-dynamizing and self-sustaining.

This restructuring must first aim at establishing an adequate balance between agricultural production for export, which is relatively abundant, and food agricultural production which is still insufficient, followed by promoting increasing productivity in both forms of agriculture. Concretely, the dominance of export over food agriculture must be gradually reduced by transferring a proportion of the factors of production (land, labour, capital and technical back-up) from the former to the latter; export agriculture benefits substantially from these factors which, until recently, were unavailable to food agriculture.

Raising the productivity of the two agricultural sub-sectors must be done in conformity with national socio-cultural requirements but in the light of the irreversible demands of scientific and technical progress; the Ivory Coast already has a number of research institutes that have achieved valuable results. This will enable both agriculture sectors to be internationally competitive while freeing land at the national level; part of food agriculture's products, once it has become self-sufficient, can be exported to other African countries whose food needs are not always being met. When well developed, both sectors will provide a solid basis for the development of the agro-industrial sector and the industrial sector.

As in most underdeveloped countries, the ills that plague Ivorian industry are numerous: excessive concentration in the city of Abidjan and the surrounding area; high costs of intermediate goods and imported raw materials, which account for some 40% of all raw materials used in the industrial sector;[26] the relatively low proportion of local raw materials processed within the country; the small national market; unequal relations between the 'dominating' exterior and the apparently 'consenting' nationals on the desirability, or otherwise, of control and national accumulation of a large proportion of the industrial surplus.[27]

Generally, it is accepted that whoever holds the majority capital of a firm has a commanding voice in all big decisions involving the firm. Thus, in 1960, faced with the weakness of Ivorian private capital, the state decided to participate on a provisional basis in financing most big firms; later to grant back its shares to the private sector when it was in a position to take over efficiently. The result was a distribution of the capital of industrial firms as is shown in Table 7.3.

Table 7.3
Distribution of capital in industry by country of origin (%) (Ivory Coast)

Year	Ivory Coast	France	Other capitalist countries	African countries
1974	35.80	39.17	23.36	1.67
1975	39.97	36.49	18.16	5.38
1981	61.81	21.29	14.31	2.63
1982	64.42	20.51	12.75	2.32
1983	66.31	19.43	12.05	2.21

Source: Special issue of *Marchés Tropicaux et Méditerranéens*, op. cit., p. 117.

In 1983 total capital was estimated at 367.4 billion Francs CFA. Table 7.3 illustrates how the Ivory Coast (state and Ivorian private capital) became the majority share-holder by 1975 and by 1983 held 66.31% of total shares. Theoretically, since 1975, the Ivory Coast has a dominant voice in the direction, management and distribution of their surplus. But, in practice, it is not as simple. In addition to control of the capital there is the effective and overriding control of industrial firms' principal strategic structures, which is achieved through current investments, technology and senior management. In the Ivory Coast these factors of production are largely supplied by international financial institutions and developed market economy countries who, therefore, ultimately have the preponderant voice in most important decisions on the choice and nature of investments, and the balance of relations between wages and profits. They are thus able to appropriate a substantial proportion of the overall surplus of these firms,[28] while remaining the favoured creditors of African countries in general and of the Ivory Coast in particular.[29] It thus appears vital that Ivorians should attempt to contribute actively to the restructuring of their economy in order to be able to participate more and participate effectively in the process of accumulating the national surplus.

Share percentages in the private and public sectors have changed between 1980 and 1983: private sector shares were, 7.9% in 1980; 13.4% in 1981; 12.4% in 1982; and 16.7% in 1983; public sector shares for the same years were 92.1%, 86.6%, 87.6% and 83.3% respectively.[30]

Although there has been an increase in the private sector's involvement it is not sufficient to permit the state's disengagement. (Disengagement by the state and accelerated national privatization are, however, conditions contained in the Ivory Coast's Structural Adjustment Plan.) In this situation any policy to increase privatization of the Ivory Coast's economy will strengthen the hold of the outside world on it. On the other hand, for African countries as for the Ivory Coast, the quest for even minimum autonomous national economic development implies strengthening and rationalizing the economic role of the state and the national bourgeoisie.[31] Thus, what is needed is for the state 1) to declare and apply the political will; 2) to conceive, prepare and follow through planning and 3) to ensure proper and profitable management of its sector. Additionally, the Ivory Coast's state must act as arbiter between the outside world and the private sector in which the bourgeoisie, conscious of its national responsibilities, must become more a producer than a consumer. But such a policy will be successful only if it meets the basic needs of the population: food, housing, health, education and adequately paid jobs. Such a policy of giving responsibility to nationals in a liberal economy is not incompatible with a real and equitable international co-operation that would enable both the developed and underdeveloped countries to benefit.

The strategy of extraverted industrialization, adopted by the Ivory Coast since political independence, initially enabled its economy in general and industry to particular to experience rapid growth, but this same strategy is partly responsible for the economic and social difficulties the country has encountered for about a decade. Consequently, a restructuring of the economy, toward even minimal autonomy, by strengthening the role of nationals, is inevitable.

Conclusion

Agriculture, up to the present, remains 'the base and the motor' of Ivorian economic development, while industry, despite some undeniable successes, has been unable to consolidate agriculture's leading role in the economy.

Despite far from adequate means of production, the food agriculture sub-sector has on the whole adequately fed the Ivorian people, but it still remains only potentially able to speedily achieve food self-sufficiency, strengthen its foodstuff industry and increase its foreign exchange receipts through exports of processed food products.

Export agriculture, despite its valuable financial surpluses, is affected internally by drought and externally by deterioration of the trade terms. A decisive policy of diversification, and local processing of its products, may enable it to continue to sustain the Ivorian economy.

Finally, only by establishing an adequately balanced relationship between the productions of the two agricultural sectors, and significantly improving their productivity can they constitute a solid starting point for establishing relations between agriculture and industry, without which there is no real autonomous development. And, in accordance with the Ivory Coast's liberal option, a rigorous industrial restructuring under state leadership, with its nationals fully in the control of the economy and the process of accumulation, are vital for embarking on autonomous growth, and resolving financial and social problems if the Ivorian people's essential needs are to be fully met.

Notes

1. Summit Conference of African Heads of State in Lagos, 28–29 April 1980, in the Lagos Plan of Action, ECM/ECCR/9, (XIV), Rev. 3, 163 pp.

2. Oil was discovered in the 1970s; two deposits are currently being exploited: the 'Bélier' off Grand-Bassam, on stream in 1980; and the 'Espoir' off Jacqueville, on stream in 1982. In 1984, combined total production was estimated at 1,100,000 metric tons against national consumption in the same year of 1,146,000 metric tons, indicating a move towards oil self-sufficiency.

3. Diawara, M. T. 'Quelques réflexions sur la stratégie du développement économique.' PDCI-RDA seminar, Abidjan 21–22 May 1971. Mimeo.

4. See my 'Le problématique de l'autosuffisance alimentaire en Côte d'Ivoire', *Annales de l'Université d'Abidjan*, Série K (Sciences Economiques), Vol. VI, pp. 56–57.

5. Ibid., p. 54.

6. Estimated from two tables in *Livre vert de l'autosuffisance alimentaire*, Abidjan, Edition de 'Fraternité Hebdo', February 1983.

7. See estimates in the Five-year Economic and Social Development Plan for the Ivory Coast 1981–85, Vol. 1, Table 21, p. 143 which places the value of food agriculture at 334.9 billion Francs CFA in 1980 and 430.8 billion Francs CFA in 1985.

8. Raymond Déniel, *De la savane à la ville. Essai sur la migration des Mossi vers Abidjan et sa région*. Paris, Aubier-Montaigne 1968.

9. See Oupoh Oupoh's doctoral thesis 'Le processus d'industrialisation dans une économie à croissance agricole. Le cas de la Côte d'Ivoire', University of Clermont I, 1979, pp. 131 ff.

10. *Bulletin d'Afrique Noire*, 1251, 29 November 1984, p. 6.

11. See Palmindustrie, *Bilan*, 1985.

12. Ibid.

13. Gérard Destanne de Bernis, 'Contribution à l'analyse des voies africaines du socialisme', course at the IEDES, Paris, 1964–65; Samir Amin, *L'Accumulation à l'échelle mondiale*, Paris, Editions Anthropos 1970; Albert Tévoedjrè, *La Pauvreté, richesse des peuples*, Paris, Editions Economie et Humanisme, 1978. De Bernis, (op. cit., p. 4) defines industrialization as 'the structuring of a whole social set under the influence of an ordered complex of machines'. See also Marc Raffinot and Pierre Jacquemot, *Le Capitalisme d'état algérien*, Paris, François Maspero 1977, 396 pp., pp. 142–7, 'La théorie de l'intégration de G. Destanne de Bernis'.

14. See, however, Marc Raffinot and Pierre Jacquemot, op. cit., which analyses the Algerian experience, its successes and shortcomings.

15. In 1983, Algeria was the ninth most indebted country in the world and the first in Africa, with a total debt estimated at $19 billion. See Mamadou Alpha Barry and Jacques Gautrand, 'Dette du Tiers-Monde, qui doit le plus?' *Jeune Afrique Economie*, No. 31, 19 January 1983, pp. 53 ff.

16. Jean-Louis Lacroix, *L'industrialisation du Congo (Zaïre)*, Paris, Mouton et Cie 1967.

17. Cacao-Barry group subsidiaries: SACO (Société Africaine du Cacao), API (Agricultural Products Industry) and CHOCODI Chocolaterie Confiserie de Côte d'Ivoire). Of the finished (Chocodi chocolate) and semi-finished products (cocoa butter and cake) 90% are sold on the European and American markets by the Cacao-Barry group and Interfood's subsidiary through their international trading networks.

18. In 1980 cement production was 1,156,000 metric tons, falling annually to only 500,000 metric tons in 1984. This continuous fall was due to the rise in price of clinker (wholly imported from the CIMAO (Ciment d'Afrique de l'Ouest) in Togo) and the economic crisis that seriously affected the construction and public works sector. See *Bulletin d'Afrique Noire*, 1263, 7 March 1985, pp. 10, 11.

Siveng (Société Ivoirienne d'Engrais), established in 1965, produces multinutrient fertilizers, with a capacity of 170,000 metric tons per annum. Production is state-subsidized but domestic demand fell from 100,000 to 50,000 metric tons in 1984; 50,000 metric tons per annum is exported. See *Bulletin d'Afrique Noire*, 1263, 7 March 1985.

19. François Perroux, 'Les couplages entre industries et agricultures dans la dynamique d'un développement multidimensionel', *Revue Monde en Développpment*, 31–32, 1980, p. 22.

20. Ibid., p. 241.

21. Ibid.

22. Louis Rousell, 'Problèmes et politique de l'emploi en Côte d'Ivoire' *Revue Internationale du Travail*, 104, 6, December 1971.

23. *Bulletin d'Afrique Noire*, 1251, 29 November 1984, pp. 5–8.

24. See Bernard Conte, 'Côte d'Ivoire, réorientation de la stratégie industrielle', *Jeune Afrique Economie*, 53–54, December 1984–January 1985.

25. See *Marchés Tropicaux et Méditerranéns*, (special issue) 2094, op. cit., p. 38, which deals with the development of oil production from these two deposits.

26. See Bernard Conte, in *Jeune Afrique Economie*, 53–4, December 1984–January 1985.

27. See Jean-Jacques Le Cat: 'Côte d'Ivoire point de vue sur le nouveau Code des Investissements, plus d'avantages, mais moins de protections', *Jeune Afrique Economie*, 53–54, December 1984–January 1985, pp. 126–7.

28. Officially available information is insufficiently adequate for fixing precisely all the elements of industrial value added, but we know, for example, that in 1982 it amounted to 277.8 billion Francs CFA against a total wage bill of 100,007 billion Francs CFA. See *Bulletin d'Afrique Noire*, 1223, 12 April 1984, p. 6.

29. The Ivory Coast's external public debt – 326,839 billion Francs CFA in 1975; 1,074,483 billion in 1979; was 2,626,100 billion in 1983. Debt servicing – 29,786 billion Francs CFA in 1975 – increased to 344,900 billion in 1983. See *Bulletin d'Afrique Noire*, 1306, 20 February 1986, p. 7.

30. *Marchés Tropicaux et Méditerranéns* (special issue) op. cit., p. 117.

31. See my doctoral thesis: 'L'importance des grands produits agricoles d'exportation dans le développement économique et social de la Côte d'Ivoire, et rapports agriculture–industrie dans la perspective d'un développement autocentré dans les conditions de l'Afrique Tropicale.' Paris 1974, especially Vol. 2, pp. 496–523.

8. Tanzania: Imperialism, the State and the Peasantry

Henry Mapolu

Introduction

In 1973–74, the government, after experimenting with a variety of 'rural development' policies, launched a 'villagization' programme for the entire mainland countryside. Basically, the programme consisted of replacing the traditional system of rural settlements, in which households are located in small isolated pockets, with the creation of large villages. This entailed moving millions of people into new areas in a relatively short time.

There has been considerable debate on the merits and demerits of the programme, and particularly on the way it was implemented. The programme's stated purpose was to facilitate the provision by government of essential social infrastructure to the rural areas – particularly water, medical services, and primary education. Whether large settlements are a necessary prerequisite for the provision of these facilities, and whether Tanzania had the resources to provide them are debatable questions.

But there has been little disagreement on the performance of rural production since 'villagization'. Agricultural output has declined in many cases and only in a few has output shown some minor increase. This poor performance may be due to many causes: climate, world commodity prices, for example. Coulson, however, has indicated that food shortages for instance cannot be ascribed to drought conditions as rainfall figures for the decade do not bear this out. Furthermore, Tanzania is a vast territory with diverse ecological zones capable of complementing each other in terms of variety of output.

> Virtually every crop known to agriculturalists will grow in one or more of these [ecological] areas. Wheat, coffee, tea, potatoes, and pyrethrum in the cool mountains. On the island plateau grow maize, rice, sorghum, varieties of millet, cotton, and tobacco, as well as sisal . . . Coconuts, cashew-nuts, rubber, cocoa, cloves, and a wide variety of spices grow on the coastal strip or on Zanzibar and Pemba. Each ecological unit produces its own fruits and vegetables.

Nevertheless, not only have food imports risen but production for export (on which the government puts strong emphasis) has also declined. In 1972–80 overall growth of food crops was 5% per annum, that of exports crops 3% per annum.

I would argue that the root causes for this poor performance lie not in natural conditions but rather in the state's social economic policies; the strategies intended to raise agricultural production have rather proved to be the fetters. Most independent African countries have elaborated policies for change in the rural areas, but Tanzania has laid particular emphasis on this aspect of development and the many policy statements regarding rural changes have stimulated considerable debate both within and outside the country.

It is, however, my contention that in substance these policies have hardly differed either from policies elsewhere in Africa or from earlier attempts by the British in colonial Tanganyika, and elsewhere.

Imperialism and rural development

The colonial powers' primary economic task was to integrate the African people into the worldwide capitalist market. As most of African colonies were considered essentially as sources of agricultural raw materials, this task basically consisted of compelling the population to produce those commodities required by European industry: sisal, cotton, tea, rubber, and so on. The methods to attain this objective generally differed from colony to colony, but usually involved coercion. Such methods led, at times, to rebellions. In German East Africa, for instance, attempts to compel the people to grow cotton led to the celebrated Maji Maji Wars of 1905–7, and in most colonies this resistance to exploitation continued despite brutal methods to stamp it out.

Force was not, however, the only form of the people's resistance. Depending on local conditions and historical experience, they devised various tricks: in colonial Tanzania, for example, they knew that boiling cotton seeds prevented germination.

With the expansion and intensification of commodity production social differentiation became inevitable and divergent vested interests began to emerge. Thus, different segments of the rural people resorted to different forms of struggle, and certain segments acquired vested interests in the new system of commodity production and exchange.

It should be noted that in each colony it was the colonial state that played the key role in these endeavours to subjugate the local inhabitants and integrate them into the world capitalist system. For example, laws were enacted compelling villagers to cultivate particular crops, the state formulated policies for all sectors of the economy, and so on.

By the time of independence this task of integrating the rural people into the capitalist market had largely been accomplished. Socio-economic structures had been built to ensure a more or less permanent flow of agricultural raw materials from Africa to Western Europe and North America and a firm dependence on the world market. Nevertheless, nowhere had the integration of rural peoples into the market economy been fully accomplished. Rural communities, often residing in inaccessible areas, or engaged in productive activities not easily penetrable by the cash nexus, continued to lead traditional communal forms of life more or less free of commodity production and exchange. In Tanzania, for instance, only in the mid-sixties did government 'discover' the Hadzape people in Singida region.

By the end of the colonial period, however, even those people who, by and large, had accepted commodity production and exchange, frequently returned to subsistence economy when it suited them. Naturally, peasants generally produce their subsistence needs outside the production of commodities and, if cash crop production endangers subsistence then more and more resources will be transferred to subsistence production. Price incentives play a key role in the movement between cash crop and subsistence production. Thus colonial rulers had the problem of maintaining low prices for raw materials while simultaneously ensuring their maximum production; this problem remains unsolved by independent governments.

Colonial rulers applied various strategies in an attempt to increase rural output *vis-à-vis* resources – from ambitious resettlement schemes managed directly by appointed officials, to more modest efforts to provide villagers with technical advice and assistance. In general, these strategies constituted the colonial governments' entire 'rural development' policies. But it has become clear that by ignoring the people's wishes, experience, and interests, these policies proved fruitless in terms of increasing productivity in rural Africa. Specifically, the resettlement schemes were a fiasco practically everywhere.

The fundamental problems inherent in these colonial policies, may be summed up in Cabral's words, as 'the negation of the historical process of the dominated people by means of violent usurpation of the freedom of development of the national productive forces'. Hence, the wish to rapidly increase African peoples' productivity while shackling them to colonialism was contradictory, and colonial governments' efforts to resolve this contradiction by enforced politico-economic measures only intensified it. At independence, governments inherited this contradiction.

Africa is overwhelmingly rural, and a first priority was to formulate policies for rural areas. In addition, Western aid donors, upon whom Africa is increasingly dependent, have constantly urged African governments to adopt strategies to increase agricultural exports (naturally in the interest of donor countries themselves). Governments have, therefore, formulated 'rural development' policies – that 'development' has been minimal is, of course, another matter. But African governments are themselves anxious to raise agricultural output, as that alone can significantly contribute the necessary funds to run the state apparatus.

Experience has shown, however, that with few exceptions, African governments have not done much better than their predecessors; in some cases, they have repeated the same mistakes and committed the same blunders; furthermore the economic relationship between Africa and imperialism is fundamentally unchanged, while the development of the productive forces remains stifled. Consequently Africa is becoming increasingly dependent on food imports and only in Africa is food production declining (see Table 8.1).

Table 8.1
Index of Food Production (1961–65 = 100)

	1972	1973	1974	1975	1976
Africa	99	92	98	96	97
N & S America	106	107	107	112	114
Europe	101	101	104	103	111
Asia	103	106	105	109	109

Pressure both by internal and external factors to improve production has resulted in constant policy changes on the part of some governments, of which one is Tanzania's.

Rural development policies in Tanzania: post-independence

Shortly after independence, in 1961, government stressed the importance of rural areas in its development efforts. Emphasis was to be placed on increasing production and on the living standards in the countryside where more than 95% of the population lived. As a result of World Bank recommendations, two approaches were adopted: 1) improvement and, 2) transformation. The former basically consisted of efforts to gradually raise output within existing rural households through extension services; the latter sought to radically transform agriculture through the resettlement in special schemes of pre-selected villagers who would then engage in 'modern' farming under the supervision and direction of officials. By the end of 1965 there were 23 such schemes with some 15,000 acres of crops and about 3,400 farming families.

These early policies demonstrate an obvious bias toward export crops. In the improvement approach concentration was almost entirely on those cash crops that had become traditional – cotton, coffee, and so on. In the settlement schemes, emphasis was on those crops that needed greater technical supervision, especially tobacco, with greater official control of what was to be cultivated totally planned by government agencies appointed for the purpose. With hindsight, it can be seen that as a result of both approaches, this was the beginning of a de-emphasis on the production of foodstuffs, and the increasing attention devoted to export crops leading to Tanzania becoming a food importing country. Grain imports have been increasing over the years currently and stand at about half-a-million tons per year.

Furthermore, the basic orientation of 'development' was resettlement of the peasants into new, larger villages, as it was considered that only 'villagization' could, in the long run, result achieve progress. I would argue, however, that the substance of 'villagization' is control. Tanzania's population density is relatively low. According to the 1978 census, there are 2.82 hectares per capita in the country – and for the rural economically capable population alone there is an average of 7.27 hectares per capita of 16.97 hectares per household. Density from region to region varies, but the vast majority of people live in areas with relatively low density: 30% with less than 15 persons per square kilometre, and half the entire population in areas with less than 20 persons per square kilometre. This is not to say that there is no pressure on the land as, despite the relatively vast landmass only a small proportion is habitable, with, at present, the entire smallholder cultivation occupying only 5% (495.033^2 kilometres, out of a total of 883,987).

This means that the peasantry is concentrated in small pockets but has considerable leeway for manoeuvre – they can and do move a great deal, opening up uninhabited areas for cultivation. During the colonial period many rural areas continued to use the shifting method of cultivation despite attempts to stamp it out. Both colonial and post-colonial governments have emphasized containing the peasantry in official settlements in order to enforce agricultural policies.

Thus, the first phase in the formulation of rural development policies in Tanzania was a logical continuation of the colonial rural policies. By assembling the peasantry into sufficiently large settlements to facilitate government supervision and control, by greater involvement in the cash economy and greater dependence on the foreign market, for their products and for their inputs, Tanzanian rural dwellers became part and parcel of the worldwide economic system.

Social consequences of rural policies

The initial manifestation of this external integration was the growth of social differentiation in the rural areas. The 'transformation' approach was explicitly intended to give birth to a landed class with vested interests in the employment of labour. But, ultimately, even the 'improvement' approach would inevitably bring about class differentiation in the rural areas by its emphasis on the 'progressive' farmer in the provision of extension services. In other words, the end result of this rural development policy was the formation of classes that would become the social basis of imperialism.

By 1966, however, it became clear that the 'improvement' approach was not producing substantial results. Although the area under cash crops production tended to increase over the years, output continued to fluctuate more as a result of climatic conditions and prices than as a result of the extension services provided by government agencies. As to the 'transformation' approach, government soon realized it was incurring enormous expense to establish and run the settlement schemes whose production continued to be minimal. It emerged that the resettled peasants tended to see themselves as government employees rather than independent farmers receiving government technical assistance. But this was by no means a matter of mere appearance, in fact there was a real change in social relations. A peasant on his own farm had control over resources – land, tools, seeds, and so on – but under the scheme, all these resources were controlled by the government agencies which had planned all production activities and called only on the peasant's labour. Furthermore, on their own farms the peasants decided on the disposal of the harvest, but under the scheme officials disposed of the harvest and paid the settler peasant whatever remained after deducting costs for all inputs (for example, chemicals, seeds, social infrastructure).

The participants in the settlements were more or less semi-workers. Not surprisingly, some often resorted to withdrawal of labour-power as a form of protest. Peasants who considered themselves underpaid often left the settlement; such protests usually forced some changes in the amount deducted prior to paying the workers. Some participants in the scheme were successful: employing labour to a greater and greater extent and thus becoming small rural capitalists dependent on, at least, seasonal labour. (Recently this group has tended to branch out into trade and come to dominate the less creditable face of business in the rural areas.) The specific relationship of the domestic to the external economy, however, militated against any but minimal discernible 'rural development'. Little could be expected from exporting raw materials from an agriculture essentially dependent on the hand-hoe.

In general, then, initial attempts to radically change the rural scene in Tanzania largely failed. In the 1960s agricultural output did register some growth, but this, as we have seen, could hardly be ascribed to the specific policies or programmes then pursued. Further, it must be noted, that as a result of many changes in the country as a whole, policy changes were becoming inevitable towards the end of the 1960s.

At independence, the reins of government were largely in the hands of the *petit bourgeoisie*: the intelligentsia, traders, bureaucrats, and rich peasants. The aftermath of independence saw ever increasing struggles between these elements and the predominantly Asian commercial bourgeoisie that controlled the economy at the local level. Steps taken by the *petit bourgeoisie* soon after independence included replacing private buyers of agricultural produce by government controlled agencies and co-operative organizations, launching of government trading institutions, and suchlike. The culmination of these endeavours came in 1967 with the proclamation of the Arusha Declaration, which led to the nationalization of all 'commanding heights' of the economy. By the end of the decade one could correctly refer to the existence of a state bourgeoisie in Tanzania – a class which, by virtue of its position in the state, controlled the major means of production in the country. Obviously, however, due to the nature of the economy itself and its relation to the world capitalist system, this bourgeoisie was, and is, a dependent bourgeoisie.

In the rural areas, the state bourgeoisie's efforts to consolidate its position in the economy began, as we have seen, with taking over the middleman's role: the purchase and sale of agricultural produce. But to attain full control of the agricultural sector required taking over at the level of production. Thus, by the end of the 1960s, with the demise of the 'improvement' and 'transformation' approaches, new strategies had to be evolved: the policies of 'state farms' and 'ujamaa villages'. State farms, due to lack of resources, were inevitably limited:

ujamaa villages conceived of as agricultural producers' co-operative institutions. Government did, however, have a considerable role in these apparently independent institutions: initiating the villages, planning and executing activities, and so on, were all to be under the direction of government officials seconded to the villages.

At the time, ujamaa villages' policy appeared quite novel and a great deal of resources were made available to implement the policy. The political campaign for setting up this programme was more intense than any previous exercise for the rural areas and, in the late 1960s, a substantial number of ujamaa villages were launched in each region. Both party and government machinery were resolutely mobilized towards campaigning for 'ujamaa', and the President himself frequently spent weeks in villages working, directing and advising. By 1973, according to official figures, more than 5,000 ujamaa villages had been established throughout the country, with some two million people.

Failure of villagization projects

Despite considerable enthusiasm for this policy, after some five years there were few convincing signs of a rapid breakthrough in the rural areas as a result of the ujamaa villages. Some showed signs of economic growth and expansion, but others, completely mismanaged, would clearly collapse. Furthermore, the ujamaa sector constituted only a small proportion of total rural economy, and there was little indication that in time this would change, since, although more new villages were started, a considerable number of the old ones died. The organization, leadership and degree of communality in the villages varied a great deal; and in some cases they were merely front organizations for kulak operations.

In themselves, co-operatives cannot guarantee rapid socio-economic development in the rural areas. Unless they are part of a larger strategy of both rural transformation and industrialization, producer co-operatives in un-developed countries simply become another instrument for continued imperialist domination of the country. Thus by 1972–73 interest in the ujamaa programme began to waver, not only among the people but in official circles too. The earlier policy of 'improvement' and 'transformation' was officially withdrawn in 1966, but the ujamaa villages policy is still officially operative. Yet, since 1973, emphasis has radically changed from communal production to village settlement. In 1973 the Tanzania government launched the largest and most ambitious programme for rural mobilization ever undertaken in the country, and its impact has been greater and more far-reaching than any other previous programme.

The villagization programme was aimed at resettling the entire rural population into large, planned centres by replacing the traditional peasant households (frequently shifting cultivation from area to area to balance resources and requirements) with fairly large settlements each comprising at least some 250 families. Between 1973 and 1975 as many as nine million rural inhabitants were shifted and by 1976 it was declared that practically all rural Tanzanians were living in these new 'development' villages.

In 1970, 531,000 Tanzanians, less than 5 per cent of the mainland population, were living in 1956 villages. These communities had an average occupancy of 271 people. By 1974, following the persuasion and inducement campaigns and after several local operations, the villagised population had grown to about 2,028,000 – 14 per cent of the population – living in 5,628 settlements with an average membership of about 360. After the first full year of compulsion, approximately 9,150,000 people, or about 60 per cent of the mainland population, were living in 6,384 villages with an average occupancy of about 1,433. At the conclusion of Operation Tanzania in 1977 an estimated 79 per cent of the 1978 mainland population and 90 per cent of all rural dwellers – more than 13 million people – were living in 7,300 villages with an approximate average membership of 1,849.

The government explained that the villagization programme's main objective was to enable the rural population to be provided with essential social services; arguing that only by gathering the people into large settlements would it be possible to provide schools, dispensaries and water facilities for all.

The way the programme was implemented left a lot to be desired. In some cases, violence was used, in others the settlement sites chosen were unsuitable, or the planning process was deficient, or too many people were settled in one village. Above all, the whole exercise was carried out too hastily. In 1973 there were 5,628 villages with a total population of 2,028,164, by 1976 the number of villages totalled 7,684 with a total population of 13,087,220.

All these factors brought about widespread resentment among the rural population, and sometimes open opposition to the party and government. Millions of people had been resettled, old homes were destroyed and new ones built, people accustomed to living in isolated homesteads now found themselves in mini-towns with, in many cases, closely built houses in straight lines. Overall, tremendous changes had occurred in the rural areas: whether these changes were for the better is questionable.

The significant factor in this programme, however, is its class character. Villagization marked the apex of the bourgeoisie's efforts to put rural production under its control. If the 'commanding heights' of the economy had been 'won' by the end of the 1960s, clearly smallholder production, in which almost 90% of the population participated, had to be tackled. But this could not be done effectively through nationalization measures. Resettlement in chosen localities with government officials to oversee production processes was the logical strategy to be adopted. Villagization can therefore be seen as the culmination of the colonialist efforts to restructure rural economic life in order to facilitate exploitation and domination of the rural masses by international capitalism. The nature of petty commodity production renders it resistant to domination, and thus resistant to exploitation of the producers; only the existence of centralized institutions that directly control the peasants can achieve those objectives. Attempts to create settlement schemes during the colonial era and the early days of independence aimed to create such institutional structures, because those participating in the schemes would be controlled directly by government agencies and yet still remain outside wage employment. In this way, capitalism, in this particular context of under-development, exerts its domination over petty commodity production.

The 'tobacco schemes', perhaps an extreme form of state control over the peasantry, exemplify the general trends. Because numerous technicalities are involved in the proper husbandry of tobacco, officials both of government and the tobacco industry make all, even the most minor decisions; the villagers' role strikingly resembles that of a worker. Officialdom decides how much land should be under tobacco, when and how to plant, weed, harvest and cure the leaf; supplies seeds, fertilizers, and insecticides; grades and, of course, markets the tobacco. The villagers provide only the labour power. Finally, officialdom decides what proportion of the turnover should be paid back to the peasant. Obviously, the largest proportions go to those who supplied the technical inputs, the administrative services, and those who marketed the crop. The villager, with virtually no control over the production process or the product of his labour, is inevitably the loser.

In the 1970s, apart from the villagization drive itself, Tanzania introduced a number of other fundamental changes to existing rural institutions. Almost all the local institutions with grass-root level participation were overhauled and new bureaucratic institutions, with direct central control, established in their place. In 1972, in accordance with an American consultancy firm's recommendations, district and town councils were abolished and central administration was devolved into the regions and districts to assume all the roles formerly played by the local government bodies. Until then these councils were directly elective with a degree of autonomy from central government. With the 'centralization' measures all powers were transferred to the central government bureaucracy, which was grossly expanded for the purpose.

In 1975, the marketing co-operative movement – then one of the most advanced in Africa – was demolished. Peasants had marketed their crops to co-operative organizations which were answerable to their members – the peasants themselves. The crops were then marketed to the appropriate government agencies which had monopoly in the export of agricultural produce. With the abolition of co-operative societies, government agencies were empowered to buy produce directly from the peasant, but the peasant is in no way involved in the activities of these agencies. Consequently the peasants have begun to suffer from yet another form of exploitation: non-payment for crops collected. For various reasons almost all government agencies are today unable to pay cash for peasant produce and instead offer promissory notes. Actual payment is very much delayed and in some cases, due to mismanagement, the peasant is either not paid at all or paid only in part.

The process of integration and control of the peasantry has finally been accomplished. In the final analysis this control and domination is most advantageous to the international division of labour characteristic of world capitalism: it ensures that peasants cannot resort to their traditional tactic of withdrawing from market forces to pursue subsistence agriculture.

These changes have not only firmly integrated the peasantry into the world market but have intensified its exploitation. Prices of primary products from underdeveloped countries bear no relation to their values: the socially necessary labour time spent on their production. Multinational companies continue to amass huge profits from the trade of raw materials from underdeveloped countries. Within the country, however, a greater and greater proportion of the peasant produce is appropriated by the state bourgeoisie. Indeed, the abolition of local government and co-operative institutions was objectively a means for ensuring this exploitation.

For example, the state has throughout paid the peasant only about 40% of its receipts from the sale of cotton, and despite occasional improvements in cotton prices on the world market, the proportion finally reaching the cotton cultivator has tended to decline.

In Tanzania, maize (the staple food) and other grains are purchased from the producers by the National Milling Corporation (NMC) – a state institution. It stores and processes the grain and sells the flour to consumers via wholesalers and retailers. The state, acting as middleman, siphons off most of what is produced and the producer is paid only about one-third of the ultimate consumer price.

The relation between the state bourgeoisie and the peasantry is one of exploitation facilitated by the existence of institutional structures that regulate the activities of the peasantry and its production; villagization has created such structures. It would, of course, be misleading to imply that in these developments the state has always had the upper hand; there has been intense opposition on the part of the peasantry. We noted earlier that peasants constantly resorted to simply leaving establishment settlements, to sabotaging official regulations and so on, and what took place during the colonial period has undoubtedly continued although in ever changing forms. It is well-known that, for example, in coffee growing regions peasants have uprooted coffee trees to plant food crops, have stopped weeding cashew-nut growing areas and instead have burnt the trees, and in most areas have been selling food crops on the black market.

A clear indication of peasant resistance is that the rural economy has been steadily declining over the years. Production of both export and food crops has at best stagnated and at worst declined absolutely. There was a small but gradual increase in the early 1970s, but production of the major export crops (cotton, coffee, sisal, tea, cashew-nuts, pyrethrum, and tobacco) has been on the decline since the villagization measures of the mid 1970s. Sisal and pyrethrum have shown the sharpest decline but even crops such as coffee and cotton have generally tended to decline. As a result of this downward trend institutional changes have had to be made, and in 1984 both local government and co-operative organizations were to be reintroduced.

Food crops have fared no better – particularly those marketed through the official system. Purchases of the main food crops have been on the decline ever since 'villagization': for example, 223,000 tons of maize for 1978–79 decreased to 105,000 tons in 1980–81; rice from 52,000 to 5,000 tons; and millet and sorghum from 40,000 and 58,000 tons respectively to nil in both cases for the same years. The result has, of course, been the now annual food crises in the urban as well as in some rural areas. In turn food imports have become essential every year.

There may be many reasons for this general decline of agricultural output, but in my opinion a kind of go-slow among the peasants is probably the key factor. Professor Mascarenhas, who praised the villagization programme as one of 'the most outstanding indigenous rural development policies in Africa', cannot but agree that 'the present agricultural picture is one of a peaceful revolt, an unwillingness to produce, or to become part of the wider system. There has been a turning back to the small farm/small plot for survival-level farming'.

At the social and political levels, institutional changes in the rural areas together with economic malaise have contributed significantly to instability in those areas. In many regions social unrest is a permanent feature, replacing the stability and social cohesion based for so long on traditional relations.

Conclusion

I have argued that neo-colonial situations entail the continuation of colonial policies, and that such policies represent an attempt to incorporate the peasantry firmly into the ambit of world capitalism. In countries such as Tanzania, where feudalism in any real sense has never existed, and where uninhabited land is still largely abundant the process of integrating the peasants into the world market is long and arduous.

9. Tunisia: The State, the Peasantry and Food Dependence

Mahmoud ben Romdhane

The purpose of this chapter is to analyse state policy towards agriculture over the last two decades and its impact on the peasantry and agricultural production. The essential conclusions that emerge and will be developed, are that, with the exception of the market gardening and fruit sub-sector, in which the state made major investments and where the beneficiaries of investment in irrigation gained substantial advantages, Tunisian agriculture has been used as a reservoir from which to extract an increasingly large surplus to the benefit of extra-agricultural capital. As a result of the continuous depreciation of the main agricultural products' prices the peasantry has been unable to save enough to finance productive investment, and capital, 'the bearer of capitalist rationality' has simply fled agriculture whose share of investment has diminished drastically period by period. Consequently, agricultural production has improved only extremely slowly and, from being an agricultural surplus country, Tunisia has gradually become a deficit country, particularly in strategic food products (cereals, milk, sugar for example).

This was the situation up to 1979. Since then, the food deficit has continued to worsen, but it seems that since 1980 there has been a turn-about in agricultural policy which is reflected both in a new emphasis on agricultural products and in the financial and institutional resources made available (or in the process of being made available) to farmers.

But this turn-around has not yet been taken up with the required determination. It remains in fact dependent, 1) on a domestic social situation in which urban actors' threat to reduce the margin of manoeuvre necessary for the implementation of a new agricultural policy is all the greater because the confrontation with them is occurring against a tense economic background; and, 2) on an international situation in which the *downward* fluctuations of international prices threaten to reduce the urgency of a policy of encouraging agriculture simply because the turn-around itself was dictated essentially by the sudden rise of the international prices of the leading agricultural products between 1979 and 1981.

But if this turnaround were to succeed in establishing itself and giving way to a policy that did not exclude agriculture, is there not the risk of a deployment of capital in agriculture with all its attendant consequences – or alleged consequences: further concentration of landownership, development of the wage nexus and rejection of the peasantry? For if the policy, that for two or three decades has consisted in reducing the prices of the main agricultural products, has helped remove agriculture from the field of capitalist investment and keep it basically a world of peasants, a policy of encouraging agriculture may indeed lead to an improvement in the standard of living of the peasant masses and keeping them on their holdings, but it may also lead to an extension of the spatial and social area of capital within agriculture and the eviction of at least part of the peasantry.

That is the real issue in coming years: everything will depend on the concrete implementation of the new policy – if the turnaround does indeed prove to be permanent. In order to put an end to food dependence, two paths are practicable: one based on capital, out-and-out resort to mechanization and rejection of the peasantry, the other, on the promotion of the peasantry and the rural areas.

The state and the peasantry

With regard to agriculture in general and the peasantry in particular – in so far as four-fifths of agricultural production are provided by small and medium-sized holdings based on family labour – state policy has consisted, since the eary 1960s, in systematically extorting a larger and larger surplus, except from farmers in the irrigated sub-sector. In fact, whereas farmers in the non-irrigated sub-sector have seen the prices of their products (cereals, livestock, olive oil) fixed by the state at a low level, farmers in the irrigated sector have received special treatment: in addition to enjoying sometimes very considerable higher land values, hitherto achieved at no cost to themselves, thanks to investments in irrigation carried out and financed by the state, the prices of their products (market gardening and fruits) are 'free' and have increased considerably.

Such a brief outline needs to be elaborated. First, farmers who have benefited from state investments in irrigation are a very small minority (some 20,000 out of a total of 355,000) and, among them, no more than 6,000 have plots larger than five hectares. Second, those who have undertaken irrigation works and installations at their own expense number some 30,000 and most of them have holdings of less than five hectares; the sole 'advantage' they derive from their situation is that they benefit from generally rewarding prices (in the sense that they include, in addition to the strict cost of production, a land rent and a 'normal' rate of profit). Finally, among farmers in the non-irrigated sector almost 4,500 have holdings larger than 100 hectares and, through the use of hired labour, they enjoy incomes several times higher than those of a medium-sized irrigated farm.

Holdings in the non-irrigated sector: state policy
State policy with regard to the 305,000 farmers in the non-irrigated sector in Tunisia (out of a total of 355,000) has consisted in continually reducing the prices of their products. In the early 1960s the state was already establishing

specialized National Boards or Companies that monopolized the marketing and/or importation of agricultural products and thus provided itself with the institutional tools which were to enable it to carry on a policy of dictating the prices of the main agricultural products and extracting an increasing surplus from agriculture.

This role was entrusted to the Office des Céréales for cereal products; the Société Tunisienne des Industries Laitières (STIL) for milk and dairy products; the Société ELLOUHOUM for meat; and (after 1967 only) the Office de l'Huile for oil. Only the market gardening and fruit sector (to be examined later) was excluded from this process.

After the early 1960s, the state fixed producer prices for cereal and livestock (meat and milk) products at the beginning of each season and, after 1967, for olive oil. Since then the prices of these products have continuously declined.[1]

Cereal prices: Between 1961 and 1972, producer prices for hard wheat, soft wheat and barley were changed only once – in 1967 – when they were raised between 12% and 24.5%. Successive adjustments after 1973 and up to 1980 increased prices on average 50% for wheat and 80% for barley, but compared to the general wholesale price index or the manufactured goods price index, the changes look rather regressive. Over 18 years (1961–79), the general wholesale price index recorded an increase of 171% and the manufactured goods price index 165%. By deflating the nominal prices of cereal products by these two indices the following figures emerge: in constant prices, hard wheat fell from 4.2 dinars per quintal in 1961 to approximately 2.850 dinars in 1979, a fall of over 47%, soft wheat from 3.450 dinars to approximately 2.6 dinars, a fall of over 31%, and barley from approximately 2.5 dinars to 2.050 dinars, a fall of over 22%.

This uninterrupted price decline reached such a level that few holdings succeeded in producing while realizing the rent and a profit margin comparable to that of other branches of the Tunisian economy.

From a Ministry of Agriculture study[2] relating to the production costs of cereals in 1975 – obtained from a sample of 262 holdings – we have prepared a table of the production costs of the three main cereal products: hard wheat, soft wheat and barley. Three types of holding varying in terms of their degree of mechanization were examined and compared with tranches by size of holdings –20 hectares, 20–100 hectares and + 100 hectares.

The results are summarized in Table 9.4, which distinguishes three production costs: 1) excluding rent and profit margin (estimated at 15%); in this case the farmer is treated similarly to a self-employed earner of the guaranteed minimum agricultural wage; 2) including profit margin, but excluding rent, which is treated as taken by urban capital but the profit margin is more or less the same as that realized in other branches of the economy (about 15%); 3) including rent and profit margin; in this case the cereal sector is not the object of any extraction of value, and landowners enjoy the fruits of their ownership in the form of rent passed on to the prices of agricultural products.

Table 9.1
Production costs of cereals

Type of holding	Ordinary hard wheat			Ordinary soft wheat			Barley		
	Not inc. profit	Inc. profit but not rent	Inc. profit and rent	Not inc. profit	Inc. profit but not rent	Inc. profit and rent	Not inc. profit	Inc. profit but not rent	Inc. profit and rent
Mechanized:									
+100 ha	5d.968	6d.993	7d.980	4d.497	5d.172	6d.087	4d.599	5d.289	6d.174
20–100 ha	5d.556	6e.188	7d.054	6d.090	7d.003	8d.326	4d.339	4d.990	5d.917
–20 ha	6d.946	7d.973	9d.928	6d.652	7d.650	8d.345	5d.348	6d.190	7d.190
Semi-mechanized:									
+100 ha	6d.993	5d.615	6d.218	5d.158	5d.943	7d.668	5d.488	6d.311	6d.930
20–100 ha	7d.317	8d.415	8d.940	8d.904	10d.240	10d.620	7d.153	8d.226	8d.605
–20 ha	9d.793	11d.272	11d.841	9d.021	9d.224	10d.577	9d.256	10d.644	11d.471
Animal traction									
+100 ha	—	—	—	10d.660	12d.262	13d.540	10d.498	12d.061	13d.241
20–100 ha	9d.949	11d.326	12d.970	—	—	—	8d.195	9d.424	10d.439
–20 ha	11d.901	17d.125	18d.792	—	—	—			

The results are not perfect,[3] but they still reveal that: no type of holding, however mechanized and of whatever size, achieves, given the prices set by the state, a capitalist-type profitability (including land rent and 'normal' profit margin). Only some large holdings are able to extract a profit margin without however managing to secure the ground rent. The small and medium-sized farms fail to cover the production costs narrowly defined (except for the mechanized medium-sized holdings specializing in producing hard wheat), which means that the farmers and their family are earning less than the minimum guaranteed agricultural wage (SMAG).

Dairy livestock prices: As with cereals, the producer price of milk, fixed by the STIL, saw only 5 increases in 18 years. It rose from 48 millimes per litre in 1961 to 51 in 1966, 54 millimes in 1967, 65 in 1973, and stabilized at 90 millimes per litre between 1976 and 1979. Its 'real' price (compared to the general wholesale, and manufactured goods price indices) fell, in constant 1961 millimes, from 48 millimes in 1961 to 31–32 in 1979, a decline of almost 50%.

According to a study conducted by the Ministry of Agriculture[4] in 1976 – a year in which the milk producer price had just been set at 90 millimes as against 65 millimes in 1975 – the cost price of milk (not including any profit margin) varied between 91.4 millimes for an integrated stock farm and 114.7 for a semi-integrated stock-farm[5] whereas at the same time the stock farmer was getting only 82 to 84 millimes per litre of milk delivered to the Centrale Laitière (Dairy Centre) in Tunis (90 millimes less six or eight to cover transport costs and various taxes).

Faced with this situation, the technicians in the Ministry of Agriculture were already writing as early as 1974:

> Given the official price of milk . . . milk production still remains marginal and the rate of profit zero. The only incomes currently being earned by some producers marketing their production at the official prices can only arise from payment for family labour or the use of buildings that have already been fully amortized. . . . This explains . . . the lack of enthusiasm or even disaffection on the part of some stock farmers and, . . . the ever-growing deficit in milk and dairy products.[6]

And more recently, in the framework of the preparation of the Sixth Plan, the sub-commission's Report on prices and marketing stated:

> This price rigidity has had negative repercussions not only on milk production but also on the development of the sector since there has been a total abandonment of dairy farming . . . This is all the more serious because our imports of dairy products have reached unacceptable levels, placing a heavy burden on our balance of trade.[7]

Beef and veal: Although officially approved, the producer price for beef and veal has not been reduced; in relation to the general wholesale or the manufactured goods price indices it has even undergone some upgrading. Between 1965 and 1979, the price of one kilogram of cattle on the hoof saw a nominal increase of 167% (rising from 221 millimes to 564 millimes) whereas over the same period the general wholesale price index rose by only 110% and the manufactured goods price index by 91%.

But this rise in prices does not indicate an improved situation for stock farmers – far from it, for there has been a dramatic change in the structures of production of both cattle and sheep farming. Whereas until recently, the bulk of cattle fed free, getting most of their food intake from natural vegetation – meadows, pastures – stock farmers are more and more constrained, as a result of the reduction of meadows and pasture and the increase in the number of cattle, to turn to the market to purchase necessary feed for their herds.[8] This led an official of a beef and veal development project in northern Tunisia to state that:

> It is currently asserted that intensification of production must be accompanied by a reduction of unit production costs; this assertion is false since it is obvious that a bull fattened along the roadside costs less than a bullock fed rationally in a purpose-built unit. In fact, it is well known that producer prices are higher in countries where stock farming is most intensive.[9]

Moreover, Ministry of Agriculture studies show that cattle raising is not a rewarding activity. A note from the Office de l'Elevage et des Pâturages reads:

> In order to estimate the production cost of a kilogram of fattened bullock meat, the various studies allow us to suggest a cost price of 0.476 millimes per kg of meat. The sale price for a profit margin of 10% would be 0.524 per kg. However, given the dues paid to middlemen, the Tunis market price ought to be about 0.575 D per kg live weight.[10]

But in that year (1976), the wholesale price of 0.516 was maintained until May 1979, despite the not insignificant rise in production costs.

Sheepmeat: Like cattle meat, producer prices for sheepmeat have risen faster than the general wholesale and the manufactured goods price indices without this rise reflecting any improvement in sheep farmers' situation. The change in the structure of production explains this fact since during 1976 the wholesale price was 691 millimes per kg whereas the cost price (not including profit margin and transport costs) varied according to the type of farming between 583 millimes and 791 millimes.

Olive oil: The regulations governing the marketing of olive oil were reformed in November 1967. From that date, the collection and export of all olive oils on the local market were entrusted to the Union Centrale des Coopératives Oléicoles (Central Union of Oil-growing Cooperatives). Armed with this monopoly, the UCCO (which subsequently became the Office de l'Huile (Oil

Bureau)) was now the sole authorized purchaser of olive oil from the producers on the basis of a 'season price' fixed in advance. Between 1967 and 1979, the producer price rose from 45 millimes per kg of oil olives to 83 millimes, a nominal increase of 84%, whereas between these two dates, the general wholesale price index recorded an increase of 95%.

A Ministry of Agriculture survey on the production costs of oil olives during the 1976–77 season[11] on a sample of 363 farms reveals that the cost price of this product is much higher than producer prices.

On the basis of a cost including expenses for olive trees in production, young olive trees and the site value of the land (ground rent) but excluding both the financial expenses arising from loans incurred and a profit margin, the results reached by the survey were: expenses for olive trees in production, 36.8 million dinars: expenses for young olive trees, 9.5 million: for a total of 46.3 million dinars for a total production of 450,000 metric tons of olives, which represents an average cost of 109.2 D per metric ton. If a gross profit margin is taken into account (including financial expenses) comparable to that of the non-agricultural sectors, a minimum of 15%, the producer price for a metric ton of olives should be: 102.9 D x 1.15 = 118.3 D. That same year, however, oil-growers received only 66 D per metric ton.

In total, state policy towards farmers in the non-irrigated sector consisted in subjecting them to a brutal extortion of surplus labour, with the prices set only rarely covering production costs: not only are profit and rent not allowed for but the labour of the peasant and his family is paid below the SMAG. In this context, landownership plays no more than an ideological role. It contributes to tying the peasant to his land and making him live a fiction, that of having the rent, which is in fact taken from him by urban capital. Deprived of rent and even of reward for his investments, the peasant is reduced to a role of underpaid home worker.

And the overall volume of the amount extorted from him by urban capital reaches immense proportions.

Amount extorted from agriculture: In order to estimate the amount extorted from agriculture, the year 1975 will be taken as a benchmark. Production costs – as determined by the UNA – will be compared to producer prices. Taking account of the UNA's production costs has the following advantages: 1) without exception, they all refer to a single year (1975) whereas the Ministry of Agriculture's costs refer to 1975 for cereals, to 1977 for olives and to 1976 for livestock: 2) for each product they provide a single cost whereas the Ministry of Agriculture provides multiple costs (four for milk, six to nine for cereals, four for sheepmeat): 3) they include the farmer's remuneration (profit) whereas the Ministry's costs do not take it into account.

It should also be stressed that, while the costs determined by the UNA generally appear to be higher than the Ministry of Agriculture's, this is essentially because they include profit and financial expenses whereas the Ministry does not. The production norms, quantity and unit price of inputs scarcely vary from one source to the other.[12]

Table 9.2 shows the production cost in dinars per metric ton of products for 1975, the production prices observed that year and the volume of the amount extorted per metric ton.

Table 9.2
Production costs and producer prices, by agricultural product (1975)

Products	Production costs (dinars per mt)	Production price (dinars per mt)	Amount extorted (dinars per mt)
Hard wheat	75.0	66.0	9.0
Soft wheat	71.5	60.0	11.5
Barley	61.0	45.0	16.0
Oil olives	119.0	83.0	36.0
Beef and veal	550.0	490.0	60.0
Sheepmeat	750.0	617.0	133.0
Milk	120.0	65.0	55.0

Taking account of total production for each of these commodities in 1975, the total amount extracted from agriculture that emerges, in 1975, is 54,815 thousand dinars. In the same year: agricultural production reached 340.7 million dinars and the value of the amount extorted to 194.1 million dinars; gross fixed capital formation reached 467 million dinars, amortizations 98.3 million dinars (21% of CCF) and net capital formation 368.7 million dinars. Gross fixed capital formation in agriculture reached 51.3 million dinars, which, assuming an amortization rate of 21.3%, gives a net capital formation of 40.5 million dinars, while in the manufacturing industry it reached 83.3 million dinars, which, assuming an amortization rate of 21.3%, gives a net capital formation of 65.8 million dinars. In public utilities (education and training, public utilities, health and urban water supply) gross fixed capital formation reached 45.8 million dinars, which, assuming an amortization rate of 21.3%, gives a net capital formation of 36.2 million dinars.

With reference to these figures, the amount extracted from agriculture represents: 16.1% of total agricultural production and 28.2% of the value of cereal, stock farming and oil olives production; 14.9% of the country's total net investment; 135.3% of net agricultural investment; 83.3% of net investment in manufacturing industries; 151.4% of net investment in public utilities. That gives an order of magnitude of the transfer of value that Tunisian agriculture bears each year.

Holdings in the irrigated sector: state policy
State policy towards the 50,000 farmers in the irrigated sector has been quite different from that pursued in the non-irrigated sector. Not only have prices of fruits and vegetables risen continuously, but some 20,000 current farmers are, owing to state investments in irrigation, enjoying an often considerable increase in land values and a water supply at prices at least a quarter of their costs.

Rise in fruit and vegetable prices: Unlike other products whose prices have been fixed officially, the products of the irrigated sector (fruit and vegetables essentially) have been subject to a 'free prices' regime. And, unlike cereals, livestock products and oil olives, their prices have undergone marked increases higher even than those recorded for other non-agricultural products.

Over 14 years (1965[13] to 1980) the fruit price index was above the general wholesale and the manufactured goods price indices and, compared to the base year 1965, fruit prices rose 3.08 times whereas those of manufactured goods and other products rise by a factor of two.

Prices of market garden crops have undergone a generally similar movement: between 1965 and 1979, they went up 2.44 times, but during the four years 1966, 1968, 1971 and 1972, their level was below that of the prices of other products, essentially due to large harvests.

Unlike the products of the non-irrigated sector, comparison of production costs and producer prices of fruit and vegetables shows that market gardening crops and fruit represent a rewarding activity in general, although from year to year, the prices of this or that product may collapse, either from the effect of a relative 'over-production' (especially for tomatoes and pimentos) or from the effect of massive imports (this is sometimes the case with potatoes and winter fruits).

A comparison of the costs[14] and prices of the 13 principal fruit and vegetables (which represent three-quarters of the total production of these products) shows that while for potatoes, pimentos, oranges and apples the production cost is higher than prices, for onions, melons, watermelons, clementines, lemons, pears, peaches and grapes, the producer price is higher than the production cost and the profit margin varies between 6% and 167%.

Weighting the prices and costs by the quantities produced in 1975 shows that total producer prices were 55,280,200 dinars, total production costs 47,493,800 dinars, thus producing a profit of 7,786,400 dinars. The average profit margin after realization of the rent – for this was included in the production cost – is 16.4%.

Apart from 'freedom of pricing' which has enabled farmers in the irrigated sector to avoid suffering a transfer of surplus labour, the state has enabled some 20,000 of them to enjoy increased land values, sometimes on a very considerable scale. Of the 227,600 irrigable hectares in Tunisian agriculture in 1982, 151,400 were in private perimeters (meaning that their layout and equipment for irrigation were carried out by the private farmers themselves, essentially through the construction of surface wells) and 76,200 in public perimeters (laid out and supplied by the state from dams, pumping stations and deep wells).

While the private perimeters merit no particular attention in so far as the increased land values acquired by the plots reflect the investments made by the producers themselves, it is quite different with the public perimeters where state expenditure is estimated at 2,400 dinars per hectare.[14] Although the laws governing the public perimeters[15] suggest a contribution to investment costs of 80 to 600 dinars only per hectare, depending on the perimeters and the agronomic properties of soils (five to 25% of actual investments), they have not always been enforced.

Today, some 20,000 farmers thus benefit from increased land values gained from public expenditure at no cost to themselves. While some two-thirds of them have plots smaller than five hectares, 6,000 have holdings larger than five hectares; in several cases, the holdings even exceed 50 hectares. A ceiling on holdings has been proposed by legislation but it has still not been applied; thus a study of the lower Medjerda valley in 1977 shows that of 1,288 holdings belonging to private persons, and covering 8,922 hectares, 25 farmers (2%) held 2,250 hectares (24% of the total area) or an average of 86 hectares whereas the ceiling fixed by the law is 50 hectares.[16]

Of all agricultural sectors only the irrigated sub-sector has been encouraged by the state: between 1962 and 1971, investments in agricultural irrigation amounted to 80.6 million dinars (29% of agricultural investment), between 1972 and 1976, 23%, and between 1977 and 1981, 254 million dinars or 43.6% were also devoted to it although the existing potential was greatly underutilized.

Table 9.3
Utilization of land in state irrigation schemes

	1980	1981	1982
Irrigable area (ha)	67,800	70,300	76,200
Irrigated area (ha)*	37,900	37,500	40,900
Area cultivated (ha)†	40,100	39,500	42,400
Utilization rate (%)	56	53	54
Intensification rate (%)	59	56	56

* Irrigated area is the physical area irrigated.
† Area cultivated includes both the physical area irrigated and the area cultivated more than once during the year.

Source: Enquête périmètres irrigués. Campagne 1981–1982, Ministry of Agriculture, Tunis January 1983.

Thus then, the intensification rate (which measures the ratio between the area cultivated and the irrigable area supplied) is only 56% whereas the accepted norm is nearly 130%. This manifest underutilization of existing potential is explained in part by the water shortages that sometimes occur at some dams but the major obstacle is represented by the structure of landownership. Surveys have revealed the existence of an inversely proportional correlation between the size of holdings and their intensification rates. In the public perimeter in the lower Medjerda valley where the average size of holdings is 10–11 hectares, the irrigation rate is only 63%, whereas in that of Nebhana where the average size is 3.5 hectares, the intensity of irrigation is above 100%. This correlation is also confirmed within a single perimeter.

In the lower Medjerda valley the intensification rate up to 20 hectares is over 50% but above 20 hectares it is below 50%, reaching only 30% for holdings over 50 hectares.[17]

The situation in the private perimeters is generally better: during the last three years, the intensification rate has varied between 85% and 90% (as against 56% to 59% for the public perimeters) so that on average, for private perimeters and public perimeters combined, the intensification rate is 78%. Given the capacity available today, irrigated perimeters' production could rise by 50%. Without even questioning the current structure of landownership (although legislation provides for that) by simply asking farmers, especially those owning over 20 hectares, to develop their land fully either by themselves or by hiring labour, the country's total agricultural production could be increased by 10 to 15% – even without any further irrigation capacity.[18]

In addition, greater respect for the purpose of the various perimeters would make it possible to reduce food dependence for livestock and sugar products considerably. While market gardening and tree crops take up a lot of space (122,000 hectares), forage crops and industrial crops (sugar beet) (23,000 hectares) are neglected, although there is the most urgent need for these.[19]

Why, of all the sectors that make up agriculture, is the irrigated sub-sector virtually the only one to enjoy remunerative prices (including in addition to ground rent, a rate of profit approximating that of other non-agricultural branches) and various inducements from the state?

The hypothesis that we adopt at this stage is that, unlike other agricultural sub-sectors, the state is here deprived of the essential weapon that enables it to extract a surplus. What enables the state to set prices at a low level is the possibility of importing similar products at a price lower than the domestic price: this is the case with cereals, meat, milk and dairy products as well as olive oil, which can be replaced by imported soya oil.

But, this recourse to imports that enables the state to exert pressure on prices is hardly possible for fruit and vegetables for, unlike other agricultural commodities: they are perishable, and between the place of production abroad and the final Tunisian consumer, the risks of damage are very high; generally, those produced in Tunisia are priced much lower than in other countries; and transport, packing and processing costs are often higher than the market value of those commodities.

The state therefore has very little margin for manoeuvre in this area; in the framework of capitalist accumulation, it must ensure that these staples are produced at prices that are not too high since they represent a not insignificant proportion of the cost of reproduction of the labour force.

The only effective means available to the state is to increase production rapidly so as to avoid demand exceeding supply and the creation of a shortage (of which producers would take advantage to extract a superprofit) and – why not? – to bring about a situation of relative over-production that would make possible a reduction in prices.

The tool it must use is irrigation since that alone can make possible a rapid intensification of production that would affect prices.

Consequences of state agricultural policy

Except for the irrigated sub-sector, with fewer than 50,000 farmers, state policy has consisted for over two decades in extorting a growing surplus at the expense of the vast majority of the Tunisian peasantry, so that:

a) the peasantry has been kept in a sometimes tragic situation of poverty where it is unable to set aside the necessary savings to preserve and improve its means of production. The 1980 national household budget survey reveals that almost half the rural population is living below the poverty line and that, out of a population of 1,865,000 persons living below this threshold (set in 1962 at 50 dinars per head per annum, equal to 120 dinars at 1980 prices), 1,473,000 live in the rural areas and 392,000 in the urban areas. This means that four out of five 'poor people' live in the rural areas whereas the rural population represents less than half the country's total population. How then can it produce the incomes necessary for productive investments?

b) capital, 'the bearer of capitalist rationality', has invested less and less in agriculture as a result of the fact that the prices of essential agricultural products barely cover production costs.

The consequences of this situation are a significant falling-off of investment, a virtual stagnation of production, an increased food deficit and a retention of small and medium-sized family holdings.

Falling-off investment, stagnation of agricultural production and food dependence
Whereas the rural population represented almost 45% of the total population during the 1960s and 35% in 1980, agricultural investments represented barely 20% of the total in the 1960s and 12% between 1970 and 1979. As a result, agricultural production virtually stagnated: the balance sheet drawn up on the occasion of the preparation of the Sixth Plan for 1982–86 reveals that agricultural value added rose in constant prices by only 1% per annum between 1962 and 1971 and 2% per annum between 1972 and 1981.

Since homogeneous statistical series for the last two decades do not exist, the movement of the production of each of the leading commodities can be reliably measured only for the period 1971 to 1981. During that period, the production of commodities, whose prices are officially fixed, virtually stagnated: that of cereals rose at an average rate of 1.1% per annum, of meat (not including poultry) at an annual rate of 1.7% and that of oil olives even declined by 1.1% per annum, while production of vegetables experienced an annual growth rate of 5.3% and that of fruit 6.2%.

During the 1960s, the growth of production was even slower since agricultural value added grew half as slowly as during the 1970s. Consequently, from being an agricultural surplus country, Tunisia was transformed increasingly into a deficit country: immediately after independence, the country had a rate of cover of its food imports by its exports of over 200% until 1960; after 1961, and until 1966, this rate of cover fell to an average of 150%; after 1967, the deficit became structural, the rate of cover, except for 1972, was around 80% but after 1977, the situation became serious since less than half of

Tunisia's food imports were covered by its agricultural exports.[20] During 1980, 1981 and 1982, the rate of cover fell below one-third and the deficit rose to 141 million dinars per annum.

Given that during these three years the value of agricultural production reached an average of 642 million dinars, it emerges that the food deficit equalled 22% of national production by value. But what must still be pointed out is that this food dependence forms an essential part of the country's financial dependence since the deficit in question represents no less than 60.5% of the deficit in the current account balance and 66.7% of that in the balance of payments.

Apart from the amounts, what is particularly serious is that the dependence relates to strategic food staples: today, national production covers only 55% of cereal needs, 40% of dairy product needs and a tiny part of those for sugar. Moreover, these three leading products alone represent over two-thirds of total food imports and nine-tenths of our deficit.

Retention of small and medium-sized family holdings
After two decades of extracting a growing surplus from the essential products of agriculture, small and medium-sized holdings based on family labour have been consolidated. This is a major trend, due not to some imaginary 'resistance' by a pre-capitalist sector to the development of the capitalist mode of production, but to state policy. In fact, if it is happening, it is because profit-seeking capital has hardly been attracted to a sector where the fixed prices cover only the strict production costs and because it is this peasant agriculture – subject to fixed prices and unable to avoid production even where these prices are particularly low – which best facilitates this transfer of value to the benefit of non-agricultural capital. For, unlike capital, the peasant and his family are obsessed neither with realizing a profit nor with realizing a rent but quite simply with surviving.

Stabilizing agrarian structures and keeping wage labour in narrow limits are typical features of the evolution of the agricultural world: the principal contradiction is not between the agrarian bourgeoisie and the agricultural proletariat (or poor peasantry) but between the vast majority of the peasantry and 'urban' capital (through the continual decline of the prices of essential agricultural commodities and the reduction of the farmer to the status of a home worker on sub-minimum wages). On top of this formal subjection of the peasantry to urban capital, the agricultural world is also witnessing the exploitation of a proletariat and semi-proletarian peasantry by big capitalist farmers and the development of new forms of surplus extortion through the ownership of mechanical means of production (tractors, harvesters and so on).

Stabilization of agrarian structures: Thanks to the survey of agricultural structures conducted in 1961–62 and the series of basic agricultural surveys that have been carried out annually since 1976, it is possible to analyse the broad changes occurring in the agricultural world.

Tunisian agriculture is still characterized by a very unequal distribution of land: between 1961–62 and 1980 the number of farmers has increased only slightly (from 326,000 to 355,000, at most 9%); small and medium-sized holdings neither in number nor area (less than 20 ha and 20–100 ha) have declined, but their numbers rather increased (320,700 in 1961–62 to 350,600 in 1980, from 98.4% to 98.8%) and the area they occupy also increased from 3,572,000 ha to 3,779,000 ha (74.1% to 81.5%); large holdings (over 100 ha) seem to have lost some importance both absolutely and relatively: the area they cover fell from 1,250,000 ha (1961–62) to 858,000 ha (1980) (from 26% to 18.5%) and the number of farmers (5,100 in 1961–62, 4,400 in 1980) fell both relatively and absolutely.[21]

On average, the size of large holdings fell from 245 ha to 195 ha while that of small and medium-sized ones stabilized (at 6.2–6.3 ha[22] for the former and 36–37 ha for the latter).

Relations of production: Within agriculture these relations have become more complex; wage labour does not seem to have increased much, indeed rather the reverse. What strikes one first is an absence of the development of capitalist relations of production involving an ever-rising number of capitalist farmers (or bigger capitalists) and wage labourers with only their labour power to sell. But a new dynamic has made its appearance: it is no longer crystallized through ownership of land but through mechanical means of production: tractors, harvester threshers, harvester binders for example.

The fact is that small producers have found themselves more and more driven to deal with the continuous decline in the prices of their products by turning to modern means of production. Lacking the means to acquire them, they are obliged to hire them. And precisely behind this 'hiring' relationship lurks a new relationship of exploitation, from which the owners of these means of production extort a large part of the surplus produced by the peasantry.

Comparison of the 1961–62 survey with those carried out in recent years also reveals a stabilization or even a diminution of the number of wage-earners in agriculture.

Thus, during the four years 1977–80, the average number of permanent wage-earners was 54,200 as against 72,600 in 1961–62, although there was an increase in the size of the permanent labour force (546,300 in 1961–62, 593,200 over 1977–80): more and more, it seems that agriculture relies on family labour (473,700 in 1961–62, 539,000 over 1977–80) which now represents nine-tenths of the permanent members of the labour force.[23]

Clearly the consolidation of independent family agriculture and the failure of wage-earning to become the norm. Recognition of the fact that this 'inevitable creation of a minority of capitalist agricultural holdings based on wage labour' and the concomitant polarization between proletarianized peasants and a rural bourgeoisie are just not happening is unavoidable. But because their land does not support them, many farmers have to sell their labour power to obtain some extra income. Wage labour is thus not a separate status; the majority of the peasantry has recourse to it more or less partially. And today almost two-fifths of smallholders devote most of their time to outside work, usually as wage labourers.

It must, however, be noted that this 'semi-proletarian' character of the peasantry seems to have diminished since 1961, as the proportion of small peasants devoting more than six months to activities other than their farms fell from 53.7% to 38.1% in 1980. The number of big absentee farmers seems to have diminished too.[24]

In 1961–62, only 18.5% of farmers had recourse to mechanical means of production; today, almost two-thirds of them do.

The users of these means of production are not only the big farmers: the proportion of smallholders using them rose from 13.2% in 1961–62 to 52.2% in 1980 and of medium-sized farmers from 38.2% to 77.7%; in the space of two decades the number of smallholders using mechanical equipment rose by a factor of 4.5 and that of medium-sized farmers by 2 to 2.5.[25]

The vast majority of these users, however, is made up of people who hire the equipment. While in 1961–62, there were 9,560 owners of such equipment and 44,290 hirers (or one owner for 4.5 hirers), today there are 11,700 owners and 187,800 hirers, or one owner for 16 hirers.[26] And behind this 'hiring' lie concealed relations of production through which the owners extract part of the surplus peasant labour and pass on to the 'hirers' the price loss that they themselves suffer (when they are farming at the same time) as farmers.

Studying the village communities in the region of lake Alaotra (Madagascar) where the state has carried out an 'agrarian reform' (redistributing land to small and landless peasants and banning dealings in land), J. Charmes[27] shows that because the problem of providing small peasants with equipment has not been solved, they have been unable to liberate themselves from their former masters, 'who soon realized that the monopoly of capital had become the new channel through which the old relations of domination were to be perpetuated'.

> The progressive disintegration of ground rent led to some redistribution of clienteles, i.e. of the labour force creamed off by those with power; in particular, a rising class (the class of owners of mechanical equipment) has made its appearance, it has been able to carve out a niche for itself at the expense of the former landowners who have not always known how to grasp the opportunity of adapting themselves as the situation required.

Closer to home, in Tunisia, Khalil Zamiti, studying the village of El Menara (55 km south-west of the city of Kairouan), highlights this extraordinary form of surplus labour constituted by the 'hiring' of agricultural equipment by the owners at the expense of the peasantry.

> At a rate of 1.70 dinars per hour for ploughing and 2 to 6 dinars for towing the water tanks intended for irrigating the olive groves, each tractor hired for 300 days a year, within the *cheikhat*, brings in for its owner a net profit of 10 dinars a day, after deducting the costs of repaying the price of the machine and the costs of fuel, maintenance, etc. Repayment of the supplier of the tractor is completed by the end of the third year.

Far more than owning and farming the land, owning modern agricultural equipment is tending to become the essential form of surplus extraction within the agricultural sector.

The monopoly of land is tending less and less (or has even ceased altogether) to be realized economically. It is more and more in the monopoly of machine capital that the extraction of surplus labour and the new contradictions in the agricultural world are crystallizing.

To summarize, Tunisian peasants are suffering a double extraction of surplus labour, 'personal' extraction by the owners of machinery and 'impersonal' extraction by extra-agricultural capital through the under-pricing of their products whose prices do not even remunerate their labour power at the minimum agricultural wage.

Current situation and prospects

Such was the situation in agriculture broadly speaking up to 1979. Since then, new trends seem to be appearing. These are shown in the unprecedented revaluation of commodity prices previously held down and even the freeing of some of them as well as in the enhanced role that the Sixth Plan for 1982–86 gave agriculture in the country's economic activity and the institutional and financial means now made available to farmers.

This turnaround, it must be stressed, was not dictated either by pressure from the peasantry or by any change in the composition of the ruling bloc. The peasantry, atomized and with no real power to make demands, does not strictly speaking represent a social force. Behind the new agricultural policy – or what is just its early beginnings – there are in fact the unprecedented upsurge of the world prices of agricultural products, the level of which has, in some cases since 1979–80, risen above domestic prices, and the dramatic deficit in the food balance. This last is fundamental since government's attitude towards the rural areas depends on how it moves: any collapse in world prices threatens to lead to a reconsideration of the policy of encouraging agriculture embarked on over the last two or three years while a rise in them may well lead to a consolidation and reinforcement of this turnaround.

The new agricultural policy and its content

Until 1979, as we have seen, the prices of the main agricultural products (cereals, beef and veal and sheepmeat, milk, olive oil) were set by the state and, from the early 1960s, were continually undervalued. And, although employing two-fifths of the total economically active population, agriculture was attracting a smaller and smaller share of investments: one-fifth during the 1960s and one-eighth during the 1970s. After 1979–80, all this changed.

Revaluation of the prices of agricultural commodities: Whereas they had remained virtually stagnant from 1975 to 1979, the nominal prices of the main agricultural commodities – except for fruit and vegetables – were substantially increased after 1980.

Table 9.4
Changes in cereal and livestock producer prices: (in current dinars)

Products	Annual increase 1975–79	1979	1980	1981	1982	1983	Annual increase 1979–83
Hard wheat (quintals)	4.8	7.6	8.6	9.6	11.0	12.8	13.9
Soft wheat (quintals)	5.3	7.0	7.7	8.7	10.0	11.7	13.7
Barley (quintals)	6.9	5.5	5.9	6.9	8.0	9.5	14.6
Milk (litres)	0	0.090	0.130	0.150	0.200	0.200	22.1
Sheepmeat*	5.8	0.910	0.983	1.061	1.400	fluctuating	17.9
Beef and veal (Kg)	4.1	0.564	0.630	0.675	0.880	1.020	16.0

* The price of sheepmeat was freed in 1979. The calculations given here relate to the period 1975–78 on the one hand and the period 1978–82 on the other.

Cereal prices experienced an average annual increase of 14%, milk prices over 22%. After an annual increase of 16.0% the prices of beef and veal were freed at the end of 1982 and those of sheepmeat were freed at the end of 1979; since then they have risen dramatically.

In recent years, inflation has been higher than in the past: prices of industrial products have increased some 10% per annum and prices of the principal agricultural inputs have also increased substantially. Nevertheless, it emerges that farmers' incomes have improved considerably.

For cereals, on the basis of an identical cost structure and the same yield per hectare by type of holding, calculations show a significant rise between 1979 and 1982–83.[28] whether including remuneration of the labour force (treated as

Table 9.5
Movements in real income (in constant dinars) per hectare of cereal land (1979 = 100)

Cereal/farming type	Index of net income			Index of net income and remuneration of labour		
	1979	1982	1983	1979	1982	1983
Hard wheat:						
Intensive	100.0	140.8	199.1	100.0	133.3	163.7
Semi-intensive	100.0	125.7	322.0	100.0	123.7	202.0
Traditional	—	—	—	100.0	102.5	147.9
Soft wheat:						
Intensive	100.0	116.1	147.3	100.0	117.5	139.1
Semi-intensive	100.0	128.2	162.8	100.0	127.0	151.5
Traditional	—	—	—	100.0	92.6	159.3
Barley:						
Intensive	100.0	134.8	204.4	100.0	128.3	156.4
Semi-intensive	100.0	—	—	100.0	206.0	314.3
Traditional	—	—	—	—	—	—

income in so far as, for the most part, this labour force is that of the farmer and his family) or treating it simply as a cost.

Dairy farming changed from being an activity that remunerated the work of the farmer and his family at a level even lower than the guaranteed minimum agricultural wage to one that is now a profitable activity. Finally, stock farming constitutes an increasingly significant source of income, especially since the freeing of prices in November 1982.

Table 9.6
Changes in real income from stock farming (in constant 1979 dinars)

Product/farming type	Net income			Net income + remuneration of labour		
	1979	*1982*	*1983*	*1979*	*1982*	*1983*
Milk:[a]						
Integrated[b]	−24.2	41.8	—	22.6	99.2	—
Non-integrated	−52.5	5.6	—	5.7	62.9	—
Cattle meat:[c]						
Integrated without ensilage	29.4	29.4	45.3	35.6	36.9	52.1
Integrated	21.1	33.2	44.8	27.3	40.7	51.7
Non-integrated	21.5	20.2	35.7	27.7	27.8	42.6

a Income per cow per annum.
b In integrated stock farming, the farmer produces the grass and hay and purchases the concentrate, in non-integrated farming the farmer produces the grass, but purchases the hay and concentrate.
c Income per fattened bull calf.

Growth of investment in agriculture: During the 1970s, agriculture attracted only 12.5% of total investment. But during the Sixth Plan, 1982–86, this proportion was to be increased to 17.3%: investments were set to rise from 543 million dinars between 1977 and 1981 to 1,420 million dinars between 1982 and 1986. The attention thus given to agriculture was something new: previous plans gave it only 12% to 14% of total investment. To achieve this target, new financial and institutional measures were proposed:

– financially, it was proposed that the state set aside 929 million dinars, 25% of its capital budget, excluding debt, for financing (as aginst 20% during the previous plan) and mobilize 178 million dinars in external credits for this sector; it was also proposed that the volume of credits granted by the banking system and the FOSDA should reach 487 million dinars as against only 173 million dinars during the Fifth Plan, 1977–81.
– in terms of institutions, a bank specializing in agricultural financing (Banque Nationale de Développement Agricole [National Agricultural Development Bank]), with capital of 40 million dinars was to be created and an Agence de Promotion des Investissements Agricoles [Agricultural Investment Promotion Agency] responsible for identifying projects and aiding agricultural promoters has already started operations.

Determinants of the new agricultural policy

The change in the political orientation towards agriculture is due essentially to the upsurge of world prices for agricultural food products. Until 1978, these were generally lower than domestic prices: including transport costs, imported cereals and livestock products were generally 20% cheaper than local products. But, after 1979, the situation was reversed, especially as regards the basic commodity: cereals.

World cereal prices which, despite sometimes large swings, had been slowly increasing up to 1978, began to rise sharply in 1979; by 1981 they were twice the 1978 level. The food deficit, which remained contained within a limit of 50–60 million dinars at most, reached 85 million dinars in 1979, 144 million dinars in 1980 and over 173 million dinars in 1981.

Even from capital's viewpoint, the situation had become alarming and despite the raising of domestic agricultural prices, international prices remained very high: encouragement of local agricultural production became vital to avoid a sharp rise in wage costs.

Prospects

The analysis made above reveals how far policy towards the rural areas is dependent on the international situation. Significant measures have, it is true, been taken for agriculture but it is by no means assured that they will be continued and pushed farther. Today, world prices have fallen[29] and the domestic economic situation is very tense: the external vice which lay behind the turnaround in agricultural policy is loosening and the pressure of urban actors – workers and the extra-agricultural bourgeoisie – for a larger share of the national income seems to be too strong to allow a real consolidation of the policy of encouraging agriculture.

The institutional and financial reforms contemplated for two or three years are being undertaken slowly and, in some cases,[30] farmers' incomes are falling. But even if we suppose that a policy of encouraging agriculture is pursued, the essential question which then arises is: for the benefit of which farmers?

So far, paradoxically, the marginalization of this sector has contributed to maintaining a large peasant population: but will not raising the prices of agricultural commodities and the various measures to encourage agricultural investment lead to an unprecedented deployment of capital – as a social relation – in agriculture and the eviction of the peasantry?

The prospects are not yet clearly defined but the orientations that are gradually becoming clear seem to indicate that the path entered on is not a peasant, but a capitalist path: the volume of credit set aside for small and medium-sized farmers, who represent nine-tenths of the total and account for 80% of production, represents only one-third of the total, and the chief purpose of the established institutions (Banque Agricole and Agence de Promotion des Investissements Agricoles) is to support large farmers.

If this orientation is confirmed, the country's food security might be more or less assured but the problems that will then appear (migration from the rural areas and rapid urban growth) may prove to be uncontrollable.

Notes

1. At least until 1979. as since 1980. the price of cereals. milk and olive oil has been increased while the price of beef and veal and sheepmeat was freed (in 1979 for sheepmeat. in 1982 for beef and veal).

2. Study entitled: 'Prix à la production des céréales et du fourrage dans la Tunisie du Nord'. by A. Mabrouk. for Bureau du Plan et du Développement Agricole. Tunis 1975.

3. A 1977 survey of cereal production costs by the Agricultural Statistics Division of the Ministry of Agriculture confirms these conclusions. It shows that the cost of production of a quintal of hard wheat (excluding the profit margin) is seven dinars in the north of Tunisia and 11.3 in the centre and south whereas the net price received by the farmer is 6.5 dinars and the cost of production of a quintal of barley (excluding the profit margin) is eight dinars in the north and 6.6 dinars in the centre and south whereas the net price received by the producer is 4.5 dinars. For soft wheat. the sample survey turned out not to be representative.

4. *Coût de production des produits de l'élevage*. Office de l'Elevage et des Pâturages. Tunis 1976.

5. In integrated livestock farming. the farmer provides the grass and hay but purchases the concentrate. and the level of production is such that one cow produces 3.000 kg per milking: in semi-integrated livestock farming. the farmer provides the grass but purchases the hay and concentrate and the level of production is 2.500 kg per milking.

6. 'Note relative aux problèmes posés au secteur de la production laitière'. Office de l'Elevage et des Pâturages. pp. 2–3. Tunis 1974.

7. Ibid.. p. 47.

8. The farmer is increasingly forced to turn to the market because holdings smaller than 10 hectares. which have most of the cattle. cover only 14% of forage areas whereas holdings larger than 50 hectares. which cover only 7% to 9% of the national herd. cover 56% of the forage areas.

9. FAO-SIDA Project. 'Développement de la production de viande bovine dans le Nord de la Tunisie'. Tunis 1976.

10. *Coût de production de l'élevage*. op. cit.

11. 'Enquête sur les coûts de production des olives à huile pour la campagne 1976–1977'. Ministère de l'Agriculture. Tunis. November 1980.

12. UNA costs and ministry costs compared (adding to these latter a gross margin of 15%) shows that there are virtually no gaps between the two sources:

Products	UNA costs 1975 (dinars per metric ton)	Ministry of Agriculture	
		Benchmark year	Costs
Hard wheat	75.0	1975	62.1 to 118.4*
Soft wheat	71.5	1975	60.9 to 106.2*
Barley	61.0	1975	59.2 to 114.7*
Oil olives	119.0	1977	118.3
Cattle meat	550.0	1976	587.0 to 642.0
Sheepmeat	750.0	1976	670.0 to 910.0
Milk	120.0	1976	105.0 to 132.0

* Excluding non-mechanized holdings.

The only product whose UNA cost is higher than the Ministry of Agriculture's is oil olive: 119 dinars per metric ton in 1975 as against 118.3 dinars per metric ton in 1977. But this, negligible, gap is more than made up for by the difference in producer prices: in 1975, oil growers were paid by the ONH on the basis of 527 dinars per metric ton, whereas in 1977, they received only 400 dinars (83 millimes per kg of oil olives in 1975 as against 60 millimes in 1977).

13. Unlike other products for which the statistical price series goes back to 1961 and even earlier, the fruit and vegetables price statistical series only goes back to 1965.

14. See 'Rapport préparatoire au VIe Plan 1982–1986: Périmètres irrigués'. Tunisia, Ministère de l'Agriculture', April 1981. A study carried out by the Centre National des Etudes Agricoles estimates that the real cost of infrastructure within the irrigated public perimeter at 3.500 dinars per hectare for the new Testour Medjez perimeter. This cost rises to 4.600 dinars if the value of the dam and delivery canal are included.

15. The first law dating from 11 June 1958 concerns the Basse Vallée Medjerda perimeter, the second, dating from 27 May 1963 and amended by the law of 16 February 1971 relates to the other perimeters.

16. See the study by M. Fekih, 'Structures agraires dans la Basse Vallée de la Medjerda'. OMVVM, Tunis 1977.

17. *Note relative aux problèmes de l'irrigation dans les périmètres publics irrigués de l'OMVVM*. PDI, p. 2.

18. Since the production of the irrigated sub-sector today represents some 25% of total agricultural production.

19. Source for figures: *VIe Plan de Développement Economique et Sociale 1982–86*. p. 100. Cf. the food deficit in industrial crops and cattle products (meat and milk).

20. For more details see the appendix: food exports and imports.

21. See *Structures des exploitation agricoles*, Ministère de l'Agriculture. Tunis, December 1981.

22. 'Pressure on the land' would be less pronounced than might appear since in the 0–5 ha band there are almost 36.000 irrigated holdings.

23. See *Structures des exploitation agricoles*, op. cit., p. 62 (for 1961–62), pp. 17ff (for 1977–80).

24. Ibid., p. 18 (for 1961–62), p. 24 (for 1980).

25. Ibid., p. 73 (for 1961–62), p. 32 (for 1980).

26. Ibid.

27. Jacques Charmes, 'Evolution des modes de faire valoir et transformation des structures sociales dans la région de l'Anony (Nord Ouest du Lac Alaotra)', *Cahiers ORSTOM*, XII, 3, 1975.

28. For 1983, we have used an increase in the official cost of living index of 10%, although we know that during the first quarter of 1983, the index remained below the level reached at the end of 1982.

29. The prices of hard wheat moved from 12.690 in 1981 to 10.612 in 1982, of soft wheat from 9.956 dinars to 9.522 dinars and of barley from 9.051 to 7.800 dinars.

30. Thus the price of feed for milch cows was increased by 50% on 22 November 1982 without the milk producer prices being raised. The result was a collapse in farmers' incomes.

10. The State and Rural Development 1960–85

Sidi Kane, Baba Ba and Pap Sow

Introduction

On 4 April 1960, Senegal became independent. In August 1960, the short-lived Mali Federation broke up, and its remaining components – Senegal and Mali – went their separate ways. Senegal now embarked on its economic and social development alone. In the beginning, the Senegalese state had far more advantages than many other newly independent African states. Industrialization could build on foundations that were already relatively extensive, accounting for 18% of GDP, and this GDP, at the time, was higher than that of the Ivory Coast or Cameroun.

By 1983, Senegal's per capita income of US$ 440.00 was scarcely half that of those countries. 'The GDP growth rate – 2.3% – was moreover the lowest of all African States not afflicted by war or civil conflicts'.[1] Whatever indicators are used, and whatever sectors are analysed, the economic crisis the country is experiencing is apparent at all levels: indebtedness, stagnation or even recession, unemployment, and so on. An assessment mission stated baldly: 'In Senegal, the crisis is now such that a priority policy is short-term adjustment of the imbalances in the balance of payments and public finances. Senegal is living beyond its means.'[2]

Overall, groundnut production has stagnated in recent years. As GDP and exports have risen, so the role of groundnuts seems to have been reduced. But this observation seems to be incomplete. This is because, 1) Groundnut production's share in GDP has rarely been more than 10%, except between 1960 and 1966, when it was slightly above 10%. After 1967, the decline began and reached its nadir at 5% in 1971, after which it fluctuated between under 5% and over 10%. 2) The decline of groundnuts exported occurred in stages, but was continuous throughout the period 1960–84. From 80% of exports in 1961, the decline was very slow until 1967. From 1968 the fall accelerated and in 1971 groundnuts accounted for only 35% of exports. After 1971, there were good years (1972, 1976, 1977) and bad years (1978, 1980, 1981) but the downward trend continued.

The presence of Agences de Développement Rural [ADRs, Rural Development Agencies] and especially those more specifically responsible for the groundnut basin (SODEVA since 1968) has thus apparently failed to bring about any significant change in achieving the development plans' targets.

In the late 1970s there seems to have been a growing awareness of this situation. Industrialization was postponed; the Sixth Four-year Plan was one of 'recovery and consolidation'. The 1980–85 Economic and Financial Recovery Plan (PREF) and the 1985–92 Medium- and Long-term Structural Adjustment Programme (PAML) were intended to carry out this declared policy of adjustment. Consequently, the need for a New Industrial Policy (NPI) and above all, a New Agricultural Policy (NPA) seemed inevitable.

The crisis was most manifest in the rural areas, and it was there that the state aimed to secure what was intended as a radical turnaround. During the 1960s and 1970s, the state aimed to carry out economic development itself as far as possible. In the rural areas, these years were also marked by the appearance of a whole series of Sociétés Nationales d'Economie Mixte and d'Etablissements Publics. In 1965, there was the Société d'Aménagement et d'Exploitation du Delta (SAED), in 1966, the Office National de Coopération et d'Assistance au Développement (ONCAD) and, in 1968, the Société de Développement et de Vulgarisation Agricole (SODEVA). And, during the 1970s, the parastatal sector continued to spread with the creation of other Sociétés Régionales de Développement Rural and Sociétés d'Interventions (SRDR, SI).

The programme for the 1980s began with the dissolution of ONCAD in 1980; the Société des Terres Neuves (STN) and the Société Nationale d'Approvisionnement du Monde Rural (SONAR) were abolished in 1985, while drastic cuts were made and proposed by SODEVA, SOMIVAC and the rest.

Between the 1960s and 1980s, the state was thus proposing to carry out a sharp change of policy. The policy for the rural areas pursued since independence was thus, a quarter of a century later, challenged by the very people responsible for carrying it out.

In order to understand the reasons for this volte-face, it is important to look back at the results of the policy, to know why it led to an impasse and the need to change it. Perhaps only then will it be possible to know what is necessary in order to pursue a different policy, by setting out the outlines of the new strategy or, at least, what is no longer a viable policy. This should lead – beyond a critique of the results of policy in the rural areas, and the factors that have hindered their development – to a grasp of the structural causes, both economic and organizational, and political and social, that underlie rural development policy in order to grasp the possibilities or limitations of a different strategy.

The essential purpose is to establish, in broad outline, the balance sheet of agriculture – rural development – 25 years after independence in an attempt to identify, through the economic, social and institutional processes set in train, the context in which to set any new agricultural strategy.

This chapter examines the impasse into which rural development policy had led; the features of this impasse: effects of agriculture's economic dynamic, inefficiency and cost of institutional back-up, economic and social confiscation of rural production; and the situations and dynamics created (impoverishment of the rural areas, destruction of agrarian systems, increased indebtedness) that any new strategy must deal with.

Management of rural development

The management of rural development in Senegal, from independence to the time when the objectives of disengagement were really put into effect, was above all a state matter. This was due to the position of agriculture in the country as well as by rural supervision through the state and parastatal structures for intervention. The results obtained and the factors leading to them thus also involve the state's responsibility.

Situation and importance of agriculture

In 1962, agriculture occupied 87% of the total population and 74% of the economically active male population. At independence, 'The cultivation of groundnuts occupied half the population and provided the bulk of monetary incomes. With its derivatives (oils and pastes) they represented 80 to 85% of the total value of exports.'[3] Today 70% of the economically active population are still employed in agriculture, and it will 'necessarily remain the principal source of employment for the majority of the population during the next 20 years.'[4]

The country's whole economic life still remains strongly dependent on the primary sector, as the Conseil National des Employeurs Sénégalais (CNES, National Council of Senegalese Employers) stressed in observing that the decline in industrial growth between 1976 and 1984 was indeed due to the various oil shocks but *first and foremost* 'to the successive "shocks" suffered by the Senegalese economy as a result of several consecutive years of drought (on average one year in two between 1977 and 1984)'.[5] And *finally* to 'the deterioration of agricultural production leading to the decline of several sectors of industrial activity (oil mills, construction materials, plastics etc.) directly linked to the success of the Agricultural Policy'.[6]

Industrialists thus clearly recognize the importance of agriculture. Its unmistakable primacy in economic life was manifested following the droughts of 1973–74 and 1977–78. The growth of GDP reflects the strong fluctuations that correspond to those of agricultural production.

The success or failure of an economic development policy is, therefore, played out essentially on the rural development front. Consequently, immediately after independence, the government involved itself directly in promoting development in this sector, setting objectives and recording results with each Four-year Plan. Rural development policy was thus the fruit of state supervision.

Rural development or rural supervision policy

From this angle, it is possible to distinguish, aside from the vagaries of the country's political life, two phases of the same strategy of state organization of the rural areas.

The 1960s: bureaucratization: The main aim of this movement was the desire to put an end to the *économie de traite*.[7] To this end administrative structures were established putting the rural areas under the state's and its ministries' wing. Thus the following structures were established in 1960:

The Animation Rurale programme (AR, Extension Service), responsible for organizing and mobilizing producers and raising their consciousness towards attaining development objectives.

The Centres d'Expansion Rurale (CER, Rural Expansion Centres), multipurpose technical teams to make possible implementation of development programmes at the district level by helping the peasants.

The Centres Régionaux pour l'Assistance au Développement (CRAD, Regional Development Assistance Centres) responsible for managing seeds, fertilizers and equipment.

The Office de Commercialisation de l'Arachide (OCA, Groundnut Marketing Board) and the Banque Nationale de Développement du Sénégal (BNDS, Senegalese National Development Bank) to manage internal and external trade and ensure the financing to facilitate breaking with the *économie de traite*.

The creation of the Office Nationale de Coopération et d'Assistance au Développement (ONCAD, National Office for Cooperatives and Development Assistance) in 1966 completed this movement by bringing together within it the tasks assigned to the OCA and the CRADs.

Following the establishment of these structures, in the 1960s a whole series of Sociétés Nationales d'Economie Mixte and d'Etablissements Publics were set up to replace the colonial companies.

In 1965, the Société d'Aménagement et d'Exploitation des Terres du Delta (SAED), replaced the Organisation Autonome du Delta.

The Société de Développement et de Vulgarisation Agricole (SODEVA) replaced the Société d'Assistance Technique et de Coopération in 1968.

The Société pour le Développement des Fibres et Textiles (SODEFITEX) replaced the Compagnie Française pour le Développement des Textiles.

The 1970s: strengthening supervision: The 1970s saw the development of this parastatal sector continue. Without making a proper assessment of this replacement phase, despite the failure to achieve the objectives set by the four-year plans, the state continued to set up Sociétés de Développement Rural and Sociétés d'Interventions at each regional level.

The SRDRs had the job of developing their region, notably the planning, execution and co-ordination of development activities. The Sociétés d'Interventions were responsible for given projects. During the 1970s, the rural areas were thus covered by a whole institutional network of supervisory companies formed by the ADRs of the parastatal sector: SAED, mentioned above, for the Fleuve region; SODEVA, for the groundnut basin; Société de Mise en Valeur Agricole de la Casamance for the Casamance (Lower and Middle Casamance above all); SODAGRI, Société de Développement de l'Agriculture, for the Anambé basin; Société des Terres Neuves for the agricultural settlement of eastern Senegal; SODEFITEX, for the development of cotton in Haute Casamance and the Tambacounda region; Société pour le Développement de l'Elevage dans la Zone Sylvo-pastorale (Fleuve region); Société d'Exploitation des Resources Animales du Sénégal (SERAS).

Last twist of the ADRs – food self-sufficiency: The 1960s and 1970s thus saw the establishment by government of a whole institutional network to supervise the rural areas. A more or less non-capitalist statist perspective – inaugurated by Senegal's first government (led by Mamadou Dia in 1960–62) – continued and maintained by the four-year economic and social development plans of the progressive and Third-Worldist Father Lebret can thus be seen in agricultural development policy. This more or less spontaneous form of ideology of the early days of independence seemed to imply that it was enough to set up state or parastatal structures (national sector) to replace private foreign companies, and to replace expatriates by nationals to achieve the objectives of rural development.

Results of rural development policy
At the end of the Sixth Plan, an examination of the results obtained for the chief crops should provide some idea of the efficiency of the institutional supervisory network's contribution to rural development.

Groundnuts: The cultivation of this crop had developed in Senegal since 1860. It remains the dominant product of the country's economy and in 1986, a leader of the groundnut oil industry stated: 'Groundnuts will probably remain a vital product for Senegal for at least another one or two decades, unless the current situation changes drastically.' Each year, groundnuts earn 60 to 70 billion Francs CFA in foreign exchange.[8] Since independence, material and institutional resources have been repeatedly mobilized primarily for this crop's benefit.

Nevertheless, groundnut production targets continued to vary. During the first six Plans, the target dropped from 1,350,000 to 830,000 metric tons, with an average of some 1,100,000 metric tons.[9] More seriously, the out-turns themselves fell short by an average of 26%. Even reaching 750,000 metric tons each year still remains an illusion; the groundnut harvest has reached this target only seven times since 1970. If 100 is taken as the base of the target and fulfilment of the First Plan, the target fell some 13% and fulfilment 10% between the First and Sixth plans.

The presence of Agences de Développement Rural [ADRs, Rural Development Agencies] and especially those responsible more specifically for the groundnut basin, SODEVA since 1968, thus seems to have resulted in no significant change in attaining the development plans' objectives.

Cereals: Even though the cereal deficit is tending to worsen, it is structural: it is inherited from the colonial policy that aimed to promote groundnut production at the expense of local cereal production, the cereal deficit having been reduced through the cheap import of Indochina's surplus of broken rice.

Visible consumption of cereals over the period 1960–85 increased by about 3% per annum, whereas population increased by about 2.5%; however, uncertainty regarding the production of millet and sorghum makes this comparison of little significance. The extreme variation in harvests, and the little-known phenomena of stocking and destocking make analysis of recent trends difficult.

Whereas at the beginning of the 1960–85 period imports (rice + wheat) represented only 20% to 30% of cereal consumption, by the end of it they were nearly 50%, due to imports growing steadily by some 4% per annum, whereas local production (rice, millet, sorghum) stagnated. Only maize experienced rapid growth, but it accounts for less than 10% of consumption. The cereal deficit currently represents about 500,000 metric tons, of which almost 350,000 is for broken rice. To reduce or even eliminate this deficit, in due course, will be difficult.

The principal cereal crops will be analysed below, taking account of the available data.

Table 10.1
Cereals: domestic production and imports (selected years)
('000 metric tons)

| Year | Senegalese production | | | Imports | | | |
	Rice	Millet	Maize	Rice	Wheats*	Total	% imports
1960	41	320	20	(100)	(60)	(541)	30
1965	72	532	37	179	61	881	27
1970	101	623	49	119	112	1,004	23
1975	76	795	43	102	102	1,118	18
1979	83	795	47	352	123	1,400	34
1980	79	496	45	303	97	1,020	39
1981	42	545	57	353	122	1,119	42
1982	67	736	79	320	106	1,308	33
1983	62	585	82	350	114	1,193	39
1984	66	352	52	360	(110)	(940)	49

* Wheats and flours.
Figures in parentheses = extrapolations, figures not available.
Source: République Française, Ministère de la Coopération, *Déséquilibres structurels et programmes d'ajustement au Sénégal*, 1985, p. 103.

Millets and sorghums: These constitute the main traditional food crops, and the success of the policy of agricultural diversification and especially that of the national target of food self-sufficiency should be evident here. The production target varies over the six Plans from 475,000 to 750,000 metric tons, with an average of 665,000 metric tons.

But fulfilments remain below targets by some 20%, with sharp falls in production each year: 795,000 metric tons in 1974–75; 621,000 in 1976–77; 590,000 in 1982–83;[10] 386,000 in 1983–84.

The still very low yields also show that all means are not yet being used to ensure that production reaches an optimum level. This also raises a question as to the effect of the ADRs' presence in the crop regions since the First Plan. In fact, since that Plan, its fulfilment rate of 97% has scarcely ever been reached. The average rate of increase of 2.50, or 0.62 per annum, is lower than the rate of population growth. The applies to other cereals.

Paddy rice: The production target during the six Plans was 174,000 metric tons on average. The fulfilment rate was 38% lower. The average annual growth rate of 0.50% per annum also remains lower than that of the population, 2.8%.

Maize: The average production target was some 64,000 metric tons per annum. Average fulfilment still remains 27.80% below that. Annual growth of 2.20% also remains lower than total annual population growth.

Clearly, food dependence is getting worse, not better.

Cotton: Cotton is one of the few areas where the targets (which have risen from 4,000 to 52,000 metric tons) have not been underfulfilled. The Second Plan, which launched the crop, was fulfilled by 150%, and fulfilment rates have remained high, almost 90%. Cotton thus increased by some 28% from Plan to Plan, or 7% per annum, a rate higher than the annual population growth rate of 2.8%.

Is it because cotton is less dependent on the vagaries of the climate? Is there better knowledge of how to grow it? In any case, here, the presence of an ADR, SODEFITEX, goes hand in hand with good results. If part of the explanation lies there, it ought perhaps to be asked what type of supervision is needed to have a positive influence on the production targets to be attained.

Apart from cotton, agricultural production remains on average always below the targets set, particularly for the main crop, groundnuts, but the same holds for the other main food crops. Results are not only mediocre but have fluctuated wildly over the six four-year Plans.

Between the Fourth Plan and the Fifth Plan, the fulfilment rate for groundnuts varied from 89% to 50%. For cotton, a fulfilment rate of 150% was reached during the Second Plan, but for the Fifth Plan it was 75%. For millets and sorghums, it fell from 77% for the First Plan to 69% for the Third. For paddy rice, the average fulfilment rate was about 60%. For the Fourth and Fifth Plans the rate bottomed out at 40% to 43%.

The erratic fluctuations at the level of forecasting and fulfilment during the six Plans are also matched by a fall in areas cultivated, production and yields varying markedly from year to year. Between 1976–77 and 1983–84, food crops fell by 16%: the area cultivated in 1979–80 was 8% less than in 1969–70. The diminution was 20% for groundnuts, 10% for millets and sorghums and 22% for maize.

Obviously, neither the presence of the so-called traditional structures of agriculture,[11] nor that of the SRDRs and the Sociétés d'Interventions with greater means, resulted in mastery of agricultural production. And that was equally as true at the level of forecasting targets as it was of production achieved. It remains then to identify the chief immediate obstacles.

In order to account for this inefficiency two series of factors are usually adduced. One, the area's ecosystem, natural factors such as poor rainfall, droughts, and soil impoverishment and desertification. Two, technical factors are invoked, associated with the supply of the rural areas and with the attention paid to problems and needs in research.

Natural obstacles

Climatic variations, notably the very inadequate rainfall, are among the first reasons for these results falling short of forecasts. The years of drought or poor rainfall (less than 700 mm) are always reflected in falls in agricultural production. Thus, in 1972–73, groundnut production was 545,000 metric tons; there was the same fall in production with the drought of 1978–79 and the poor rainfall in 1983–84: 544,000 metric tons.

Nevertheless, these fluctuations are no longer exceptional. Since 1970, rainfall has remained poor, less than 700 mm at least one year in two. One function of the supervisory network formed by the SRDRs and the agricultural research institutes should since have been to develop and disseminate short-cycle varieties as well as better exploitation of regions potentially favoured by the rainfall, such as the Casamance and western Senegal, to avoid these fluctuations and assure production.

Soil impoverishment and desertification are realities. But only in soil exhaustion and the non-replacement of the plant cover does drought and rainfall play a role. Man-derived causes are also at work: deforestation consequent upon towns' high demand for firewood, and/or extensive farming; decline of organic and mineral manure; disappearance of fallow; the extent of soil exhaustion in the groundnut basin and the beginning of the same phenomenon in the newly settled lands similarly exploited – a 'strategy based on an increased consumption of space'.[12] These also are the responsibility of supervisors, who either fail to take preventive measures or worsen the situation created by natural obstacles.

Technical factors

Supplying rural areas with such factors of production as fertilizers, seeds, agricultural equipment and agricultural research might constitute one of the main ways for the supervisors, the ADRs, to reduce the problems associated with poor rainfall and soil impoverishment.

One particular role given to the SRDRs and the parastatal sector was to supply the rural areas with agricultural equipment, fertilizers and seeds; to date it seems this function has been very ill-performed. ONCAD, which had a monopoly of it from its creation, was dissolved in 1980. This co-operative bureau functioned primarily to the advantage of the big producers, and failed to fulfil its tasks of providing assistance or supplying producers with the necessary inputs at the right time; and furthermore disappeared leaving debts of 94 billion Francs CFA. SONAR, which succeeded it, also failed to fulfil its role of supplying the rural areas. It too was dissolved in 1985.

The rural areas remain underequipped and what agricultural equipment there is is outdated. The average age of sowers and hoes is 17 years. The average rate of replacement is 15 years. In addition, with a halt to the Agricultural Programme in 1979, no new equipment has appeared since the 1980–81 season, except for the cotton-growing area (SODEFITEX).

Resistance to marketing fertilizers and fungicides remains stubborn although peasants are aware of their usefulness. Moreover, they use them much more on cash crops. The peripheral regions (strongly oriented to cereals) received only some 155,000 metric tons (17%) between 1961–62 and 1980–81. Over the same period the groundnut basin received 784,000 (83%) metric tons.[13]

Groundnut seeds increased by 11% per annum while area sown grew by only 1.5% per annum. Apart from the problem of seed varieties better suited to the poor rainfall cycle, at the technical level a problem of fraud and speculation remains to be dealt with to dry up the 9.5% of seeds put to other uses. At the financial level, cost remains worrying. The management of the state's seed stock led to a loss of earnings from the groundnut sector of the order of six or seven billion francs CFA for seeds.[14]

For other species, seed policy reflects neither the objectives of agricultural diversification nor the priority of food self-sufficiency. Needs for millets and sorghums were only 15% covered, for maize 4.6% and for rice 11%.

Research and rural development

Agronomic research in Senegal, the legacy of colonialism and its interests, became involved only belatedly and more slowly in crops and growing methods other than groundnuts, an export crop.

In common with other classic components of higher education and scientific research, programmes and proposals relevant from the technical and scientific point of view – agronomic rationality – are not always the most operational and practical from the point of view of local populations and conditions; the 'technological packets' offered to ensure maximization of yields are often difficult to make compatible (because they are too complicated or the economic cost or risk in the event of drought) with the minimal economic profitability of which the peasants would like to be assured. 'The theoretical bases of the "packets" proposed by research often have an exclusively agronomic rationality.'[15]

The problem of an effective link between research and rural development thus remains open. The Memorandum on the economic situation in Senegal states: 'For a long time the research bodies have not developed reliable and profitable technologies for rainy areas'[16] but Senegalese agriculture is still based almost entirely on rain-fed crops.

It is understandable that after independence, the government wanted to manage this sector in order to ensure the success of its economic and social development plans. The nationalist perspective of the 'sums of independence' led to the replacement of colonial and foreign firms by the state and parastatal sector, private stocking agencies by Centres d'Expansion Rurale Polyvalente (Multipurpose Rural Expansion Centres), Sociétés Rurales de Développement Rural and Sociétés d'Intervention in order to win the battle for development.

The results show that the achievement of rural development during the period was very slight: 'Since independence, the inhabitants of this Sahelian nation [Senegal], most of which is poor, rural and semi-arid, have not for the most part been able to raise either their productivity or their real income.'[17]

Production remained uncontrolled, subject to wide fluctuations according to rainfall or drought, and to soil impoverishment and advancing desertification. Under-equipment of the country, under-consumption of fertilizers and fungicides and non-dissemination of short-cycle varieties or operational farming techniques signalled the failure of rural development policy. After 25 years, the state was unable to ensure this development, or mitigate or contain the effects of poor rainfall or soil impoverishment – even by providing the peasants, in sufficient quantity and quality and at affordable prices, the necessary inputs to intensify and secure the harvest.

The reasons for this crisis must be sought over and beyond simply a changing concatenation of circumstances or ecological imponderables. That means locating the structural causes of the crisis of rural development policy.

Structural causes of the crisis

The government itself, contrary to the options of the 1960s and 1970s eventually decided that a New Agricultural Policy was required.[18] To establish that it was necessary meant, first of all, realizing the failure of the previous policy by ceasing to explain it essentially in terms of such factors as poor rainfall, soil impoverishment or gaps in supplies to the rural areas,[19] relating these obstacles to their underlying structures. First, were the effects of the structure of Senegal's mode and dynamic of economic production on rural development. Then, the burdens of inefficiency and cost of the state and parastatal sector. Finally, the political and social project that underlay this kind of rural development.

The effects of extraversion

The economic system is part of the mode and dynamic of extraverted capitalist production. The laws and trends that govern such economic production and reproduction are those that give agriculture its place and value in relation to other spheres of the production and exchange of commodities at the world level: the subordination of agriculture to industry, of the countryside to the towns and of the peasants to urban workers.

Senegal's continued integration into the world capitalist system after independence was reflected in its acceptance of its place in the capitalist international division of labour as a country chiefly supplying raw materials – groundnuts and phosphates.

The choice of agriculture and groundnuts as the basis of economic development thus in any event meant mortgaging development by having articulated it around this commodity. Groundnuts, like all, especially agricultural, raw materials, are subject to the downward trend of their values on the world market as shown by falling share prices. The state's pursuit of the option for groundnuts thus expressed and reinforced the Senegalese economy's extraversion and dependence in relation to the outside world, where the prices of commodities are fixed in terms of the degree of productivity in the centre (socially necessary labour time) and not of the periphery. This reinforces the effects of the deterioration of trade terms between the centre (the capitalist metropoles) and the periphery. Indeed, the economic history of 25 years of independence illustrates this fact better than any theory. Even when production of the main export crop rises, falling groundnut prices caused value to collapse, whereas the price of (manufactured) imports rises; this has been the case since the mid-1970s (see Tables 2 to 5).

Additionally, this downward trend in the value of primary commodities, agricultural and groundnut exports particularly, is aggravated by a similar trend in the quantity produced (see p. 174ff). In *L'Afrique en panne*, I. Giri establishes that this fall in production exists for virtually all raw materials in sub-Saharan Africa.[20] Rural development in Senegal has, therefore, been permanently involved in a crisis rendered the more acute in that its effects had not been mitigated by industrial structures.

Burden of structures of agro-industrial processing

In the framework of an economy 'walking on both legs', the fluctuations of agricultural production due to the vagaries of the climate may be more or less compensated for by the industrial sector's dynamism, particularly one articulated on the main agricultural crops.

In the Senegalese context, the balance sheet of industrial policy shows that in no way is agriculture sustained by industry. A ministerial communication elucidating the New Industrial Policy showed that 'the earlier industrialization policy was . . . based on import substitution and has not produced the results anticipated of saving foreign exchange, increasing productivity and accumulating capital, . . . profits and rents have often been transferred . . . only rarely has there been reinvestment'.[21]

Such an industrial sector, comprising more nearly a juxtaposition of industrial structures rather than an industrial fabric, not only makes it impossible to balance the effects of the crisis of rural development, but exacerbates it.

First, because, as the report by the Inter-ministerial Council recognizes, agriculture has been used and drained to serve the industrialization policy. 'The development of import-substitution activities has been promoted and made possible by the establishment of a major wall of protection which led to major transfers of resources from agriculture and consumers to industry.'[22] Next, because it was then billed for the failure or the very heavy operational deficits of the agro-industrial structures.

Since 1981, the deficit of the groundnut sector has become chronic . . . From 22 billion in 1981–82, it moved to 17 billion in 1983–84 and 12.4 billion last year, the sector has been experiencing a loss of earnings of 10 billion per annum on average . . .'[23]

The report goes on to observe that, at the industrial level, the deficit is essentially due to the disproportion between the husking capacities of the four factories, in which the state is the majority share-holder, and the groundnut crops reaching scarcely 600,000 to 700,000 metric tons.

Failure is also due to over-ambitious agro-industrial projects, as was the case with the Société Nationale des Tomates Industrielles in which capacity here too was way beyond that of the local supply. Failure, too, due to the management problems in market gardening in southern Senegal.

There were also excessive running costs for the Compagnie Sucrière Sénégalaise.

> Although the duty on imported sugar is less than 15%, quantitative restrictions have kept the domestic retail price over 300% above the world market price; in 1982, this resulted in a rent of the order of 10 billion Francs CFA ($US 30 million), according to estimates, for the company that had the monopoly on domestic sugar.[24]

The primacy of agriculture (in the framework of an economy and dynamic of capitalist production) is thus reflected in enhanced dependence and extraversion, reinforced by the failure of the industrialization policy and particularly that of agro-industry with regard to the targets set.

The institutional framework for implementing rural development added an extra burden to this negative account.

Inefficiency and ineffectiveness: supervisory and 'traditional' structures

Apart from the SRDRs and the Sociétés d'Interventions, the rural development services described as traditional are those of the agricultural department, the plant protection, seed, and the co-operation departments, the executive secretariat for the CERs and so on. This latter service serves to illustrate the limits of these structures' activities.

The Centres d'Expansion Rurale were formed by a multi-skill team, theoretically made up of a dozen technicians, but actually on average only four or five agents: one each for agriculture, stock farming, water and forests, and family and rural economy.

The reduction in the team's size seriously undermined its multi-skilled character. Lack of logistical and financial means meant an inability to respond to the tasks of development and grass-roots co-ordination. In practice, therefore, apart from data collection, these structures intervened very little on the ground. Lacking the means available to the SRDRs and the Sociétés d'Interventions they were thus rendered parasitical.

Timely supply of seeds, fertilizers and pest control products continued to be decidedly unsatisfactory. ONCAD, which had a monopoly of it, was dissolved in 1980. SONAR suffered the same fate in 1985, and in the 1985–86 season, there were still shortcomings in the supply and quantity of inputs available to the peasants at the right time.

Dissemination of technical information and intensification of production through research and popularization continued to be poorly done. These research shortcomings also existed in the area of dissemination work performed by the supervisory companies. The companies' services were often poorly performed or not performed in time – for example, the distribution of inputs – and were also very costly. Thus, peasants were forced into debt and the ADRs' deficits, given the low rates of recovery due to the peasants' low purchasing power, were increased.

At the time they were dissolved, ONCAD was employing some 5,000 agents and SONAR 1,200. SODEVA was able to cut its staff by 55% (755 agents), SOMIVAC by 38%, SODAGRI by 35%. These operations had no noticeable effect on production, and plainly illustrate the excessive number of the ADRs' staff. The Agences de Développement Rural running costs also absorbed almost 60% of government subsidies.

In 1981–82 SONAR received 7.8 billion Francs CFA in share capital and subsidies for running costs and 5.82 billion in 1982–83. SAED, SODEVA, and ISRA received subsidies for running costs of between two and 2.5 billion Francs CFA per annum.[25]

In 1984, of the 12 ADRs only two, SODEFITEX and SEPAS occasionally turned in profits. This inefficient and bureaucratic management can also be blamed for the cases of misappropriation of funds and the misuse of public office for private gain, of which ONCAD often provided illustrations.

The responsibility for these dysfunctions and rural supervision management burdens cannot be laid on the mode and dynamic of capitalist production. The political and social management of rural development must share responsibility for the fundamental reasons for the difficulties of the rural areas.

Political project of rural development or economic confiscation

World prices for raw materials, including groundnuts, are not determined by the state, which itself decries the deterioration of trade terms. From there to denying it any share of responsibility in the crisis of agriculture is but a short step. The state is *not* a neutral entity.

The state is, as we have seen, responsible for the establishment and strengthening, at national and regional levels, of companies to supervise and intervene, whose inefficiency and exorbitant cost weighs so heavily on the rural areas. The state fixes producer prices of main crops (groundnuts in particular) and consumer prices (of inputs and factors of production in particular) and in this way, can stimulate or penalize rural producers. The state also determines the budget for rural development, and whether to increase or reduce investments there.

The state's acts – the political project – show that it has embarked on economic and social confiscation, or rural development to the benefit of the dominant class – the bourgeoisie and particularly its political and technico-bureaucratic fraction – and its allies – the big rural producers, notables, and the urban *petit bourgeoisie* – at the expense of the rural areas and the peasantry.

Organizational bottlenecks: The supervisory companies deter and forestall any powerful autonomous peasant organization. Even the co-operatives fall under organized supervision. decreed and fixed by the state. Crowning this takeover by the state in 1966. ONCAD, following CRAD and the OCA, was made responsible for supervising co-operatives and marketing groundnuts. It stood between the peasants and the suppliers of inputs. It also intervened in the marketing of millet and other agricultural produce, as well as in the distribution circuits of rice and other consumer products of national importance. It also stood between the peasants and financial bodies. This position as a monopoly and unavoidable middleman essentially benefited only the big producers, big marabouts, chairmen of co-operatives and their henchmen, and the political and bureaucratic supervisory apparatus. Even after the dissolution of ONCAD leaving a bill of 98 billion Francs CFA to be paid by the country as a whole[26] the task of supervising the co-operatives was entrusted to the SRDRs.

This institutional blockage is to be found too at the level of rural projects. Once more, state structures seek to be their mandatory managers, such as GOPEC when it is not the SRDRs, the Ministry of Social Development even endeavours to exercise a right of overviewing the NGOs. The struggle and the dealings of the Conseil des Organisations Non-Gouvernementales d'Appui au Développement (CONGAD) can also testify to the state's determination to prevent any autonomous peasant organization outside its own apparatuses.

Economic confiscation: The operation of eliminating the private stocking agencies until 1985, the closing of PETERSEN, the purchase of the three oil mills in Dakar, Lyndiane and Ziguinchor, the opening of the SEIB in 1981, the creation of ONCAD, SONAR and the supervisory companies, signified the establishment of state monopoly over the whole groundnut sector: from seeds to oil production. The state, therefore, was enabled to fix producer price below the world groundnut price, thus demonstrating a clear political will to control the economic surplus derived from the difference between world prices and the price paid to groundnut producers.

Data from the Caisse de Péréquation et de Stabilisation des Prix show that the net out-turn of the groundnut/oil and other products balance was in surplus until 1979 with an overall sum of 49.4 billion Francs CFA. This means that the rural areas had, until 1979, been subsidizing the other sectors.

The surplus produced by agriculture is not reinvested in that sector. Instead, the state used the exceptional receipts derived from primary products, particularly from groundnut exports, up to the mid-1970s, mainly to extend the parastatal sector, majority shareholding in over 30 companies[27] and thus to increase public sector employment.[28]

Wages made up almost 50% of current expenditure and, between 1975 and 1982 the number of public officials grew at an annual rate of 6%. It must also be noted that while public enterprises represented a falling share of GNP from 1978 onwards, they contributed to increasing employment and paid increased wages and remuneration.[29] The audit commission report shows, between 1977 and 1981, wages had risen by 78% in the main enterprises.

The development crisis also results from the fact that rural producers are increasingly conscious of not benefiting from their efforts. They see that since independence the end product of these efforts has been the steep increase in the number of state officials who are paid their wages whatever the vagaries of the climate, soil impoverishment or the supply of production factors to the rural areas.

The producer price policy, use of the surplus generated in agriculture, breakdown of state subsidies and investments, confirm that until the decision to embark on the New Agricultural Policy rural development essentially served to increase the number of petty offices and state agents and guarantee them good living conditions.

Rural development and groundnut production has largely served to form and maintain a bureaucracy of the *petit bourgeoisie* and the strata allied to it than to maintain the actual producers. The creation and strengthening of supervisory structures despite their admitted inefficiency, the misappropriation and the heavy deficits that burdened the management of the ADRs like ONCAD and SONAR, the enormous proportion of the wages budget, all indicate this political and social function of rural development.

The prospects of a different rural development strategy, such as the New Agricultural Policy would like to be, thus depend essentially on its capacity to confront or remedy the situation produced by the three structures of causality that determine rural development.

The first, which is diachronic and structural, concerns the mode and dynamic of economic production, particularly the downward trend of the value of agriculture, and its subordination to industry. Can the New Agricultural Policy go against this dynamic?

The second, which is functional, relates to the inefficiency and cost of supervision. Can the New Agricultural Policy forestall their effects and deal with the reasons for them?

The third, which is super-determining, is the social and political option: confiscation to the benefit of bourgeois fractions, the intellectual and technocratic *petit bourgeoisie* and its allies, the urban *petit bourgeoisie*, the big producers and notables of the fruits of agricultural production. Can the New Agricultural Policy oppose and limit it?

Prospects for a different rural development strategy

To grasp the conditions and limits of a different rural development strategy may now devolve upon seeking out and setting out the processes and the situation that must be changed twenty-five years after independence, if the 'New Agricultural Policy' is to be, President Abdou Diouf's words, 'for the sole benefit of the producers, the true actors in and beneficiaries of agricultural development, by liberating them from the various negative structural constraints and making them masters of their destiny'.

Impoverishment of the countryside
'Rural income is inadequate . . . One can only observe the general stagnation of the peasant condition despite (or because of) the marked stepping-up of government action on agriculture'.[30] That is how the introduction to an official ILO report begins its discussion of the situation in the rural areas.

A 'negative structural constraint' with the subordination of agriculture to industry means impoverishment of the countryside. The remuneration of ordinary rural labour in the framework of the capitalist mode of production is below the average real remuneration of urban manual and white collar workers.

'Income inequality [in Senegal] is such that the average income of 70% of the total population is one-third that of the average income of the remaining 30% living in the urban centres.'[31] The effect of such an imbalance is obvious, notably for Cape Verde. Dakar, which had only 16% of the total population, sees an extra 200.000 coming in each year. According to a statement on the New Agricultural Policy, 'those who leave are mainly the young and the most economically active, the ones least resigned'.[32] The ILO report concluded: 'Rural income is inadequate and there is a more or less permanent exodus towards the urban areas, on top of the annual seasonal migration.'

In the framework of the capitalist mode of production, the development of agriculture and its modernization tends to draw the labour force from the countryside to the urban areas. This migration, fuelled by the rural–urban income differential, is further increased by the fact that the vast majority of people depend on rain-fed agriculture. After three or four months of activity, the vast bulk of the rural population is condemned to under- and unemployment and hence migrates out of the rural areas.

There is, then, impoverishment in the countryside, with underemployment, unemployment and rural exodus, and enrichment in the urban areas – the income of the 30% in the towns is three times that of the 70% in the countryside. The countryside is thus made dependent on the towns. The maintenance of the precapitalist structures of mutual assistance within the community which still survive, mitigates the social consequences of rural conditions. 'On average, each employed urban worker supports 2.6 individuals with no regular occupation [1976]. How, for example, can it be justified that in the rural areas where about 70% of the population live, no structures have been set up to promote the integration of young rural dwellers whose general educational level it is sought to raise?'[33] Six years later, the New Agricultural Policy provides no answer to this question.

Destruction of traditional production systems and capitalist reconstruction
Generalization of commodity economy and monetarization, in short the development of capitalism, has destroyed any possibility of living in the countryside without becoming involved in growing cash crops and particularly groundnuts. This activity is the leading source of monetary income for 46% of the population. Rural craftsmen have all but disappeared. Food crops have had to make way for groundnuts. Ultimately, the rural areas can no longer support

the country, and the food deficit is such that some 400,000 metric tons of cereals have to be imported annually; a clear indication of a structural food dependence.

Destruction of the production system also signifies subjection to the capitalist system of production and exchange, international division of labour and to the capitalist reconstruction of agrarian production systems. The 'Letter on development policy' indicates that the New Agricultural Policy's aim is less to deal with the effects of a cash crop such as groundnuts than to make all other crops into cash crops. Official speeches sometimes give the impression of a dilemma between developing groundnut production and developing food crops, but the major concern remains to ensure the priority of groundnuts, the economic profitability of which, according to the World Bank, is high. The New Agricultural Policy's approach therefore is not to oppose the destruction of agrarian systems and their capitalist reconstruction but rather to develop them and thus to accelerate integration into this system.

Indebtedness

The cost in subsidies for running costs of the supervisory structures was high: 4,033 billion Francs CFA in 1977–78, 6,924 billion in 1980–81; 10,920 billion in 1981–82.

Taking over the dissolved companies' debts also remains a heavy burden: 98 billion Francs CFA for ONCAD, to which must be added the billions in running costs of other structures or the failure of others such as SONAR; the ADRs debts would also have to be added in. Overall, to see the function of the burden of state apparatuses on the rural areas as formidable structures to create indebtedness for the nation would not be invidious. Debt servicing today amounts to 160 billion Francs CFA with arrears of 30 billion. Total rural debt was zero in 1972, nine billion in 1975 and 24 billion in 1980. Foreign capital also receives its share in the form of repatriation of profits on this capital or net factor incomes.

The process of indebtedness thus makes it possible to develop economic subjection, ensure and tighten the links of extraversion and dependence between Senegal and the states in the centre. This explains why the World Bank, the IMF, the suppliers of funds are always ready to support either a 'stabilization plan', an economic and financial recovery plan, a structural adjustment programme, or a medium- and long-term adjustment programme . . . and always ready with the next one too.

Conclusion

In the final analysis, rural development policy provides no grounds for easy optimism. Yet, even in the framework of an open economy such as Senegal's, the results for rural producers appear better in the Ivory Coast or Kenya. Possibly, however, the choice of groundnuts, which face strong competition from other types of oils such as soya and sunflower, does little to help the country.

Retaining, even developing the groundnut option, at the expense of food crops, however, is a development policy option chosen by the state. Agriculture in itself is not at all a curse that consigns those who work in it to poverty and ruin, the responsibility for this situation lies principally with the 'statist path' of development chosen.[34]

In Senegal, this statist mode has consisted, through money creamed off from agriculture, in enabling other sectors of production to survive and proliferate, and above all to ensure the growth and development of the intellectual and political fraction of the bourgeoisie and its allies. This is the political choice that explains the maintenance of parasitical supervisory structures that forestall any autonomous initiatives and forms of organization by the rural masses. It is this political will that leads to the destruction and increased impoverishment of the countryside which is reflected in increased food dependence and indebtedness tying the fate of the national economy to the will and choices of fund-donors. Possibly, however, these latter, more conscious of the risk of a social explosion that maintaining such a policy threatens to precipitate, may demand a different alternative.

The Berg Plan, the World Bank's measures and programmes for Senegal, seem to indicate such a variant. Envisaging the dissolution of the parasitical supervisory structures, calling for the promotion of food self-sufficiency, asking for the rural producers' purchasing power to be raised, are today the minimal measures to halt the deterioration of living conditions in the rural areas. But can such a series of measures be enough when it is essentially motivated by the prospect of ensuring repayment of debts and ensuring the liberal character of economic systems? Can the interests that have lived off this money extracted from rural producers carry out and agree to follow a different policy? Can they be forced to?

The future of agriculture, the success or failure of a different rural development strategy or New Agricultural Policy depends on the answers that the next quarter of a century will give to these questions.

But it can already be asked whether the targets set by the New Agricultural Policy are not compromised as a result of the political strategy that underlies the current reform.

Was not the New Agricultural Policy set out following the Paris meeting in 1979 between the government and the creditors dictated rather by financial imperatives in a context of the restructuring of international finance capital? This would mean that the reform of agricultural policy flows less from a domestic will to change its focus and a dynamic that takes full account of the urgent need to lay the bases of an autocentred policy, than from the demands imposed by the state's creditors.

In addition, the New Agricultural Policy set out to promote and liberate the producers. What tools and what framework exist to ensure that this necessary emancipation comes about? The co-operative system was conceived by Mamadou Dia's Circular No. 32 as a weapon of peasant self-emancipation. But as a result of successive shifts, it turned out, as we have seen, to be the key instrument for dragooning and stifling peasant initiative. In short, it became an institution at the service of the bureaucratic bourgeoisie.

The reconstruction of the co-operative system, which resulted in the creation of village sections, does not yet seem to have given the producers their freedom as decision-making economic agents in the rural areas. Was it not an attempt to resolve the peasant discontent against excessive indebtedness?

Peasant self-development requires that the producers' autonomous organization are encouraged and their acceptance as fully accredited participants in deciding on policies and the exchange system.

Table 10.2
Output of industrial crops (selected years)
(hectares/metric tonnes)

	Groundnuts				Cotton	
	Oil		Edible			
	Area	*Production*	*Area*	*Production*	*Area*	*Production*
Total: 1983–84	965,502	559,828	21,963	9,000	33,653	31,000
1982–83	1,121,180	18,198	18,244	42,018	47,400	
1978–79	1,154,000	1,050,300	21,100	17,100	48,200	33,800
1977–78	1,161,000	508,100	23,700	11,200	47,100	37,100

Sources: NPA, op. cit. (adapted).

Table 10.3
Output of food crops (selected years)
(hectares/metric tonnes)

	Millet/sorghum		Maize		Paddy rice		Niebes	
	Area	Production	Area	Production	Area	Production	Area	Production
Total: 1983–84	783,619	351,812	70,512	60,594	52,006	108,540	39,433	12,857.5
1982–83	990,865	585,223	86,241	82,148	68,165	95,025	45,886	10,889
1978–79	1,054,700	301,700	56,700	44,800	91,400	146,000	—	22,500
1977–78	942,800	420,000	53,600	33,100	63,300	62,000	—	11,719

Source: WPA. op. cit. (adapted).

Table 10.4
Growth in agricultural investments by sector (%)

	81–82	82–83	83–84*	Annual growth rate
Agriculture	7.9	16.5	22.2	18
Livestock	1.4	1.6	2.8	
Forest	1.7	2.8	4.4	
Fishing	2.1	2.5	4.7	
Water	6.3	4.1	9.3	
Total primary	19.4	27.5	43.4	18
Agricultural investment: primary/total investment:	41/9	60/13	51/14	

* Estimated.
Source: NPA, op. cit. (adapted).

Table 10.5
World prices of Senegal's principal exports and imports: actual and forecast
(constant US$/mt)

	Annual average			Forecast	
	1960–70	1971–78	1979–83	1990	1995
Exports:					
Groundnut oil	981	1,245	787	685	670
Groundnut cakes	293	326	208	183	182
Cotton	2,040	2,234	1,740	1,730	1,750
Fertilizers	46	211	145	170	170
Imports:					
Rice (Thai 5% broken)	500	500	349	339	327
Wheat (Can. No. IWRS)	211	226	173	153	149
Sugar	240	461	302	315	315
Petroleum products	32	91	206	190	265
MGPI* (1983 = 100)	31.49	62.5	103.7	165.0	220.8

* MGPI = manufactured goods price index.
Source: World Bank; Price forecasts, July 1984.

Notes

1. World Bank, Report No. 5243. *Sénégal. Memorandum Economique*.
2. Pierre Thenevin. *Quelques réflexions pour des politiques de développement au Sénégal*. May 1980.
3. *Situation Economique du Sénégal*. 1962, p. 32.
4. *Sénégal, Memorandum*, op. cit., p. 99.
5. Ibid.
6. CNES. *Réflexions sur la Nouvelle Politique Industrielle*. April 1986, p. 3.
7. *Mémoire d'un militant du Tiers Monde*. Premier Mamadou Dia explicitly said 'That was the touchstone of my policy, my objective: the end of the *économie de traite* in Senegal' (p. 120).
8. *Le Soleil*. 20 June 1986, p. 3, 'La filière arachide'.
9. NPA. *Réflexion Association Sénégalaise des Ingénieurs de l'Agriculture*. 1986.
10. *Situation Economique du Sénégal*. 1976, p. 83.
11. Inspectorates of Agriculture, Livestock and CERP.
12. See A. Lake and E. Seydou N. Touré, *L'Expansion du Bassin Arachidier*. Dakar, IFAN 1981, p. 61.
13. El Hadji Omar Touré, *Analyse des incidences des politiques adoptées depuis 1960 sur la situation alimentaire du pays*, July 1985.
14. *Le Soleil*, 'La filière arachide', op. cit., p. 3.
15. El Haji Omar Touré, op cit.
16. Ibid., p. 26.
17. *Memorandum*, op. cit., p. 1.
18. *Nouvelle Politique Agricole*. Dakar, March–April 1984.
19. See 'Les Facteurs directs', in *NPA*, p. 23.
20. *L'Afrique en panne*; see 'Des greniers qui sont vides', p. 39 and 'La fin des eldorados', p. 117.
21. 'Communication sur la Politique Industrielle', p. 4, Conseil Interministériel of 10 February 1986.
22. Ibid., p. 2.
23. 'La filière arachide', op. cit., p. 3.
24. *Memorandum*, op. cit., p. 80.
25. Ibid., p. 68.
26. Banque Centrale des Etats de l'Afrique de l'Ouest, *L'endettement bancaire de l'ex-ONCAD*, p. 8.
27. *Rapport général sur la gestion des entreprises publiques*, CVCCEP.
28. *Memorandum*, p. 54.
29. Ibid.
30. Preface by Abdou Diouf, president of the Republic, p. 2 in *NPA*, op. cit.
31. ILO, *Pour une politique de l'emploi au Sénégal*, 1982, pp. 73, 21.
32. *NPA*, op. cit., p. 21.
33. ILO, op. cit., p. 23.
34. To use Samir Amin's terminology.

11. Agricultural Development Without Delinking: Lessons to be Drawn

Bernard Founou-Tchuigoua

The nature of the problem

In Africa, which has virtually only its agricultural commodities to export, agricultural products are increasingly insufficient to feed its inhabitants.

An agricultural crisis must not, however, be confused with famine, and this chapter does not focus on the problem of famine, but on the crisis of agriculture. In order to avoid the spread of famine agriculture must undergo three series of transformations: of its functions, techniques and the ways in which accumulation is controlled.

Transforming agriculture's functions involves a radical reconsideration of colonial agriculture. During the colonial period, the principal function of agriculture was to sustain the economy of the metropole. Independence may have led to minor changes: one consequence of a new policy may be to require local agriculture to sustain both the local economies and those of the developed capitalist countries. The primary function of agriculture is to feed a growing population, and other functions should be subordinated to that. But this prior function must not entail neglect of export agriculture which, I consider is by far the best means for most African countries to acquire foreign exchange today apart from their mineral riches.

Transformation of agricultural technique is essential. African agriculture must become technologically oriented, but this must not be confused with mechanization and the introduction of chemicals, both dominated from outside. Technical transformation must be compatible with the requirement of ensuring full employment at the earliest opportunity, since industrialization would be unable to rapidly absorb workers freed from agriculture by the agrarian reforms and capital-intensive techniques. In short, labour-intensive agriculture is essential in virtually all African countries. Extensive mechanized production could be justified only in cases where it proved to be the only way to deal with a real threat of famine.

According to Samir Amin, complete control of accumulation is defined as control by the local ruling class and the state over five essential conditions of the accumulation process: (1) local control of the reproduction of the labour force, which presupposes that at a first stage state policy ensures that agriculture develops in such a way as to be capable of producing sufficient food surpluses at prices compatible with the demands of accumulation; (2) local control of the centralization of the surplus, which supposes not only the formal existence of national financial institutions but also their relative autonomy from the flows of transnational capital, guaranteeing national capacity to determine how it is invested; (3) local control of the market (largely in fact reserved for national production, even in the absence of high tariff or other protection) and the complementary capacity to be competitive on the world market, at least selectively; (4) local control of natural resources, which supposes, beyond formal ownership, the nation-state having the capacity to exploit them or keep them in reserve; in that sense, the oil countries, which are not, in fact, free 'to turn off the tap' do not have this control; (5) finally, local control of technologies in the sense that, whether locally invented or imported, they can be rapidly reproduced without indefinitely relying on importing essential inputs.[1]

The so-called economic and social development plans of the periphery are specific in that: they claim to lead from extraversion and poverty to control of accumulation, sustained rises in incomes and improved living conditions of the masses. Without the certainty that this transition would take place, the peoples' sacrifices in national liberation struggles would be meaningless. The experiences fall into two main categories.

First, there are the experiences guided by the Rostowian philosophy of development by stages. Priority is given to maximizing the GNP per capita growth rate; problems of controlling the conditions of accumulation and employment are deemed to be resolved if growth is maintained. The mode of integration into the capitalist system is set by the outside world and economic policy consists in taking advantage of this integration by realizing the maximum growth rate in the prevailing competitive situation. In Africa, that generally consists in only slightly modifying colonial agricultural practices without radically challenging them.

Secondly, are the experiences of countries where the objective of economic and particularly agricultural policies was to carry out the revolution without delinking, something which has not happened since the advent of contemporary imperialism in the last quarter of the 19th century. These experiences have sought to stress both growth and control of the conditions of accumulation in agriculture.

The results obtained in agriculture seem entirely independent of strategies adopted and implemented over successive plans. Taking the chief criterion of performance as the agricultural GDP growth rate, we find that in comparable conditions of climate and political stability, countries falling into the first category (for example, the Ivory Coast, Cameroun and Malawi) have often achieved the best results. The defenders of the status quo exemplify these countries as models to follow. In my opinion, however, if these countries' strategy aimed at gaining control of the conditions of accumulation does not replace current strategies, they too will ultimately suffer acute agricultural crises; that is the lesson of both historical experience and theory.

The future thus lies in autonomous agriculture that radically challenges colonial agriculture, even if short-term growth rates are lower and attempts at gaining control have aborted. That is why it is important to examine the specific conditions of this category of experiences. Tanzania and Algeria, whose agricultural policies have had considerable impact both at the social and political level, and in theoretical and empirical analysis, despite obvious differences of context, have been chosen here as examples.

Algeria

Algeria inherited an agriculture that was dualist in its objectives: first, to produce wine and wheat for export; and second, to produce foodstuffs for the majority of the population. It was also dualist at the technical level: alongside a sector with modern techniques producing for export, was another with archaic techniques producing for the people's subsistence. There was dependence at all levels, and the majority of the rapidly growing rural population lived in abject poverty. But these people had fought doggedly for independence and demanded development, meaning, relieving poverty. According to the FLN's (National Liberation Front) doctrine developed during the national liberation war decolonizing agriculture would contribute to the achievement of this objective. Its principal purpose would be to assure the reproduction of a growing labour force, through a much higher rate of growth of food crops than the rate of population growth. Next, it would be integrated into an upstream industrial complex in order to avoid technological dependence. These objectives appeared to be realistic. The country is well endowed with natural resources to supply steel and engineering, as well as agro-chemical industries, with raw materials. Finally, intensification of production techniques and an appropriate redistribution of land and income would maintain a rate of rural out-migration compatible with the rate of economic, particularly industrial, growth and hence with the rate of job creation in those sectors. What is the balance-sheet?

When Algeria became independent, its agriculture was serving the French economy. The revolutionary character of the liberation struggle and the determination to industrialize rapidly led it to carry out a swift process of reallocating productive forces to sub-sectors producing for the domestic market. Colonization had specialized the country in the export of wines, produced on the best lands with the most skilled agricultural manpower and the most advanced management techniques.

The most spectacular reallocation affected the vineyards whose area fell from 500,000 hectares in 1962 to 233,000 hectares in 1975–76, a reduction of 53.4%. This reorientation, one of the most radical in the history of agricultural decolonization, is doubtless to be explained less by a Muslim country's aversion to wine, or the desire to reduce dependence, than by the difficulties of finding outlets (Bedrani) and, above all, the possibility of replacing export receipts from agricultural commodities in general by oil receipts. Thus between 1972 and 1977, the food, beverages and tobacco head fell in volume from

900.000 to 580.000 metric tons and in current value from 664 million dinars to 550.[2] In 1970, agricultural commodities contributed 20.5% and hydrocarbons 70.5% of export receipts, in 1978 the percentages were 2.45% and 96% respectively.[3]

Clearly, a drastic reduction in wine's place in the economy and exports was necessary; but why it was replaced by oil, is not clear.

For Algerian planners, the reallocation of productive forces was not to be done at the expense of the growth of production. But, during the 1970s, there was no upward trend of production – quite the reverse. Thus, on the base 1974–76 = 100, the production index was 97 in 1982, after being 109 in 1980 and 102 in 1981. The per capita index went from 93 in 1978 to 80 in 1981 and 88 in 1982. The indices of foodstuff production moved even more negatively, the index for 1982 being 77.[4]

Nevertheless, physical accumulation, notably through mechanization was considerable. Between 1970 and 1978, the quantity of agricultural machinery increased considerably. Over these eight years, the quantity of tractors and harvesting, ploughing and transport equipment increased by 3.17, 2.76, 2.18 and 3.85 times respectively. In 1979–81, with 43.000 tractors, Algeria was the leading mechanized country in Africa (after South Africa) and well ahead of Tunisia (34,000) and Egypt (25,000).[5]

This divergent evolution between growing fixed agricultural capital accumulation and stagnation of production is not unconnected with a process of nationalization unaccompanied by any increase in the social and perhaps also technical capacity to ensure effective planning. At the time of independence, the French settlers owned over two million hectares of agricultural land in the country; 95% of their holdings averaged over 100 hectares. These lands were confiscated by the people and formed the socialist sector. In the early 1970s, the Agrarian Revolution (the official expression) made it possible to take 400.000 hectares from Algerian private ownership. S. Bedrani[6] shows convincingly that the workers in the self-managed sector, also called the socialist sector, as well as the 'agrarian revolution' sector, are really state employees, the allocation of the product and the means of production being carried out by the state and not by the workers. In other words, the vast agricultural sector owned by the state is dependent upon the state for the means of production. But, its demand for mechanized equipment is greater than the private sector's; in 1978, for example, the figures for the state sector were: tractors, 32,443; equipment for: harvesting, 29,594; for transport, 19,056, for other purposes, 22,997. Those for the private sector were: 10,053; 54; 20,135; 10,103; and 15, respectively.[7]

Since the USSR's experiences in the 1970s, the coexistence of a large quantity of agricultural machinery and low productivity on nationalized lands has been a common phenomenon in the agricultural history of the world; an experience shared by Algeria too.

The option in favour of intensification was, however, unavoidable in a country where each year erosion is responsible for a considerable loss of top soil, a 3% per annum population growth rate in 1960, (among the highest in the world) and where no model of industrialization makes it possible to foresee the rapid ending of unemployment. But neither was the objective of intensifying production reached. Between 1967 and 1977, cereal crops yields (which account for 30% of the weighting in the agricultural production index) fluctuated around six quintals per hectare, as in 1955. No sustained upward trend of yields of pulses emerged in the early 1980s; they were rather diminishing. It is only in the case of so-called industrial crops that, despite fluctuations, yields have increased considerably, rising from 38.8 quintals per hectare in 1967 to 86.5 in 1977.

These meagre results in the evolution of yields partly explain the instability of the demand for fertilizers and pesticides. In a country which has chosen the Western rather than the Chinese model of accumulation in agriculture, the consumption of commercial fertilizers is an important indicator of their effects on yields. But in Algeria, per capita consumption was unstable during the 1970s, with a very marked downward trend for phosphate and nitrogenous fertilizers. For the years 1972–74 the consumption, in metric tons per inhabitant was: Nitrogenous fertilizers, 7.82; phosphates, 6.75; potash, 5.53; and insecticides, 0.23. For the years 1979–81, consumption was: 8.10; 5.53; 3.01; and 0.25, respectively.[8] It is also a feature of nationalized agriculture to consume agricultural equipment more easily than the components that combine to increase greater intensity of labour time (not to be confused with greater intensity of labour).

The failure of intensification led to the failure of employment. By 1977, the employed rural population represented only 53.5% of the total employed population, whereas in 1966 58.23% of male employment was in agriculture, a percentage that fell to 31% in 1977. In the rural areas, agricultural activity occupied only 50% of the population. Rural processing industry was still embryonic since it employed only 7% of this population as against 16% in construction and public works and 10% in administration and services. That is better than in many African countries. Nevertheless, here is an agriculture whose quest for accelerated growth through mechanization has led to a very rapid reduction in the rural agricultural population, but the growth of industrial employment has been insufficient to absorb all the working age population. Emigration remains one solution to the problem found by the ruling elite. According to the 1955 French census, the total economically active Algerian population in France was 308.575, representing 13% of the employed population in Algeria, this latter being estimated at 2.336,972 in 1977.[9]

The government also applied an incomes and prices policy, quite favourable to agriculture so as to limit the drift from the rural areas. Trade terms, unfavourable to agriculture before 1974, subsequently became favourable. Compared to 1969 = 100, the wearing apparel and footwear price indices (168.2) were decidedly lower than those of agricultural commodities, including the cereals (189.2). After 1974, the daily or monthly wage indices (134) for unskilled administration workers rose less rapidly than that of agricultural products (213.4).[10] This incomes and prices policy failed to counter the effects of the rapid mechanization of agriculture and even faster industrialization.

One essential condition for controlling accumulation lies in achieving self-sufficiency and reducing the proportion of food imports and, particularly, by multiplying links upstream with engineering, agro-chemical and agro-biological industries.

On neither aspect is the balance-sheet satisfactory:

1. The rate of cover of food consumption by national production has continued to worsen.
2. The quality and quantity of statistical information provided by the Ministry of Planning and Regional Development are remarkable. Using those contained in the table of inter-industrial exchanges in 1974, it is possible to see the degree of agriculture's integration in industry in the mid-1970s. The year 1974, however, was exceptionally favourable to raw material prices. The effect of the quadrupling of the oil price suddenly overwhelmed the importance of other products in the national economy. Nevertheless, the orders of magnitude are respected.

We shall distinguish self-provisioning by the agricultural sector, intermediate industrial consumption and machinery, and finally the linkages with the foodstuff and other industries. Table 11.1 enables us to make the following observations. In value, agricultural self-provisioning is far ahead (41%), followed by the chemical industries (20%) and engineering industries (11%). The modest share of hydrocarbons and water (8%) is largely explained by the fact that these products are delivered to agriculture at subsidized rates.

Table 11.1
Agricultural inputs by type (1974)

	Values (million AD)	%
Self-provisioning	489.8	41.2
Hydrocarbons and water	98.8	8.3
Chemical industries (fertilizers)	246.5	20.7
Transport and services supplied to enterprises	93.6	7.8
Food and agricultural industries	112.3	9.4
Steel, engineering and electrical industries	133.4	11.2
Various	12.8	100

Source: Algeria, Ministère du Planification, *Annuaire Statistique de l'Algérie 1977–78.*

What is the rate of self-sufficiency upstream? In 1974, Algeria imported some 2,181 million dinars of agricultural machinery and equipment, or 24% of the value of steel and engineering products imported, and over 16 times the value of amortization of the agricultural machinery used the same year. In short, the upstream linkages from agriculture to industry were stronger with foreign agro-industrial complexes than with Algerian industry; and that was the case despite steel industry growth rates of 17% between 1963 and 1973 and 8% between 1973 and 1981. While it did not result in financial dependence, because of the large volume of petroleum rent, it still remains the case that they involved a heavy technological dependence.

Table 11.2
Fertilizer production as % of consumption, 1972–74 and 1979–81

	Algeria	Cameroun	Ivory Coast	Tanzania
1972–74:				
Nitrogenous	26.8	2.2	8.8	4.5
Phosphate	48.5	65.4	63.2	Nil
Potash	Nil	Nil	Nil	Nil
Pesticides	18.3	–2.3	52.6	—
1979–81:				
Nitrogenous	8.5	2.8	20.3	9.5
Phosphate	35.6	24.1	69.7	Nil
Potash	Nil	Nil	—	—
Pesticides	18	0.01	24.9	—

Source: UNIDO, *Handbook of Industrial Statistics, 1984* (adapted).

The objective of circulating constant capital was rapidly to raise the level of self-sufficiency, through the manufacture of chemical fertilizers from the plentiful raw materials available within Algeria. Table 11.2 clearly shows that the objective of improving the level of fertilizer self-sufficiency receded whereas in the Ivory Coast it improved. But self-sufficiency must not be confused with an adequate level, and rate of self-sufficiency and 'rate of control' of accumulation. The self-sufficiency rate seems higher in the Ivory Coast, but it must not be forgotten that production there is directly under the control of multinational companies and that, compared to Algeria, the level of use per capita is also lower. Nevertheless, it is clear that Algeria is far from being self-sufficient in fertilizers.

In the last analysis, then, the decolonization of Algerian agriculture has failed either to achieve high growth rates to deal in the short-term at least with population growth, urbanization and rising incomes, nor to make any appreciable move towards controlling accumulation. We have suggested that the nationalization of agriculture without effective planning has a major share of responsibility for this situation. Another factor that may be even more important is the existence of oil rent, a source of wealth not arising from labour. Without it, the ruling class fraction and the state would, in order to satisfy popular aspirations born of the national liberation struggle, have been obliged to adopt a more autonomous path of accumulation and a more labour-intensive strategy, or failing that, give way to other fractions which might do so. This approach would have consisted, first, in aiming at full employment, including employment of women, and simultaneously financing imports principally by exporting products produced by national labour. The importance of this last point will be considered later.

Tanzania

Tanzania became independent in conditions quite different from those in Algeria. In particular, it had not had to wage an armed struggle nor to mobilize the poorest strata of the population. Nevertheless, by 1967, important events had led the ruling strata and the state to formulate a development strategy that was rather unusual in the region. In 1967, when the dominant development theory reigned unchallenged over Africa, and before the publication (or wide diffusion on the continent) of works that were subsequently to become dependency theory and autocentred development classics, the Arusha Declaration proclaimed the need for self-reliance and African socialism. The ruling Tanganyika African National Union (TANU) noted the failure of the planning strategies implemented during the early years of independence and declared its determination to ensure that Tanzania controlled its process of accumulation, and became a socialist country simultaneously realizing high economic growth rates and a fairer distribution of access to wealth. Agriculture and the rural areas were chosen for the application of the new policy as well as for their relations with the rest of the economy and society. In what are known as the 'Dar es Salaam debates',[11] there was no debate on control of accumulation in the context of the strategy and specific economic policy of African states. The debate on the economic plan remained at a very general level and concerned the nature of capital and its transformations. Tandon distinguishes three phases, not combined but successive: the first saw a debate between progressives and reactionaries which ended in the elimination of structured reactionary thought in the University; the second saw a debate between advocates of dependency theory and supporters of bourgeois political economy, which ended in the latter's defeat; and the third, a debate within the left, ended in the return of classical Marxist thought, dependency theory advocates being classified among the neo-Marxists. In criticizing these debates, an Indian scholar saw them as taking place purely between intellectuals without concrete practice. My own opinion is that above all the debates missed a good opportunity to draw up a balance sheet of the experience from the viewpoint of the left, not only at the general but also at the sectoral level and, specifically, the level of agriculture.

That the left critique did not bear directly on the Tanzanian development strategy left the field open to international big capital to make its own diagnosis of the crisis and propose solutions to its own advantage. That is the meaning of the critique of the right which, although it had left the University, as Tandon stresses, is still very active in practice: through pressure on the government from institutions such as the IMF and the World Bank; in theory: by making new proposals to maximize growth rates, especially by giving priority to export crops.[12]

In so far as this domination by the interests of capital both in theory and practice hampers the development of struggles for a more autonomous and popular type of development, the left critique must show the real limits of the endeavours of TANU and its state. This was an invitation to the protagonists in the 'Dar es Salaam debates' to engage in a more detailed but theoretically oriented examination of the balance sheet and prospects of the Tanzanian experience. Noted here, are simply the results of these attempts: a) to reduce the extent to which agriculture simply acts as a provider of foreign exchange; b) to gain control of the segments of the process of accumulation; c) to change production relations in agriculture in the direction of nationalization.

Attempts to reduce the role of the export sector: Since in Africa, specialization in the export of raw agricultural produce had been established by the colonialists, with all the disadvantages that involved, it seems relevant to decolonize agriculture by giving priority to those functions, linked to expansion of the domestic market and consumption. Tanzania had specialized particularly in sisal and coffee production, accumulation giving pride of place to this largely settler-controlled sector. The sub-sector producing for mass consumption, in both urban and rural areas, comprised first, cereals, accounting for 30% (primarily maize, followed by sorghum and millet consumed mainly in the rural areas) and pulses; second, roots and tubers (mainly consumed in the rural areas). Fresh vegetables, fruit and meat consumed in the towns can be classified as luxury items, although the size of the livestock population in Tanzania makes meat less scarce than in many other African countries.

Once the leaders had decided to reorient agricultural activities towards these latter two sectors, what happened to the evolution of production?

During the first decade of independence, that is, before the decisions arising from the Arusha Declaration had been implemented, the overall product increased regularly, while agriculture GDP and food agriculture GDP stagnated. During the second decade, the product fell by 1.9% per annum on average; per capita agriculture GDP and food agriculture GDP collapsed. On the whole, the crisis in production for the domestic market was less acute than that for export crops. In use value, production of everyday consumer goods increased remarkably.

Among cereals, production fell only for sorghum and millet despite the fact that they are the best adapted to the difficult climatic conditions. The difficulty of increasing supplies is not the cause of the decline in production, but inadequate outlets: urban dwellers do not like them. In my opinion, as I have recommended for Senegal,[13] rehabilitation of these relatively easy to produce cereals (compared to others) is vital.

In common with virtually all African countries, there have been high growth-rates in the import-substituting foodstuffs group (fruits and vegetables, sugar, meat, and so on). Conversely, the export sector's production has totally collapsed, with the exception of cotton and tea (see Table 11.3).

Differences in growth rates primarily result from the redirection of means of production. Despite declarations in favour of a highly labour-intensive agriculture, in reality the agricultural labour force has been reallocated over wider areas. Thus, the areas devoted to cereals, roots, tubers and pulses increased by 61% (from 2.75 to 4.46 million hectares) between 1975 and 1980; the area under cereals alone accounted for 1.2 million hectares (43%) and 2.5

Table 11.3
Tanzania: Main export crop production – target and actual – 1969–74 and 1976–81 (% growth per annum)

	First five-year plan (1969–74)		Second five-year plan (1976–81)	
	Target	Actual	Target	Actual
Coffee	6	–3.1	7.5	2.5
Cotton	16	–2	14.4	–0.1
Sisal	0.2	–6	17.5	–0.7
Cashewnut	10	7	14.2	–6.9
Tea	9	5.8	12.1	4
Tobacco	25	10	18.8	0.1
Pyrethrum	4	1.6	25.2	–4.4

Source: Ellen Hanack.

million hectares (56%).[14] This extension took place with a marked shift in the deployment of labour from the externally oriented, to the domestic consumer goods sector. In 1974–76 export crops covered 647,000 hectares, but in 1983 only 602,000 hectares, a 7% reduction in five years. This shift owed more to the peasants' determination to meet their own food needs than to the authorities' determination to reduce the proportion of exports.

In fact, as Table 11.3 shows, if the government's export sector target, set in the two five-year plans, had been reached, clearly, the declines we have noted would not have occurred. Industrialization, too, through the creation of agricultural processing industries was a priority targetted in the 1976–81 five-year plan.

The fall in export production was not as a result of a political choice made possible by, for example, oil rent, as in Algeria. In Tanzania, the peasants' choice of producing for the domestic market resulted from their determination to give priority to their own subsistence needs, and the government's difficulties in easily importing cereals. Consequently, between 1974–76 and 1983, yields per hectare increased in the production of mass consumer goods and some vegetables, but export crop yields fell. This fall was accompanied by the reallocation of the most fertile land at the expense of export crops.

Nevertheless, it should be noted that increased yields in food crops were due less to intensive techniques and manpower than to the fact that, as a result of the villagization policy, mechanization was being applied to relatively virgin lands. The collectivization policy of the years 1969–73 and the villagization policy moved toward mechanization, at least for land clearing and ploughing. First, because mechanization was intended as an incentive for people to join the ujamaa collective farms; and secondly, because villagization would have led to the adoption of intensive techniques only if resettlement had been carried out on irrigated lands, and this was not possible on a significant scale.

Therefore, despite the decline in the quantity of imports (partly because of the balance of payments crisis) the number of tractors increased by more than

1,000 between 1970 and 1980, keeping Tanzanian agriculture among the most highly mechanized on the continent. In 1980, there were 18,600 mechanized units in Tanzania, almost as many as in Zimbabwe (20,000 units) and nearly four times those in the Ivory Coast (3,000 units), Malawi (1,200 units) and Cameroun (572 units) combined.

As a result of the very large quantity of arable land available per inhabitant in Tanzania, the adoption of low-intensive land-use techniques can, in the long run, be beneficial. For an African government to increase agricultural production within a reasonable time-span, without involvement with transnationals that dominate the fertilizer and high yield seed markets, it cannot avoid temporarily adopting such land-use techniques.

The fall in agricultural and food production during the second decade of independence meant of course that food dependence increased. In 1970, Tanzania was largely self-sufficient in food and food imports represented only 9.5% of exports by value of agricultural produce. The situation deteriorated seriously between 1975 and 1980, and by 1980 the ratio had fallen to 37%, with more and more imports of cereals. At the same time, the capacity to finance these imports fell sharply: in 1982, the grant element in the quantity of imported cereals was 70% as against 34% in 1974–75.

Attempt to control segments of accumulation: If the growth of products and yields was not very strong, it can be argued that this was not the most important objective. According to Y. Rweyemamu, the Arusha Declaration and Mwongozo saw development not simply as a process of accumulation, that is as increasing the Tanzanian economy's capacity to produce, but as a process of realizing an overall project with self-reliance and socialism as its twin pillars.[15] What happened to self-reliance? In a young agriculture self-reliance can be applied either at the level of self-sufficiency in what is produced or at the level of self-sufficiency in the conditions of production. Thus, export receipts were diminishing, dependence on food imports was continuing; this was associated with a dependence in the process of accumulation. To understand this, it must be recalled that the model of industrialization envisaged in the Arusha Declaration is very close to the Algerian model.

The launching of the Second Five-year Plan 1976–81 was preceded by major debates within TANU, in which supporters of a strategy guided by the concept of 'industrializing industries'[16] (as in Algeria at the time) were pitted against advocates of a strategy based on processing raw materials (an alternative never seriously contemplated in Algeria). Analysis of the available statistics indicates that the advocates constructing 'industrializing industries' won out, without the policy of processing for export being abandoned or even considered as non-priority.

The fact that between 1967 and 1979 the proportion of fixed capital (other than transport equipment) in imports rose from 23.7% to 46%, while the proportion of final consumption fell from 35.6% to 13.8%,[17] not only shows the development of the first stage of an import-substitution industry but also reflects the desire to build up basic industry.

Yet in no sense was this an industry in the service of agriculture; the most one can note is a small chemical fertilizer industry. Both consumption and production of chemical fertilizers remain very limited, which explains why the rate of cover of consumption by national production (40–50%) may appear comparable to Algeria's, while the absolute figures are very different. This industry's crisis is particularly serious: 3,000 metric tons in 1982–83 as against 65,000 metric tons in 1981–82.[18]

Generally speaking, the foreign exchange cost of agricultural inputs rose from five million in 1970 to 32.5 million in 1981. The country's energy bill, even taking re-exports into account, remains very high, accounting for 21% of imports in 1981; due to mechanization agriculture was a significant imported-oil consumer. But moving from inputs to equipment, it can be noted that no policy of an optimal combination of mechanization and full employment of the labour force existed. The reduction in the rate of mechanization after the 1973 collectivization policy was abandoned did not lead to a reduction in the value of imported tractors, which rose from $4.7 million in 1970 to $17 million in 1981, thus increasing by a factor of 3.6 in eleven years whereas it was 2.5 in Malawi and four in Cameroun that initially, had been far less mechanized.[19] In short, it cannot be said that even a beginning had been made in gaining control of the technological conditions of accumulation.

The Arusha Declaration laid great stress on the need to gain control of the financing of accumulation by emphasizing the dangers of dependence in these terms: 'Independence cannot be real if a nation depends upon gifts and loans from another for its development . . . It is true that loans are better than "free gifts".'

But Tanzania is one of the Third World countries most dependent on external financial flows and technical assistance on favourable terms. UNCTAD points out that 'over the last decade, 40% of Tanzania's public expenditures have been covered by external resources'.[20] In 1982, it received 10% of all aid for the 36 'least developed countries' (LDCs). In the same year, external aid represented 75% of imports as against 43% for LDCs as a whole. Even on a per capita basis, Tanzania came first that year with US$ 44 as against 36 for Mali and 24 for Malawi.[21]

External debt service figures for 1970 compared to those for 1982, looked modest with a not too rapid increase compared to that of underdeveloped countries as a whole and even less than that of the LDCs (Table 11.4).

Unlike debt servicing, compared to 1970, the balance of payments had considerably deteriorated. The main reason for this was the particularly favourable terms of the financial flows into Tanzania. This 'generosity' in aid had three harmful consequences: 1) it allowed Tanzania to pursue an investment policy not necessarily in accordance with the imperative of full employment; 2) it enabled the avoidance of proper integration of debt service into planning; and 3) with this external aid diminishing, the country had to accept its creditors' conditions, which demanded that the socialist features in the agricultural policy must be abandoned.

Table 11.4
Tanzania: Current account balance and external public debt service in comparative perspective: 1970 and 1982

	Current account balance (US$ millions)		Debt service			
			% GNP		% Export receipts	
	1970	*1982*	*1970*	*1982*	*1970*	*1982*
Tanzania	–36	–268	1.2	1.1	4.9	5.1
LDCs' average less China & India			1.5	1.6	5.7	9.9
Middle income oil-importing countries' average			1.5	3.8	9.2	15.9

Source: World Bank, *World Development Report 1984.*

Attempts to nationalize agriculture: The socialist doctrine of TANU, is one aimed at exploitation – against private capital and for state capitalism. This doctrine does not imply peasants' and workers' political control of the state apparatus. During an interview some months after the adoption of the Arusha Declaration, Julius Nyerere said: 'for us nationalization means socialism.'[23] Socialism would thus exist with the surplus contributed directly to the state, or foreign private capital in the form of transnational corporations, and sees itself as incompatible only with the formation of a stratum of nationals living off the surplus in the form of rent (from land or other property) or profit. The concept of rentier employed to bar nationals from business is indeed very close to the narrow meaning given it by Joan Robinson: that shareholders who are not managers of companies are in fact rentiers, just like the holders of bonds and the owners of immovable property. It is thus natural to say that 'a genuine TANU leader must not live off the sweat of another man, nor commit any feudalistic or capitalistic actions'.[23]

According to Nyerere's doctrine, it is not necessary to be a rentier or a capitalist to exploit other men or women; some inequalities may be the same as exploitation.

> There are two possible ways of dividing the people in our country. We can put the capitalists and feudalists on one side, and the farmers and workers on the other. But we can also divide the people into urban dwellers on one side and [rural dwellers] on the other. If we are not careful we might get to the position where the real exploitation in Tanzania is that of the town dwellers exploiting the peasants.[24]

The principal means of eliminating the three possible forms of exploitation (capitalist, feudal, and exploitation of the countryside by the towns) is the formation of a dominant state sector, with nationalization being synonymous with socialization. To what extent principles been was this effected, and what have been the results in agriculture?

In 1958, three years before independence, on the subject of private ownership of land Nyerere wrote: 'if we allow land to be sold like a robe, within a short period there would only be a few Africans possessing land in Tanganyika and all the others would be tenants.'[25] At that time, the most fertile African lands had been appropriated by foreigners. In 1959, European and Asian settlers, who formed barely 1.3% of the total population, owned 1,270,000 hectares and the Africans 1,800,000. And, 'since the most fertile lands went to the Europeans, the Africans were driven back to the areas least suited to crops',[26] as in the settler colonies.

At the same time, African agrarian capitalism was developing in regions where commercial crops were widely grown. In the Imani region, for example, where this movement began in the early 1950s, Awiti has demonstrated the existence of three quite distinct social classes: capitalists, petty capitalists and poor peasants. He showed how, in this region, where maize is the principal cash crop, the big kulaks (9% of the 349 households counted) took 53% of the 7,230 cultivated acres, all the 24 working tractors in 1970, employed 99% of the 1,175 paid labourers and took 76% of the monetary income estimated at 2,740,000 Tanzanian shillings.[27] According to Awiti this capitalist class also had ideological power and was 'opposed to socialism for both material and ideological reasons'.

Private capitalists (Arabs and Indians) who controlled the marketing networks for agricultural products as well as big international capital did not favour the abolition of exploitation. Forces in favour of state capitalism (African socialism, according to TANU) had, however, successfully procured the adoption of the 14 February 1962 law abolishing private ownership of land; in short, ground rent and land dealings were prohibited. But the great period of Tanzanian socialism was from 1967 to 1973, marked by the formation of ujamaa villages, with a strong trend towards voluntary collectivization. The state promoted collective farms by indirect means: priority in securing credit, state assistance, provision of technical services, tractors on credit, and so on.[27] Prior to the Arusha Declaration, the first priority was to state farms, followed by private capitalism. Moreover, before the implementation of the Arusha Declaration's principles, the World Bank played a leading role in the country's development strategy by drawing up basic development texts.

The ujamaa village is one in which the community spirit prevails and villagers participate in economic and political decision-making. Collectivization of the means of production was voluntary, obviously therefore it was the poor peasants who were most interested in its extension and expanded reproduction. This presupposed that the class struggle would be intensified and lead to a great social upheaval, and also that the means of production would be mainly of national origin. Finally, it presupposed that the law of value did not operate in all relations with other sectors of the economy, notably in marketing and supplies. In short, the success of the experiment presupposed delinking and a decisive intervention in political life by the poor in the framework of an autocentred development strategy. But, the leaders did not choose this alternative option. Perhaps conditions were not ripe for it. Whatever the case, the question that arose was, what agrarian system should follow that of the ujamaa villages system? A return to the pre-Arusha model? Or further nationalization?

The official objective of villagization was, as has already been noted, to regroup an excessively scattered population in order to reduce the costs of providing basic communication services, drinking water, education and health services. The idea of collectivizing production in the framework of these villages was rejected. Stress was put on the need to increase production through agricultural policies typical of developed capitalism, prices and exchange rate policies. In short, in future there would be no further basic questioning of the principle of capitalist agricultural production; advocates of ujamaa socialism were thus beaten on this front too.

What about the problem of the capitalist middlemen with whom the state had no desire to share the agricultural surplus? The state could have won its gamble only if production had increased considerably, and this did not happen. In a situation of shortage, the parallel market developed – particularly in the marketing of food crops – and became if not legal at least legitimate. As Table 11.5 shows, the proportion of food crops delivered to the official marketing channels continued to fall as people turned to private channels.

Table 11.5
Tanzania: Food product deliveries to official marketing channels ('000 metric tons)

	1978–79	1979–80	1980–81
Maize	223	160	105
Rice	52	30	5
Wheat	28	26	26
Millet	40	17	
Sorghum	58	21	

Source: H. Mapulo, *Imperialism, the State and the Peasantry in Tanzania,* UNITAR, Dakar 1984.

In the last analysis, if the development of private capitalism is synonymous with the development of exploitation, it can be said that according to TANU's own criteria, the policy of reducing exploitation has failed. However, it must be noted that there is no unanimous agreement on the notion of a proletariat. Mapulo's opinion that the trend is towards turning peasants into *de facto* wage-labourers in the development villages, must be further qualified. Is this a *de facto* state wage-labour force or private capital (both local capital and transnationals) labour-force? More fundamentally, as Tanzania remains in the capitalist system, is it right to allow kulakization to develop? In my opinion, even when delinking is achieved, a limited and controlled kulakization must not be condemned on a priori grounds, as it is not necessarily opposed to a well-managed process of socialization.

Failing the development of socialist relations of production, is there at least a tendency towards socialism in distribution? Since, overall, labour productivity has not risen and yields have only marginally increased, the objective of raising the monetary incomes of the peasantry has not been attained, indeed quite the reverse. The fact is that trade terms were very unfavourable to small producers during the 1970s (23% between 1969–70 and 1978–79).

This regression of rural incomes was not necessarily accompanied by any relative deterioration in living conditions in the countryside. Thus compared to some African countries with comparable income levels, Tanzania led in achievements such as literacy, primary school enrolment, access to drinking water, calorie consumption per diem, relatively low infant mortality rates.[28]

The villagization policy obviously played a stabilizing role by reducing the costs of delivering certain services. Mapulo[29] considers this to be the most ambitious programme ever carried out in Africa. It has no equivalent in Africa and few countries in the world have succeeded in carrying out such an operation so rapidly. If, however, it may be considered that the villagization policy reduced the relative gap between the rural areas and Dar es Salaam achievements remain fragile, with the decline in external aid, combined with the stagnation or even regression of economic activity as serious threats. Privatization might well accelerate the process of deterioration.

To conclude, in both Tanzania and Algeria even if the effort accomplished on the social level is very significant and must be preserved, the achievement of self-reliance and socialism has barely begun.

Experiences of Algeria and Tanzania: lessons to be drawn

Could these experiences, that failed to achieve the objectives the countries set for themselves, have succeeded?

Both countries' experiences were conditioned by two basic factors: 1) staying within the capitalist system such as it functions worldwide with no hope of seriously altering its basic laws. Even between 1974 and 1976, the high point of the struggle for the new international economic order (NIEO), to believe that North–South relations could be modified by the replacement of links of dependence by links of interdependence suggested either naivety or delusion. But the dominant fractions of the ruling classes that drew up the agricultural policies analysed here acted as if they could remove agriculture from the logic of the global functioning of the system into which their economies and their agricultures were integrated. They made two fundamental mistakes: they overestimated the capacity of the state to centralize the surplus; and they underestimated the role of property relations in agriculture during the transition period.

For these elites, the state could centralize the surplus and devote it to accumulation without arousing insurmountable contradictions in the global system where such a use necessarily involved capital owned by businesses competing with one another. They believed that the state's legal ownership of the means of production was enough to give it a sufficient social and technical capacity to ensure the transition from the position of peripheral economic formation to one of central formation. This was to forget that this happens only when nationalization is a part of the processes necessary for this transition (which requires delinking) and in itself is not a sufficient condition.

The second erroneous conception concerns the place of private ownership and even petty agricultural capitalism during the transition period. when three models are conceivable: large-scale state ownership, co-operative ownership of labour and hence of the land, small-scale private ownership which may include limited kulakization, the state having the means to direct production towards the realization of national and popular objectives. The essential question is: what model is best adapted to the imperative of controlling the process of accumulation? Obviously, there is no single answer, especially as in reality the three models can co-exist. In each concrete case, the problematic of the dominant model must be resolved.

If the first model is dominant in a typical African country (that is, non-industrialized and with a low and unadapted technological capacity) it will have great difficulty in ensuring technical and financial control of its agriculture. Moreover, to turn the peasants into wage workers prematurely involves costs that the economy cannot sustain.

If the collectivization of property encounters a great deal of resistance, especially in sub-Saharan Africa, the main reason is, that outside Ethiopia, communal appropriation of the land without the labour has been the rule in the history of the peoples of these areas. There has thus been no expropriation which would prepare the 'landless' to accept collective ownership in preference to private ownership.

Integration into the world capitalist system has only modified mentalities and behaviour in this respect in a few areas of southern Africa. In relation to the problem of gaining control of the process of accumulation, one advantage of collective ownership is that it facilitates mobilization of the labour force for large-scale public works, as in the people's communes in China. This model may, however, be enduringly dominant only if the whole of the social formation delinks from the dominant system. If it fails to do so, the effects may be paralysing.

While the dominant model is communal ownership and limited kulakization (with no commercial alienation of agricultural land), the fact that accumulation occurs in small plots makes rapid mechanization and mobilization of the labour force for large-scale public works rather difficult. Conversely, family ownership of the land is a powerful stimulus to the adoption of land- and labour-intensive techniques. Generally, states fear the pre-dominance of this model because of the autonomy it allows to peasants. But it has advantages, the most important of which is that it avoids the emergence of a gap between urban and rural incomes, *if* the peasants enjoy ample freedom to organize. It can, of course, co-exist with service co-operatives.

Whatever the dominant agricultural model chosen, remaining in the capitalist system whose basic laws cannot be modified, when it those very laws that block the process of an accumulation controlled in the periphery, constitutes an insurmountable obstacle.

If Algeria and Tanzania were, despite everything, able to attempt developing an autonomous agriculture in economies that were not autonomous, it is because of special circumstances: the possibility of having financial means of accumulation that did not result from national labour, whether agricultural or industrial. Algeria had oil rent, and Tanzania, as we have seen, had access to particularly large-scale external 'aid'. From this point of view, the availability of these un-produced riches led the elites to adopt development strategies in general and agricultural strategies in particular that may have postponed, rather than hastened, the objective of the transition to development.

Financing accumulation in agriculture with receipts from mineral or energy resources exports can lead only to the breakdown of agriculture. The centralized character of the rent automatically reinforces those fractions within the ruling classes that want to spend it on prestige activities, at the expense of those who want to use it as a scarce resource. In Algeria, Bedrani has distinguished two groups: within the state, an industrialist fraction, advocates of decentralizing decision-making and efficiency, and an 'agricultural' fraction (in the sense that it prepares and executes agricultural policy, not that it represents the interests of agriculture) that advocates waste. He considers that the struggle between the two fractions for control of profits or the surplus 'wins out over the logic of increasing production, which is the aim of development strategy'.[30]

In my opinion, this happens because, by its nature, oil rent strengthens the position of the fractions in favour of expenditure, since it accumulates by itself without really resulting from labour. Going beyond most Algerian researchers, I would claim that the proposal to finance accumulation by oil receipts bore within it the seeds of the subsequent crisis of Algerian agriculture. The existence of this rent made possible the political marginalization of that fraction of the population – the landless peasantry and the smallholders – which had fought most for national liberation.

It made possible the formation of the important stabilizing stratum of permanent wage-workers and co-operative members in the state agricultural sector. But, according to Bedrani, these wage-earners are not sufficiently productive since the management system established 'enables them to develop a greater range of capacities to resist the exploitation of their labour than under the lash of the settler'.[31]

Tanzania had the possibility of obtaining massive aid from abroad, this aid also acted as a rent. It strengthened the power of the class fraction that advocated ignoring both the objective of full employment of the labour force and the development of export crops. In the initial phase of the transition, Tanzania could finance its purchases abroad only by exporting agricultural commodities; that was simple common sense. This effort is perhaps all the more vital in countries that have chosen to give priority to the food sector than in those that have chosen to place the main stress on export commodities.

For a progressive African country that does not want to take the Algerian or Tanzanian path, a gradual delinking is essential. Delinking will make it possible to draw up a model for income distribution and a model for controlling consumption; it will make it possible to envisage full employment of the labour force and gradually to create new production capacities. In such a model, and in a first stage, most vital imports will be paid for by export receipts from agricultural commodities, in the broad sense, and craft products. In so doing, the country will naturally be a victim of unequal exchange, but unequal exchange causes the reproduction of underdevelopment only for countries that have not delinked. In the problematic of delinking, the use value of imported items plays a more important role than the exchange value.

From the preceding discussion, it follows that planning cannot be reduced to a global exercise and sectoral planning cannot be considered principally from a technical angle. A planning process is characterized first by the dominant mode of production and the socio-economic system of which it is part, and second by the socio-economic or even political content of its objectives; its techniques, which often change rapidly with information and the trade cycle, come only in third place.

a) Let us take the experiences of the central capitalist countries. Since the Second World War, economic policies to promote or diminish growth have been remarkably effective at the national level and even in the regional framework, as the example of the EEC shows. They enabled decolonization to succeed, and avoided an economic Bandung after 1973 by considerably reducing the growing elasticity of raw materials and energy sources. In short, those countries succeeded in overcoming the contradictions between growing socialization and maintaining decentralized decision-making over the allocation of productive forces, between the world scope of accumulation and the national dimension of political struggles. Even when they were taken by surprise by the countries in the periphery, they succeeded in turning the situation round in their favour. The same happened when the social upheavals of 1968 almost demolished capitalism in some countries, such as France. It is in this context that the effectiveness of techniques and even the relevance of theoretical analyses must be situated.

During each phase, the objective of economic policy was to maintain the mode of production and the capitalist system. The concrete objective was to ensure the local domination of a capitalist class. During the long phase of growth which ended in 1975, the tools used were above all Keynesian, and they were applied essentially nationally; the forecasts bore only on a single alternative, as if the future was known (in fact, comparable growth rates and a great expansion of trade justified this hypothesis as regards the future). Since the beginning of the present crisis, techniques have been changing. Instead of stressing those that legitimize the maximization of demand (Fordism), stress is put on those that minimize the costs of production (supply-side economics).

In planning, the fact that the laws of capitalism have a worldwide character is increasingly taken into account; an approach inaugurated by the Club of

Rome. The technique of the choice of the single alternative was replaced by the technique of the simulation of several scenarios, of which one is desirable. It is an error to deduce, as does Jacquemot,[32] from these technical changes the conclusion that there is a crisis of planning of accumulation in the centre, since we may observe that even during the current crisis, the central countries continue to control the process of accumulation at the level of the system and to produce techniques adapted to circumstances; that is the main point.

To return to agriculture. Following the Second World War, this sub-sector experienced unprecedented advances in productivity. The result was a fall in the value of the labour force, a fall favourable to accumulation. Conversely, spontaneous evolution led to the emergence of a gap between urban and rural incomes, leading to an excessively large drift from the rural areas. The solution was found in the expansion of demand through, 1) the development of an industry capable of endlessly diversifying how food was packaged; and, 2) the quest for external outlets. These policies succeeded so well that they created a phase marked by surpluses of food products, which could only be absorbed by the periphery. This new situation was one of the key causes of the crisis of agriculture in the periphery, particularly in Africa.[33]

Where does this capacity for self-regulation of accumulation, even through crises, come from? Apologists of the system put forward theoretical or technical arguments. For them, better knowledge of the workings of economies made possible by Keynesianis, for example, and more abundant and better processed statistical information played vital roles. In reality, the theories concerned and the tools that they make it possible to use, derive their effectiveness above all from the autocentred character of the economies to which they are applied. Proof of this is that technical forms of planning vary greatly from country to country. France adopted a highly formalized approach, both in the technical preparation and in the political co-operation between state, employers and trade unions. Japan has no formal plan but undeniably it is perhaps one of the most planned countries in the world, thanks to its Ministry of International Trade and Industry (MITI).[34] In the United States there is apparently neither global nor sectoral economic planning, but the press tells us every day that the level of cereal and dairy production there is determined to a large degree by the government's political decisions. The examples show, a plan need be neither formal nor public. Alongside these often informal, but effective, planning systems, are the sometimes very formal but ineffective plans of African countries.

The content of the planning system in Africa is provided by the extraverted character of the economies, and the social and technical weakness of the ruling classes in matters of accumulation. The continent specialized in the export of agricultural, mineral or energy products in the framework of very small nations. Impoverishment and the tendency towards a structural imbalance of payments and even of public finances are the result.[35] It follows that the objectives of planning are not necessarily given by a structure to be reproduced. Two alternatives are possible: to accept this subordinate specialization and impoverishment of peoples, or to challenge them root and branch.

When new leaders accept the colonial model of accumulation the technical exercises of planning at the macro-economic and sectoral level are of no interest. Absence of control of the conditions of accumulation means that the use of neither Keynesian nor neo-classical tools is legitimized. That is why the big international institutions that have become the *de facto* planners in Africa (so weak are the local social classes) propose only analytical techniques for projects that have their own logical relationship with other units of production, usually situated in the centre.

When, on the other hand, the local ruling classes want to challenge the existing status quo, their intention is not to make global planning simply an efficient exercise for creating an autonomous economic base; at the same time, however, they reject delinking. The result is confusion, for the political will for radical transformation runs up against the capitalist laws that govern the system as a whole.

Since the crisis, and above all since the worsening of the external debt situation in the early 1980s, the principal problem seems to be debt repayment. Now, there are 'structural adjustment plans', officially aimed at restoring the continent to the growth rates of the 1960s, but whose most important objective is to oblige African countries to deal with their debt by making up for the deterioration in the trade terms by increasing production. The differences between the two categories we have just distinguished are becoming blurred. The grand world-wide scenarios slot them in indifferently.

For agriculture, African planning in those countries that have chosen to continue the colonial model, has consisted in setting growth rates and seeking the means to achieve them. These rates are often irrelevant because the priorities are set by the evolution of external demand. Achievement of the rate does not necessarily mean that it results from the changes desired. 'The advantage' in this case is that the approach does not go against the underlying logic of the global system of which it is part. If it happens that the local ruling class opportunistically exploits a peak of strong external demand, success may then be wrongly attributed to the application of 'planning techniques'.

Agricultural planning in countries that have opted for 'autocentred development without delinking', like Algeria and Tanzania, also gives excessive importance to the technical exercise. In fact, these regimes are more likely to accumulate productively in industry than in agriculture, which sector is the most difficult to transform for historical, sociological and psychological reasons.

The lesson on this point is clear: planning that is technically weak but is part of the framework of an autocentred development with delinking is more valuable than technically successful planning that enhances extraversion and the risks of impoverishment of the people in the long run.

We can generalize: socio-economic or simply social revolutions have been attempted in the periphery of the capitalist system from Mohamed Ali's Egypt in the early 19th century to the Sandinistas in Nicaragua today, by way of Japan, the Soviet Union and China, not to mention Cuba or Vietnam. Some have been successful, others have failed. On the whole, projects whose realization required recourse to a surplus originating 'outside' local agriculture and industry – mining or petroleum rent, financial reserves accumulated over an earlier period, transit taxes or dues, external loans sometimes in the form of 'aid' to finance accumulation – have failed. In the same way, experiences that counted on capitalist markets to realize their products in the framework of the international division of labour have also failed. Without the illusion that 'the outside world' had a positive role to play, these experiences would not have been attempted. The Algerian project that we have examined rested on oil rent; so did the imperial Iranian project in the 1970s. Tanzania obviously counted on massive external aid. Looking at Nkrumah's Ghana shows that the external reserves accumulated by the country during and after the Second World War played an essential role in the Ghanaian import-substitution industrialization strategy and in the role assigned to the world market. The Nasserite project in Egypt would not have been attempted without the hopes based on receipts from the Suez Canal and Soviet aid.

These experiences bore within them the seeds of failure. First, recourse to an 'external' surplus, in the sense defined above, produces, or maintains, relations between classes, and nations, that exclude the popular classes from the exercise and control of power. The state is not obliged to organize labour nationally in order to make possible the production of a surplus. In particular, national production of food staples, which can only follow from the agricultural revolution, is not imposed as an inflexible necessity; and an accumulation that excludes the peasantry, and thus has a very narrow social base, is fragile and impossible to carry through.

Then, the allocation of this 'surplus' necessarily pays special attention to the needs of social strata that want a model of accumulation involving either a model of social organization imposed from outside (large-scale external aid), or a model of technical articulation that encourages the import of technological packages (equipment, organizers, management models). This simply means that this allocation 'marginalizes' rural activity. The concentration of incomes, and of the power of access to services and goods as well as political power, resulting from this deepens instead of reducing the inequalities of productivity and incomes.

Worse, the more a project for transition counting on an unproduced source of financing (Nasser's Egypt, Boumédienne's Algeria, or the Shah's Iran) is consistent, the more its implementation involves the formation of an arrogant bureaucracy or even technocracy, incapable of satisfying the popular cultural demand. The cultural content of these experiences is in general very poor, oscillating between out and out Westernization and withdrawal into the past. The people's impression may then be that not only are they failing to materially enjoy the fruits of transformations (which may indeed be very rapid), but also that they are losing their cultural identity. They may equally become a mass to be manipulated by groups with an objective interest in the perpetuation of underdevelopment, and also for the fundamentalist ideologues of all persuasions. The upshot then is that for two or three decades the state once again becomes a comprador state and the people wait for a 'strong' man to come and restore the situation.

In short, if one of the factors that we have listed as 'external' intervenes significantly in the conception of the transition strategy, the delinking will not be embarked upon.

In my view, it is thus possible to know whether a country is embarked on the path to transition out of the periphery. To do so, it is enough to observe how it expects to finance the increase in agricultural productivity, how its industrialization drive is oriented in relation to agriculture and what is its technological policy. If the increase in agricultural and industrial productivity, based on massive recourse to domestic know-how combined with selective importation of technology, is financed by the agricultural and industrial surplus, there may be reason to assume that the transition is underway. Both Japan[36] and China or North Korea did this. Is it still possible?

The principal non-social constraint lies in the size of the country. For military as well reasons of economies of scale some authors consider that a population of at least 50 million is needed. In Africa, in that case, only a few countries are in a position to delink: Nigeria, Egypt, Ethiopia, Zaire, South Africa, Tanzania and, soon, Morocco and Algeria. In reality, this constraint is not absolute. Given certain conditions, countries with smaller populations can embark on the transition; the size of the population constitutes an absolute constraint only for countries with fewer than one million inhabitants. Whatever the case, political regroupings in Africa would make it possible to remove this constraint. For this reason, pan-Africanism remains an ideology of the future, conditional upon it becoming purged of its purely demagogic aspect.

The basic constraint is, of course, socio-political. To count only on the values produced through the full employment of the national labour force is possible only if the state becomes a national one, because it rests on a broad consensus that itself results from popular participation in the exercise of power. This consensus, obtained on concrete questions touching on austerity, cultural orientation, distribution of the power of access to goods and services, is essential. Can it emerge only from a popular movement or can it be generated from the top? Because of the often repressive character of most present-day states and their subordination to the international system that sustains them, what characteristics will popular struggles, purged of all trace of funda-mentalism, take on? These are questions to which it would be presumptuous to provide answers with assurance in a situation marked by the fact that, officially and with great fanfare, imperialist states are financing movements designed to destabilize progressive governments and, unofficially, wars between countries in the South and civil wars, the objective being in some cases the dismemberment of nations. But the forces favourable to delinking and an agricultural revolution conceived in a perspective of global development are at work on the continent.

Notes

1. Samir Amin, 'Questions posées par l'analyse de l'expansion mondaile du capitalisme', UNU, Dakar, September 1985, pp. 15–16.

2. Algeria, Ministère du Planification, *Annuaire statistique de l'Algérie, 1977–78*, p. 292.

3. UNCTAD, *Handbook of Trade, 1980*.

4. FAO, *World Food Situation, 1983*, annexes.

5. FAO, *Production Yearbook, 1982*.

6. S. Bedrani, *L'Agriculture algérienne depuis 1966*, Algiers, OPU.

7. Ministère de la Planification et de l'Aménagement du Territoire, *Annuaire statistique de l'Algérie, 1977–78* p. 171.

8. FAO, *Fertilizer Yearbook, 1983*.

9. Algeria, Ministère du Plan, *Annuaire statistique, 1978*.

10. Ibid.

11. Yash Tandon, 'Arguments within African Marxism: the Dar es Salaam debates', *Journal of African Marxists*, 5, February 1984.

12. E. Hanack has applied the World Bank/IMF scenario to Tanzania in 'The Tanzanian balance of payments crisis: causes, consequences and lessons for a survival strategy', ERB paper 81–1.

13. B. Founou-Tchuigoua, 'Stratégie d'autosuffisance alimentaire et choix d'une céréle prioritaire au Sénégal', World Congress of Sociology, Mexico, 1980.

14. FAO, *Production Yearbook, 1983*.

15. Y. Rweyamamu summarized this thesis in 'A neglected relation between agriculture and industry', IDEP, 1975.

16. Ibid.

17. Ellen Hanack.

18. FAO, *Fertilizer Yearbook, 1983*.

19. FAO, *Trade Yearbook, 1975* and *Trade Yearbook, 1982*.

20. UNCTAD, *The Least Developed Countries, Report, 1984*.

21. Ibid.

22. Interview with *Jeune Afrique*, 326, 9 April 1967, p. 21.

23. Arusha Declaration, Part two.

24. Ibid., Part three.

25. J. Nyerere, 'National property', in *Freedom and Unity*, OUP 1966, as cited in A. Coulson, 1974, p. 79.

26. Sylvain Uffer, *Ujamaa, espoir du socialisme africain en Tanzanie*, Aubier, p. 45.

27. Adhu Awiti, 'Luttes des classes dans la société rurale en Tanzanie, une étude de cas de Ismani-Iringa', in *Agriculture africaine et capitalisme*, Anthropos 1975, p. 28.

28. René Dumont, interview with *Demain l'Afrique*, 45, 28 January 1980.

29. Henry Mapulo, 'Imperialism, the State and the peasantry in Tanzania', UNU, Dakar, January 1984. This paper is now Chapter 8 of this book.

30. Ibid.

31. Bedrani, op. cit.

32. Ibid., p. 267.

33. Jacquemot, 'Crise et renouveau de la planification', *Le Soleil*, 20 August 1985, previously published in *Revue Tiers Monde*.

34. Bernard Founou-Tchuigoua, 'Crise agro-alimentaire africaine', IRES,

Kinshasa, *Lettre mensuelle*, 8–9, 1983.
   35. Samir Amin, *Unequal Development*.
   36. Japan applied delinking between 1608 and 1945, China after 1945.

Conclusion

Hamid Aït Amara and
Bernard Founou-Tchuigoua

In countries with high population to land ratios, industry has a fundamental role to play in the creation of the conditions necessary for progress in agriculture. Industry helps promote growth at several levels. On the one hand, it provides the material, mechanical and chemical means to modernize the techniques used in stock-rearing and crop-growing. But through the employment it creates, it also determines, directly or indirectly, the number of agriculturally active workers, the productivity of the peasants' labour, their income level and, ultimately, the overall agricultural demand for consumer and capital goods. Industry is the basis for the growth of an internal market, an indispensable element in the dynamic of development in which agricultural demand is a fundamental factor. In Algeria, the farmers have very substantially improved their marginal income, more by employing the manpower resources of rural households and raising the price of agricultural products than by increasing the productivity of labour. The state, striving to intensify agriculture, has laid great stress on farming equipment, tractors, harvesters, crop treatment and irrigation techniques. This progress in equipment was supposed to promote the adoption and diffusion of new, more intensive production methods and to improve crop yields.

This increase in the capital provided by industry, however, was not by itself a sufficient factor in agricultural progress. Research in agronomy and the training and education system were not adequate to ensure renewal of production methods and improvement in the technical expertise of the peasants.

Despite amelioration of the level of farm equipment, stock-rearing and crop-growing methods have barely evolved and yields have increased only slightly. The relative costs of mechanization and other agricultural investment, in view of the productivity of the land, limit the use of more intensive techniques, methods of cultivation, fertilizers, weed killers, selected seeds, and so on.

In this context, extensive systems have shown themselves to be more profitable for those enterprises that gear their production to this market than systems that make more use of modern production methods, at least in low to medium rainfall areas. The relative stagnation of yields results in a tendency towards more land and resources being used for stock-rearing. This process is underpinned by a price system favourable to animal products and the high revenues expressing the associated demand. As a result, the price policy in force over the last decade to stimulate base production, wheat, milk, and vegetables, has proved powerless to reverse the tendencies observed in the structure of production.

Furthermore, it has not been possible to draw the full benefit from the conditions created by industrialization because of the system of property and labour. Structural reforms aimed at changing the size of farms and the way work is organized have only marginally affected private sector land, which has remained outside the process of agricultural modernization.

The global dynamic of employment has been sufficient to orient surplus rural labour towards activities outside agriculture in the 1970–85 period. Having access to mixed employment and income, the great majority of small peasants have stayed on the land. But now that the rate of economic growth has slowed, it seems that the question of a development process fuelled by a dynamic of internal accumulation is once again on the agenda.

Export earnings have suffered a severe decline since 1986, dropping from $13,000 million in 1983 to $7,000 million in 1987, from which debt interest and capital repayments of $4,000 million a year had to be found. There has been a sharp decline in investment, especially in the public works and buildings industry, and this has slowed economic growth. Employment has contracted seriously. Unemployment, rising fast, will probably reach about 20% of the active population by the start of the 1990s. Following the early 1980s, the brakes applied to the growth of the industrial sector now make it essential that all or part of those additional fractions of the active rural population who will not find work elsewhere remain engaged in agriculture. In other words a return to the situation prevailing during the 1960s before the industrialization plans took off.

Abbreviations

(Chapter 10)

ADR	Agence de Développement Rural (Rural Development Agency)
AR	Animation Rurale (Extension Service)
BCEAO	Banque Centrale des Etats de l'Afrique de l'Ouest
BNDS	Banque Nationale de Développement du Sénégal
CEAD	Centre Régional pour l'Assistance au Développement
CER	Centre d'Expansion Rurale (Rural Expansion Centre)
CERP	Centre d'Expansion Rurale Polyvalente
CONGAD	Conseil des Organisations Non Gouvernementales d'Appui au Développement
CSS	Compagnie Sucrière Sénégalaise
CVCCEP	Cours de Vérification des Comptes et de Contrôle des Etablissements Publics
ILO	International Labour Organization
ISRA	Institut Sénégalais de Recherche Agricole
ITA	Institute de Technologie Alimentaire
NGO	Non-Governmental Organization
NPA	Nouvelle Politique Agricole (New Agricultural Policy)
NPI	Nouvelle Politique Industrielle (New Industrial Policy)
OCA	Office de Commercialisation Agricole (Agricultural Marketing Board)
ONCAD	Office National de Coopération et d'Assistance au Développement (National Office for Cooperatives and Development Assistance)
OSP	Opération de Suppression des Organismes Stockeurs Privés
PAML	Plan d'Ajustement Structurel à Moyen et Long Terme (Medium- and Long-Term Structural Adjustment Plan)
PAS	Plan d'Ajustement Structurel (Structural Adjustment Plan)
PREF	Plan de Redressement Economique et Financier (Economic and Financial Recovery Plan)
SAED	Société d'Aménagement et d'Exploitation du Delta
SRDR	Société Régionale de Développement Rural
SEIB	Société d'Exploitation Industrielle de Baol
SERAS	Société d'Exploitation des Ressources Animales du Sénégal

SI	Société d'Intervention
SODAGRI	Société de Développement de l'Agriculture
SODEFITEX	Société pour le Développement des Fibres et Textiles
SODEPS	Société pour le Développement de l'Elevage dans la Zone Sylvo-Pastorale
SODEVA	Société de Développement de Vulgarisation Agricole
SOMIVAC	Société de Mise en Valeur Agricole de la Casamance
SONAR	Société Nationale d'Approvisionnement du Monde Rural
STN	Société des Terres Neuves

Index

Rwanda, 17, 24
Rweyemamu, Y., 202

sabotage, by peasants, 147
sacrifice, ritual, 87
Sahara war, 94
Sahel, 68; dependence of, 14; drought in, 92
Sankara, Captain, 112
SAPH company, 110
Saudi Arbaia, 43
Sawadogo, Abdoulaye, 112
schooling, 145
sedentarization of nomads, 90, 92
seeds, 110; renewal of, 59; selection of, 48; supply of, 181
segmentarism, 95
self-sufficiency in food, 30-8, 174
Senegal, 16, 18, 25, 26, 36, 77, 79, 82, 170-90; New Agricultural Policy, 179, 184, 185, 186, 187; New Industrial Policy, 180; Sixth Plan, 171, 174, 176
Sepas company, 182
Servolin, C., 23
share-cropping, 92
sheep, 70
sheepmeat: costs of, t156; prices of, 154, 165
shifting method of cultivation, 142, 144
sisal, 139, 147, t201
slave trade, 2, 36, 77, 85, 95
slavery, 87, 88, 93, 94; Moorish, 91
slaves: emancipation of, 93; sale of, 91
smallholders, 162
Société de Développement de l'Agriculture (SODAGRI) (Senegal), 173
Société d'Aménagement et d'Exploitation des Terres du Delta (SAED) (Senegal), 171, 173, 182
Société d'Exploitation des Resources Animales du Sénégal (SERAS) (Senegal), 173
Société de Développement et de Vulgarisation Agricole (SODEVA) (Senegal), 170, 171, 173, 182
Société National d'Approvisionnement du Monde Rural (SONAR) (Senegal), 171, 177, 181, 182, 183, 184, 186
Société des Terres Neuves (STN) (Senegal), 171
Société Nationale pour l'Industrialisation et la Commercialisation du Bétail (SONICOB), 79
Société Tunisienne des Industries Laitières (STIL), 151, 153
Sociétés Rurales du Développement

Rurale (SRDR), 176, 178, 181, 183
social contract theory, 95
socialism, 2, 3, 25, 121, 204, 205
socialist agricultural estates, Algeria, 64
Sodefitex company, 173, 176, 178, 182
Sodepalm company, 108-9
Sodesucre company, 110, 111, 112
soil deterioration, 3, 24, 25, 42, 63, 106, 177, 184
soil erosion, 42
soil improvement programmes, 63
Somivac company, 182
sorghum, 26, 148, 174, 175, 176, 178, 200, t206
South Africa, 33, 195, 214
South-South relations, 30
soya beans, 125
spare parts, 112
stagnation, 8
standards of living, 13
state: as trader, 53; relation to rural community, 4; relation with producers, 115-16; role of, 64, 65, 96, 121, 134 (in agriculture, 113-14); in Senegal, 170-90; in state agricultural policy, in Tunisia, 160-4
state capitalism, 108, 204
state farms, 143; in Tanzania, 138-48; in Tunisia, 149-68
steel, 19, t45, 128
Stewart, C.C., 95
stock farming, income from, t166
subsidies, 41, 56, 110, 128, 130
subsistence farming, 14, 25, 140, 147
Sudan, 18, 24, 27
Suez Canal, 213
sugar, 15, 16, 18, 81, 100, 103, 108, 110, 112, 126, 132, 159, 181; prices of, t190
sweeteners, development of, 15

Tévoedjrè, Albert, 127
Tanganyika African National Union (TANU), 199, 204, 205, 206
Tanzania, 25, 138-48, t198, 199-207, 207-16, 214; crop production of, t201
taxation, 6, 72, 78, 79, 89
tea, 139, 147, t201
technology, 10; agricultural, 4, 132; imported, 17; neutrality of, 2
Tichitt Chronicle, 94
timber, 124, 125, 130
tithes, 79
tobacco, 141, 146, 147
tomatoes, 181
Toupet, Charles, 71
tractors, t45, 46, 47, 55, 107, 162, 201, 205
trade balance, 11, 12, 81